MIKE PARKER
THE GREASY POLL

DIARY OF A
CONTROVERSIAL
ELECTION

"This book is by turns funny, thrilling and terrifying. It's the day-by-day story of idealism as it meets political reality in a Wales with a dishonest media and craven politicians. Mike Parker's colonoscopy of Welsh politics will make you laugh, and it may make you angry, but above all it will make you want to change things."

Patrick McGuinness

"An honest, no holds barred account... The fact that Mike is English born, and has learnt Welsh as a second language gives him a refreshingly different perspective on Wales and its people, but it also means that he does not suffer from the sensitivities which tends to hold us natives back from being too open and honest about each other. So Mike sails through this lively campaign diary, naming names, and telling it as it is, warts and all. It is all done with good humour and delightful candour, but no-one is spared from criticism if deserved, friend or foe.

It all amounts to a very enjoyable read which throws a new light on many aspects of present-day Welsh and British politics, and the way the press and media deal with it, and the author has some pertinent things to say about Plaid Cymru itself. It certainly rings true to me."

Dafydd Iwan

"In this portrait of the political badlands of Ceredigion, Mike Parker is at his self-deprecating, witty, outraged and excoriating best. Sharply alert to the complexity and contradictions of the constituency he hoped to represent at Westminster – its beauty and poverty, its politeness and viciousness, its rich international culture and stultifying insularity – he shows here just what we in Ceredigion lost by failing to elect him."

Dr Jasmine Donahaye

"This is a compelling, readable account of one candidate's 2015 general election. Mike Parker's account is searingly honest, most of all about his own shortcomings as a would-be politician, the strain on his personal life through two long years of campaigning, and the vitriol directed against him as the result of a particularly nasty smear by the local newspaper.

The Greasy Poll is not likely to make many people want to put themselves forwards as political candidates. And Mike Parker's experience raises particularly troubling questions about whether people who have tried to think and write seriously about society's problems can actually step into the realms of electoral politics, without having their previous words distorted out of all recognition and used against them."

Professor Roger Scully

"There is good reason for the Liberal Democrats' reputation as the dirtiest fighters in politics, as this entertaining election diary makes painfully clear. A crash course in the brutal tribalism of Welsh politics, *The Greasy Poll* is the sobering story of what happens when a gay Englishman becomes a Plaid Cymru candidate in one of their top target seats. It was never going to be easy, but no-one foresaw such a filthy fight, nor so many problems close to home. Mike Parker's book should be compulsory reading for anyone from outside of the political bubble who is contemplating standing for election. It will soon cure them of the idea."

Iain Dale

First impression: 2016

The publishers wish to acknowledge the support of
Cyngor Llyfrau Cymru

Cover photograph: Keith Morris
Cover design: Olwen Fowler

ISBN: 978 1 78461 269 6

Published and printed in Wales
on paper from well-maintained forests by
Y Lolfa Cyf., Talybont, Ceredigion SY24 5HE
website www.ylolfa.com
e-mail ylolfa@ylolfa.com
tel 01970 832 304
fax 832 782

MIKE PARKER
THE GREASY POLL

DIARY OF A
CONTROVERSIAL
ELECTION

To my fighting friend, Leanne Wood

Introduction

In twenty-five years of self-employment, I've been a writer, a stand-up comedian, a TV and radio presenter, a poet, a columnist, an editor, a lecturer, a club promoter, a tour guide, an actor, a DJ, a kids' party entertainer, an office clerk and – inevitably – several times a barman. In the general election of May 2015, I came three thousand votes short of adding Member of Parliament to the list.

This was not quite the severe career swerve it might at first seem. In almost everything I've done, politics has been drizzled through it. Writing and broadcasting from a sense of place has been my mainstay, and it seems to me impossible to do that without a strong political antenna. Power, money, class, land ownership, patronage, exploitation and corruption have shaped our landscape as thoroughly as they have moulded our imperfect democracy.

Just how imperfect *is* that democracy? Decades of activism had brought me to the suspicion that our political system is irretrievably broken, corrupted beyond repair by a self-serving elite busily tightening their grip. Challenges to that, such as rows over MPs' expenses, phone-hacking or dodgy honours, created acres of furious headlines, but seemed to deal only with the symptoms of the malaise rather than its causes. I wanted to find out for myself if things were as bad as I feared.

Despite my cynicism, I am still atavistically excited by the mechanics of democracy: the tribal loyalties of party politics, the elections, the swings and stats and storms-in-teacups. It was an interest forged in me, as for most other political anoraks, at an early age. At twelve, I volunteered to be the Liberal candidate in a school mock election, held to coincide with the real 1979 poll that swept Margaret Thatcher to power. Even as she stood on the threshold of Number 10, mangling the prayer of St Francis of Assisi, I knew that we were sworn enemies. She was everything I was growing to loathe about the suburban Middle England of my childhood: its hypocrisy and conformity, its penny-pinching mindset and purse-lipped worldview.

I signed up for real with the Liberals, and was soon the local ward secretary as well as its most prolific deliverer of *Focus* newsletters. I had a few haughty letters printed in *Liberal News* and the *Kidderminster Shuttle*, a wild weekend in Croydon helping out in a victorious by-election campaign and became the founder and Chairman (and quarter of the membership) of the Kidderminster & District Young Liberal Association.

From Young Liberal to Old Labour took only months. By the time I reached the University of London in 1985, my hatred of Thatcher had become all-consuming, and I was ripe for conversion. I pounded the streets for Neil Kinnock in 1987 (London) and 1992 (Birmingham), growing tired of the acid taste of election night disappointment. Not until I was thirty did I know the exhilaration of victory, when the Conservative government that had filled my teenage years and twenties was finally jettisoned on that glorious May night in 1997. Even that was topped two years later, at the euphoric results party in Cardiff's Park Hotel for the inaugural elections to the National Assembly for Wales.

Although I'd never yet lived there, Wales was increasingly dominating my horizon. Growing up less than forty miles from the border, my eyes had always drifted west, and in the early 1990s, I took on the job of co-authoring the new *Rough Guide to Wales*. The physical splendour of Wales was obvious, but just as big a draw for me were its culture and politics. This was a land that booted the Tories out altogether in '97, yet remained commendably suspicious of smoothie New Labour as well. Here too was Plaid Cymru: socialist, green, cultured, iconoclastic and, it seemed on that joyous day in 1999, marching to victory. A revolution was breaking, and I wanted in.

Having been such a political philanderer in England – not only had I been a member of the Liberal and Labour parties, I'd also voted Green and even Communist at one point – since moving to Wales in the spring of 2000, I've been going steady with Plaid. My first encounter with the party had been at the tail end of the 1980s, when I was a member of the NUS national executive. At conferences, I gravitated without even noticing to the Plaid crew, whose vision of the world so closely tallied with mine. More to the point in 1989, they were always far more convivial company than the shiny ranks of Labour careerists.

Welsh Labour was never an option. They are the true conservative party of Wales. Having won every significant election since 1922, they have acquired all the trappings of a divine right to rule: cronyism, corruption and a quite chilling contempt for their electorate. In the Welsh Labour heartlands, where their candidates routinely took more than three-quarters of the vote, democratic activity was dead.

I joined Plaid as soon as I moved here, and soon found my comrades. Some, such as Adam Price, I'd known since the rumbustious days of student politics; others were new to me. I first met Leanne Wood when I interviewed her for a radio series in the mid-noughties, a couple of years after her initial election to the National Assembly. We clicked instantly. We shared similar politics, history and outlook, despite coming from such different backgrounds. A similar sense of humour too: I love late nights with her, hearing the political gossip and laughing uproariously. She was one of the most ego-free and incorruptible politicians I'd ever met, the cause always far more important than her own position. When Ieuan Wyn Jones gave up the Plaid leadership in 2011, Leanne sounded many of us out on whether she should contest the election as a standard-bearer for the left of the party. It seemed an unlikely idea but why not, I replied.

All said though, parties are only one part of the political equation. The press and media's role in our disintegrating democracy cannot be overstated. In my politically formative years of the 1980s and early 1990s, the press was supine and biased, but something changed in the mid-nineties and they began to call the shots in evermore strident ways. If the papers demanded someone's head on a plate, they invariably got it.

On a few occasions, I became the story myself, and saw how far and fast it could stray from its origins. The piece that made most waves, both at the time and then fourteen years later in the Ceredigion election campaign, was one I published in 2001 in *Planet* magazine. It concerned the "white flight" phenomenon of incomers into Wales, focusing especially on the leadership of the British National Party. After being picked up very sympathetically by *Wales on Sunday*, rather more hyperbolic reactions to it made the following day's front pages in both *The Guardian* and *The Daily Telegraph*. That was on Monday, 10 September 2001. The following day of course, the world changed for ever, and with it our discourse on racism. After 9/11, crude bigotry started its creep from the shadows into the mainstream of political and media discussion. It has only grown shriller and more widespread ever since.

*

Over the past couple of decades, and especially since moving across the border, I have been given wonderful opportunities to explore Wales, and to communicate my impressions, in print and on TV and radio. There is an honourable place in any culture for the perspective of an outsider, and I've been thrilled that so many people have responded to my work. Like most writers, I'd always guarded this outsider status rather jealously, but I could see that that was changing, especially since 2011, when my partner Preds (short for Peredur) and I moved to an old farm, just down the road from where he had been brought up. Our new life started to burrow me deep into the rock in ways I'd never previously experienced.

My relationship with Wales, if not something I was born to, feels evermore like a marriage. The giddy infatuation of those early days has long mellowed into a stubborn love, warts and all. And there are plenty of those on both sides. Wales and I can both be hot-tempered and thin-skinned, prone to gloomy introspection and sudden insecurity. I'd like to think, too, that we are both instinctively kind, hospitable and creative, and with strong, enduring principles. This dawning realisation that I was no longer quite the outsider shifted my perspective radically. Perhaps, I thought, it was time to make the leap from spectator to participant. I convinced myself that the gap between them was tiny.

I was very wrong.

A division in the house . . .

It's definitely not a case of like father like son in Kidderminster estate agents David Parker's home.

When it comes down to politics they are as different as chalk from cheese — and two opposing election posters outside the house in Chester Road South prove the point.

Mr Parker is urging fellow electors to vote Conservative in the Wyre Forest District Council elections on Thursday.

But alongside is another poster put up by his 15-year-old son Michael, an active Liberal supporter.

Mr Parker said: "Michael is secretary of the Aggborough and Spennels ward Liberals and, although he can't vote, is backing them to the hilt."

He added: "There's no aggravation in the family, although my wife Anne and I have always backed the Conservatives. Michael happens to hold different political beliefs but I'm glad he has adopted a sensible attitude towards community affairs."

Kidderminster Express & Star, May 1982

FOLLOW MY LEADER

December 2011 – June 2013

Thursday 29 December 2011,
Home:
Our first Christmas at Rhiw Goch and a visit from Leanne and family, full of the usual wine, walks and Scrabble, at which both she and Ian ritually stuff me. She's very excited about the Plaid leadership election, and is heading off on a tour of meetings around Wales as soon as the holidays are over. Her only fear is that she will be heavily beaten. True to form, her concern is political, not personal. "If the left get flattened in this election, it'll take us years to bounce back," she says.

Sitting by the fire,with a full belly and several slugs of festive bonhomie, I idly promise that if she wins, I'll get more involved in Plaid activism. It's a fairly safe commitment to make, mind you, as she's the 5/1 outsider.[1]

Friday 13 January 2012,
Cann Office Hotel, Llangadfan, Powys:
An inauspicious date, but a brilliant meeting for Leanne's leadership campaign. There's a real sense of something happening out there. Although Elin Jones[2] remains the clear favourite, Leanne's odds have tumbled. It is remarkable to see thirty people out on a January night, in the frozen depths of rural Montgomeryshire. I've never seen a Plaid meeting in the county even reach double figures before.

Leanne is so good with people. Everyone melts towards her, from crusty old boys to Cymdeithas[3] activists plastered in badges. Even though she is the only non-Welsh speaker in the race, she is picking up support among many language campaigners, who share her more radical politics. Many less vociferous Welsh speakers are with her too, keen to prove that

---

1   Paddy Power odds just before Christmas were Elin Jones as favourite at 4/7; Dafydd Elis-Thomas at 10/3; Leanne Wood and Simon Thomas both at 5/1.
2   AM for Ceredigion, 1999–.
3   Cymdeithas yr Iaith Gymraeg, the Welsh Language Society.

Plaid is not just the preserve of the *Cymry Cymraeg*[4]. It's still the biggest single assumption made by people about the party, and they think that she is the one to change that.

Thursday 26 January 2012,
Home:
Nominations have closed for the Plaid leadership. It's a four-way contest, between Elin Jones, the frontrunner by some considerable margin, Simon Thomas[5], Dafydd Elis-Thomas[6] and Leanne. Despite the disappointing election result last year, it's creditable that from a party reduced to eleven AMs, there's such a solid range of talent and experience on offer.

Monday 6 February 2012,
Home:
Leanne's campaign is gathering momentum. Although Elin has the support of a majority of AMs, Leanne won the most nominations from branches and constituencies, more than the other three put together. Who saw this coming? And it's not just the language issue, nor the Valleys thing.

We're almost two years into this Tory-LibDem government, and it is beginning to bite. Labour have backpedalled themselves into terrified reticence on everything, just when we need clear opposition to the relentless austerity agenda. Plaid must make the running in articulating the alternative case in Wales. By a mile, Leanne looks like the candidate most up for that.

Tuesday 14 February 2012,
Owain Glyndŵr Institute, Machynlleth:
It's a sign of comfortable middle age that my Valentine's date this year is taking my mother-in-law to an Elin Jones campaign

---

4   The Welsh-speaking Welsh.
5   MP for Ceredigion 2000–5, AM for Mid & West Wales 2011–.
6   MP for Meirionnydd 1974–92, party leader 1984–91, AM for Dwyfor
     Meirionnydd 1999–, Assembly Presiding Officer 1999–2011, Member of
     the House of Lords 1992–.

meeting. There's a decent turnout, but it's low-key and business like, with none of the buzz of Leanne's meeting last month at the Cann Office.

Simon Thomas pulled out of the race last week, and threw his weight behind Elin. If she wins, she initially said that he would be her deputy, before it was pointed out that the post is elected by AMs and not in the gift of the boss. It looks like a stitch-up, and can only be indicative of panic in Camp Elin. Neither has she said anything about Simon's parting shot that Plaid would never "achieve government or electoral success by playing Fisher Price politics", widely seen as an artless attack on Leanne. I like Simon very much, but he is such a stirrer at times. Elin may well have acquired more of a liability than a deputy.

In a chilly room at the OGI, Elin presents a solid case for her leadership, and I've no doubt she'll do a good job if she gets it. She has a quiet authority and masses of experience; someone said the other day that she could be the Welsh Angela Merkel. On the flip side, she can come across on television as slightly hesitant, even dour. It's a shame, because I know from experience she's good fun.

I've already told Elin that I'm supporting Leanne, but that I wish her well. Her instant reply was pure politician: would I promise her my second preference vote? Yes, absolutely.

Wednesday 15 February 2012,
Morlan Centre, Aberystwyth:
A Plaid leadership hustings, and there are hundreds here. For a party that seems to be, at best, flatlining in the polls, the spirited *hwyl* of the occasion is astounding. Dafydd Êl comes out with some bizarrely baroque statements, as if he's given up any hope of winning and is now determined to make as much sport as possible. Elin is on great form in front of an adoring home crowd. Leanne does well, and from conversations I have with a few friends, she is picking up speed. I wish I'd put fifty quid on her at 5/1.

Thursday 15 March 2012,
A470, near Trawsfynydd, Gwynedd:
I've stopped the car to get the result of the leadership election. I can't find it on the radio, so take to Twitter. My timeline suddenly explodes with news of Leanne winning. She almost clinched it on first preferences, but it took the elimination of Dafydd Êl, and the redistribution of his second preferences, to get her over the line. I punch in my own tweet of congratulations, let out a little whoop, and then remember my promise to her. As I pull back into the traffic and head north to a gig in Caernarfon, I ponder what the next year may bring.

And for Leanne… will she cope? She's an amazingly strong and focused woman, and she's got a solid base at home, but this is going to test her to the hilt. She will need her comrades around her.

Friday 23 March 2012,
Ffos Las racecourse, Carmarthenshire:
Making good of my promise, I've booked in for Plaid Cymru's spring conference at the new racecourse on the site of an open cast mine near Llanelli. The sun is shining and the mood excitable. There's a wooden platform for photographs on the side of the racecourse, with a sign above it emblazoned with the word WINNER. The press photographers are trying to inveigle Leanne to pose there, but she's not having it.

Jill Evans, Plaid's MEP since 1999, sees me and scurries over for a chat. She and Leanne are old Rhondda comrades, sharing much of the same socialist outlook and heritage. I have never seen Jill this animated. She grasps my hands and chirrups, "isn't it amazing? We've[7] won! *We're* in control now."

There are a few familiar faces; none better to catch up with than Adam Price[8]'s parents. Last time I saw them was 23 years ago, when I stayed at their house as a student activist, having

---

7   i.e. the left of Plaid Cymru.
8   MP for Carmarthen East and Dinefwr 2001–10.

spoken at a Plaid training event nearby. I was remembered for years, so I'm told, as I helped with the washing up after tea, and by the sound of it was the first and possibly the last male to get his hands wet in the Price family kitchen sink. When Adam came out as gay to his parents, he used me – the fondly-remembered English boy who knew how to wield a Marigold – as a positive reference. It's really good to see them again, and Adam too. I have always hoped that he'll be First Minister one day.

For now though, the stage is all Leanne's, and she laps it up. Her arrival on stage, in a packed and hot function room, is almost messianic. We're on our feet cheering, cameras are flashing and a beam as wide as Cwm Rhondda splits her face. She gives a good speech, too – conciliatory, positive and with plenty of ideological red meat.

Thursday 29 March 2012,
Tafarn Dwynant, Ceinws, near Machynlleth:
My monthly pub quiz, and I sneak a picture of Leanne into one of the picture rounds, just to gauge how familiar she is to people who aren't political anoraks. Not very, is the answer. One team remembers her first name and one that she is that "Plaid Cymru woman". Two teams thought she was Jodie Foster.

Friday 13 April 2012,
Home:
Email from Leanne, encouraging those of us she feels are her closest allies, and who subscribe to "the project" as she calls it, to continue the spirit of the leadership campaign by working closely together on ideas, but also as a rebuttal force on social media. Right now, that's her main concern, and it's obvious why.

Before becoming leader, Leanne's highest profile media position was as an avowed republican, thanks initially to her infamous "Mrs Windsor" remark in the Assembly, shortly after she was first elected in 2003. Now that she is leader, Welsh

Labour, with their characteristic lack of finesse, have scheduled an entirely pointless debate in the Senedd to congratulate the Queen on her diamond jubilee. There's no precedent; no such debate took place for the golden jubilee ten years ago. It is just a trap for Leanne. In the email, she writes that "on 26th April, there is a jubilee celebration at Llandaf cathedral. I am coming under great pressure to attend. Senior party people are fearing a big, negative response from opposition and media (and possibly our own people), so a stream of tweeters and Facebook comments with defensive lines might be very helpful."

"Possibly our own people" must mean Dafydd Êl, never shy of a schmooze with royalty. He it was, of course, as Presiding Officer, who ordered the very pregnant Leanne out of the chamber for her "Mrs Windsor" remark all those years ago, making her the first AM to be temporarily excluded. This grudge goes back a long way, and as he is doubtless smarting after an unexpectedly poor last place in the leadership election, she is probably right to feel nervous. It's taken less than a month for the cold – and lonely – reality of leadership to bite.

Saturday 5 May 2012,
Y Plas, Machynlleth:
The third Machynlleth Comedy Festival, and already it feels like a permanent fixture. The town is buzzing. I'm chuffed to be part of the line-up with a one-man show, which sold out days ago and goes down a storm. It's the first proper stand-up I've done in years, and it's reminded me how much I love it. I really should do more, if I don't get sucked into the world of politics. That said, are they so very different? Showbiz for ugly people, and all that.

Tuesday 29 May 2012,
Home:
Carwyn Jones's love-in to the Queen in the "debate" celebrating her diamond jubilee. Leanne gives a brilliant speech, neatly

side-stepping all the traps. It is respectful, heartfelt and unexpectedly moving; she makes the point perfectly that this is "the chance to highlight the contribution, not just of one person, but that of an entire generation whose service and sacrifice we pay tribute to today."

All the other AMs (including no doubt one or two of her own) and all the journos and Twitterati were panting for her to say something they could tear to bits, but she waltzed through them all with such calm dignity. I'm so proud of her, and drop her a line to say so.

Friday 20 July 2012,
Home:
The Leanne-Dafydd Êl soap opera rolls on. Two days ago, he had the party whip withdrawn when he failed to turn up for a vote of no confidence in Health Minister Lesley Griffiths. She survived by one vote. Yesterday, Carwyn Jones cheekily invited him to join Labour. Today, the whip has been restored to him, and Leanne has issued a spectacularly furious statement. In it, she states that "the whip has never before been withdrawn from an elected member of Plaid Cymru. I do not expect, and will not accept, the party being placed in this position again." Turning to the noble Lord, she says "Dafydd's future role in Welsh politics is of course a matter for him. Whatever Dafydd decides to do we will respect his decision, but it is my wish to bring this matter, and this process to an end now and move on."

She is inviting him to walk the plank, it seems. He won't.

Friday 27 July 2012,
Home:
The Olympic opening ceremony in London, which is superb. Danny Boyle is a genius. It's the first time since I was about ten that I've seen something purportedly bigging up Britishness that sits so comfortably with me, for it is a celebration of our diversity, culture, wit and history of bloody-minded struggle. I have no problem with that take on this island's story; in fact, I

have no problem with Britishness per se. That is an inalienable fact of geography and history; it is wholly different to what might be called UK-ness. That I do have a problem with, and I wish we could more readily separate the two.

Boyle's ceremony is such a contrast with the diamond jubilee pageant on the Thames last month. Even had it not been pouring with rain, it still looked like something out of an Ealing comedy about a tinpot Ruritania. Tonight, looking at Twitter, I'm pleased to see that the Olympic ceremony has succeeded in annoying some of our least lovely public representatives. A Tory MP[9] tweets that it is "leftie multicultural crap", to which someone replies: "Can it, Tories. Your go was the Jubilee, and all you gave us was some old racists on a wet boat."

Saturday 28 July 2012,
Canolfan yr Urdd, Llangrannog, Ceredigion:
A leisurely drive down the coast to the Plaid Cymru summer school at the Urdd centre. It's my third trip to Llangrannog in as many months. A gang hired a cliff-top cottage for a few days in May, and then last month, three of us walked through doing the Ceredigion coast path. It is a magical spot.

Summer school is lively. There are lots of new and young members who have come to the party thanks to Leanne. The formal sessions are very good, particularly a blistering presentation from Adam Price about the inherent weaknesses of the Welsh economy. It is, he says, pointless even thinking about independence without getting to grips with that. Dozens of us do our bit for the local economy on the Saturday evening with a fabulous night outside the Pentre Arms, right on the beach.

Thursday 23 August 2012,
Cilfaesty Hill, near Dolfor, Powys:
A day's walking with Lynne Jones, who used to be my Labour MP in Birmingham, and has now retired to Radnorshire. I

---

9   Aidan Burley, MP for Cannock Chase. He stood down before the 2015 election.

worked on her campaign in 1992, when she won the seat from the Tories. On that grim night, when John Major confounded the polls with a surprise overall majority, Lynne's election was a rare flicker of joy. As was Cynog Dafis's startling leap from fourth to first place for Plaid in Ceredigion. Even never having lived in Wales at the time, I remember the electric thrill that coursed through me as the green flash appeared across the bottom of the screen.

In parliament, Lynne was one of the most consistent members of Labour's anti-Blair awkward squad. Little changed on the arrival of Gordon Brown as Prime Minister. As we squelch our way across the moors to the source of the River Teme, she tells me of the sole occasion she had a one-to-one meeting with PM Brown: "he fidgeted all the way through and never once looked me in the eye".

I ask her what she makes of Plaid, under new management. She and Leanne are cut from similar cloth politically, and although she's well aware of that, there is no budging her from loyalty to Labour. She – and I know, many other Labour voters – just cannot get past the N-word, nationalism. I understand the reticence, but it's just nonsense to think that there's no nationalism, of the UK variety, in Labour's history and outlook.

[Six weeks later, at the Labour conference in Manchester, leader Ed Miliband outlines his vision of "One Nation" Labour. In his speech, he uses the phrase 46 times, against the backdrop of massive Union Jacks. No nationalism there, of course.]

Saturday 8 September 2012,
Morlan Centre, Aberystwyth:
I'm speaking at a Cymdeithas yr Iaith rally in Aberystwyth, part of their fiftieth birthday celebrations. It coincides with a funeral for one of my old neighbours from Ceinws, but the rally is neatly timed between the service at Aberystwyth crematorium and the wake in Machynlleth, so I can squeeze it in.

I've thought long and hard about what to say in my speech.

As it's a birthday event, I decided to go back to the words that sparked Cymdeithas into life, Saunders Lewis's pivotal 1962 radio lecture, *Tynged yr Iaith*[10]. Right at the outset, he stated in his hypnotically wavering tone that if trends continued, Welsh would be dead as a living language by the year 2000. That belief framed his entire argument.

I wanted to take this idea on, because self-evidently he was wrong. Welsh is still with us, and despite massive pressures, is in relatively rude health. It may be that this is partly thanks to Lewis's warning all those years ago, for it fomented a boisterous revolution in public attitudes and policy, but I want to challenge the image of poor little Cymraeg coughing up blood on its deathbed, one that's been with us since at least the middle of the nineteenth century. Too many people – on both sides of the argument – are addicted to it.

Framing the debate only in terms of loss threatens to be dangerously counter-productive, for it helps fan the flames of the dreary anti-Welsh brigade and all their mutterings about having "a dead language forced down my throat". More to the point, it just isn't true. Welsh is a thing of beauty and of strength, a nonpareil inspiration to speakers of many other minority languages worldwide. This is the tone of my speech. It is listened to in polite silence, and I am given a perfunctory smatter of clapping.

A minute after I finish, and before I have to dash back to the funeral, the room erupts into thunderous applause. People stand up, cheering, as a dark, intense young man enters the hall. It is Jamie Bevan, who has just endured a fortnight in prison for refusing to acknowledge a court order sent repeatedly to him in English only. This is the stuff that has kept Cymdeithas roaring for five decades, and does so now. Jamie punches the air, and takes the stage. A workaday atmosphere has suddenly exploded into one of evangelical worship. I watch fascinated, and forgotten.

10   "The Fate of the Language".

Thursday 27 September 2012,
Old Library, Cardiff:
Launch night of *25/25 Vision: Welsh horizons across 50 years*, published to celebrate the silver anniversary of the Institute of Welsh Affairs. Edited by John Osmond and Peter Finch, the book is a fine collection of essays by twenty-five Welsh writers, me included. Our brief was to go back 25 years, and forward 25 years, and to see where that took our thinking with regards to Wales.

Always the class swot, I seem to be the only one who has taken our initial brief literally: my essay, 'Polls Apart', is about two elections, the real general election of 1987, when I was a student in London, and the imagined general election of an independent Wales in 2037. In that, I'm seventy and retired, having spent two terms as the Plaid Cymru AM for Montgomeryshire. Although the idea was tongue-in-cheek, within its frivolity there is a nugget of genuine interest, and I'm hoping someone might notice.

Monday 22 October 2012,
Home:
Leanne sends me a draft speech on heritage that she wants me to beef up. I put a little flesh on it and garland it with a few rhetorical twirls. Some jokes, too, though Leanne is not, by her own admission, the best gag-merchant in Welsh politics. Not in speeches anyway. She's razor sharp and hilarious out of school.

I'm faintly embarrassed how easily I slip into writing the "hopey, changey stuff", as Sarah Palin so memorably patronised the oratory of Obama. It comes too easily.

Saturday 3 November 2012,
Bro Ddyfi Leisure Centre, Machynlleth:
A Plaid training day with motivational guru Claire Howell. It's said that the SNP's transformation from hairy-arsed pugilists to sleek vote-winning machine is thanks to her. So

Plaid, hoping for some SNP stardust, has hired her. Leanne suggested I come along; she thought I'd find it interesting – and handy if I do indeed stand some time. I'm the only one here from Montgomeryshire; everyone else is Ceredigion or Gwynedd. Some are councillors, some branch and constituency officials.

Positivity is the name of the game. We each have to make a nameplate for ourselves, and write the words *Keep an Open Mind* on the side facing us. In the middle of the room, a pot is placed and we are told that if any negative thoughts bubble up, we are to chuck a penny into it. I have to lob one in straight away, just from hearing that. At various flashpoints throughout the afternoon, the pot pings with coins being hurled at it from all sides – though mainly from me.

We have to write down our goals and ambitions, which provokes much grunting and head-scratching. My list roams near and far, and only occasionally sounds like a 1970s beauty queen. It includes reconfiguration of the UK, a genuinely ethical foreign policy and a freshwater swimming pool dug from the spring at home. I sneak a look at the list of the young woman next to me. In big letters at the top, it says A WHITE RANGE ROVER.

Claire tells us that she worked with Alex Salmond and the high command of the SNP for years before the news leaked out. That, she says, is the kind of discipline we need. By contrast, days after her first weekend of training for Plaid[11], it was all over the *Western Mail*.

Saturday 24 November 2012,
Oriel Pendeitsh, Caernarfon:
Some readings to promote the IWA book. In front of a small but attentive audience, Bethan Gwanas, Rachel Trezise and I

---

11   Plaid's 11 AMs, 3 MPs, one MEP and Lord Dafydd Wigley attended the residential weekend course at Gregynog, near Newtown, in September 2012.

discuss our contributions. I read my chapter out, including my fanciful imaginings of twenty-five years hence as a retired Plaid Cymru AM.

"So, would you be seriously interested in being a politician then?" asks Bethan, after I finish. "You know, for real?"

I answer without hesitation, "Yes, absolutely." That it comes out so automatically is a surprise even to me, and it's the first time I've ever said it out loud in public. It hangs in the air, and no-one laughs.

Tuesday 4 December 2012,
Home:
The annual Welsh Political Awards tonight, always painful to watch. The impression is of overpaid people in a tiny bubble slapping each other on the back. Worse, the winners are always spread suspiciously evenly among the four main parties, so that every press officer has at least one good story to spin. It makes the parties look interchangeable and Welsh politics unadventurous and smug.

Before the ceremony, an email from Leanne tells those of us in "the project" that she has won the Campaigner of the Year award, specifically in recognition of her outsider-to-winner leadership campaign. She obviously feels slightly compromised by it, so assures us that "as you all helped to make that happen, I wanted to give you all a confidential heads-up ahead of it, so that you can all take something from it too". They always say that. "Award ceremonies are not my thing", she also assures us, but they always say that too – at least, until they're in the running to win one.

Thursday 3 January 2013,
Home:
A late festive visit from Leanne and family, and a terrific day out in the Dysynni valley, and then a wet walk on the beach at Aberdyfi. Although Leanne's been quite poorly over Christmas, she is bubbling with ideas and raring to get back

into the fray. I just don't know where she finds the energy.

One purpose of the visit is to persuade me to apply to go on the Plaid register of potential candidates. I don't take much persuasion. Leanne is thrilled, and will do all she can to help, though she is evidently regarded by quite a large section of the party hierarchy with considerable suspicion – and not just Dafydd Êl. There are plenty of other older men, party stalwarts for decades, who cannot quite get their heads around her youth, her feminism, her socialism, her lack of Welsh, even her republicanism. Her election after Ieuan Wyn was a seismic cultural and generational shift for the party, and seismic shifts invariably have casualties.

Saturday 2 February 2013,
Plaid Cymru HQ, Cardiff:
My interview for Plaid's register of potential election candidates. I've never been to the new Tŷ Gwynfor[12] before. It's in that no man's land between Cardiff city centre and the Bay, a dustbowl of busy roads, crumbling Victoriana, razor-wired demolition sites and Legoland modernism. The Plaid HQ is in a dispiriting modern block, overlooking the wind-whipped waters of Atlantic Wharf.

There are a few of us being screened today; we swap bright words and nervous smiles while waiting to be ushered individually into the meeting room, where a three-member interview panel awaits us. Our task is to start with a five-minute presentation, and then take their questions. After my presentation, we have an interesting discussion about the enduring problem of Plaid's public image.

It's a perception that I call "Old Testament". To many Welsh people, the personification of Plaid Cymru would be an austere chapel elder with untamed eyebrows and a lingering smell of camphor. The discussion comes after I mention a recent Stonewall Cymru poll about perception amongst LGBT people

---

12   Plaid Cymru HQ, named after Gwynfor Evans.

of the different parties in Wales: Plaid came fifth in terms of perceived queer-friendliness, beating only Respect, UKIP and the BNP. This despite the party's exemplary record over the years on LGBT issues; not for nothing did Tory rottweiler Rod Richards[13] describe Plaid as "the poofs' party".

We talk too of the specifics of Montgomeryshire. One of the panel is the redoubtable Heledd Fychan, who was the county's candidate in the 2010 general election. She did a great job in upping the vote and winning many new friends, and shares my belief that with serious graft, a prevailing wind and a candidate who can nurse it over at least a couple of elections, it is a seat that Plaid should be aiming to win at Assembly level. Up until 2010, when Lembit Öpik managed to throw it away, Montgomeryshire had been the most consistently Liberal seat in Britain, having been represented at Westminster by the party for all but four years of the last 130. The following year, they lost the Assembly seat too, and now that the Liberal-voting habit has been broken (and for many, it *was* nothing more than habit), everything could be up for grabs.

The interview goes well enough, at least until the final question: what would you do if the party whip and your own view were opposed? I was expecting to be asked this, but even so hadn't quite yet formulated a comfortable answer, so what comes out is largely impromptu. And that is that if the vote concerned an area in which I had some expertise, or felt strongly about, then there is no way I could or would toe the party line. For some reason, I feel the need to emphasize this, and possibly slightly overdo it. Threatening to denounce your party publically is a curious way to end an interview to become one of its representatives.

And that was it. Thanks, handshakes and ejected out into the barren streets. I walk distractedly back into the city centre; it is the first Six Nations Saturday, and the Irish are in town.

---

13   Colourful BBC newsreader turned Tory MP for Clwyd NW (1992–7) and regional AM for North Wales (1999–2002). Now in UKIP.

The pubs and streets are overflowing; I weave my way through the beery throngs feeling pleasantly invisible. I also feel certain that I will not be accepted on to Plaid's register of candidates, as my last answer must have rung enough alarm bells to wake the dead: *warning, loose cannon!*

Tuesday 12 February 2013,
Home:
Email from Tŷ Gwynfor: I have been accepted on the Plaid Cymru national register of candidates. They are delighted. So am I – and a little amazed. The doorsteps of Welshpool and Newtown may beckon.

Thursday 28 February 2013,
Home:
The Eastleigh by-election today, caused by the Shakespearian downfall of Chris Huhne[14]. A preening twerp he may be, but I couldn't help but feel a shiver of pity for him, in that his ruinous "crime", getting his wife to take his speeding points on her driving licence and then lying about it, had only escaped into the public sphere because their domestic life had imploded. Such liberal sympathies shrivel up the minute I see a photo of his car, number plate H11 HNE. Throw away the key.

The by-election is a battle between the Ugly Sisters of the coalition government and the even more hideous pantomime dame of Nigel Farage. My attention though is taken by Labour's candidate, writer, broadcaster, and ever-reliable satirical turn, John O'Farrell. For those of us of a certain age and political mien, his *Things Can Only Get Better* had us nodding in painful recognition and laughing at the collective lunacy of being young, left and furious in the dark days of Thatcherism.

He's stood before for Labour, as the no-hope candidate for his home town of Maidenhead in the 2001 general election, but his

---

14   LibDem MP for Eastleigh 2005–13, Secretary of State for Energy and Climate Change in the coalition government 2010–12, jailbird 2013.

eleventh-hour adoption as the Labour candidate in Eastleigh is altogether different. There's the searchlight media scrutiny of a knife-edge by-election, the fact that he is far better known now than he was then, and the booming amplification of the blogosphere and social media; indeed O'Farrell's candidature only came about when he idly expressed his interest on Twitter.

At first, almost everyone welcomes this apparently new-fangled way of doing politics. Some commentators even foresee a surprise Labour leapfrogging of both coalition partners to produce John O'Farrell MP, and proof that under Ed "One Nation" Miliband, Labour could start to win once again in southern England.

The papers, of course, have something to say about that. They trawl through his various memoirs and find passages that they know will inflame their apoplectic readership. One describes O'Farrell's youthful ambivalence about the 1984 Brighton bomb, and the survival of Margaret Thatcher that night; the other his similarly off-message views of the Falklands conflict two years earlier.

This is the rocket fuel they crave. O'Farrell's ancient comments are ritually disemboweled of context, magnified and shrieked over. "Is Ed's pal the sickest man in politics?" howls a headline in the *Mail on Sunday*, the weekend before polling. An acquiescent Tory MP[15] lands the first question at PMQs the day before the by-election: "Does the Prime Minister agree that it is totally unacceptable for Members or prospective Members of this House to say anything that supports terrorism?"

Cranking his outrage dial up to the max, David Cameron does indeed agree: "Frankly, it is absolutely staggering that someone is standing for public office who has said this: 'In October 1984, when the Brighton bomb went off, I felt a surge of excitement at the nearness of Margaret Thatcher's demise. And yet disappointment that such a chance had been missed'. Those are the words of the Labour candidate in the Eastleigh

---

15 Richard Drax, Tory MP for South Dorset.

by-election. They are a complete disgrace and I hope that the Leader of the Labour party will get up and condemn them right now." It's fine though, presumably, to have spent the same era trashing Oxfordshire restaurants in a morning suit over a *Hang Nelson Mandela* T-shirt.

The LibDems, having thrown absolutely everything at the campaign, squeak home in Eastleigh with 32 per cent of the vote. UKIP are second, the Tories' third, both scoring over a quarter. In fourth place, John O'Farrell nets just under 10 per cent. In interviews after the result, he looks exhausted, haunted even, and a whole ten years older than he did a little more than a fortnight before, when he was selected. Sadly, a candidate with an extensive hinterland in both writing and comedy seems to provoke just one likely outcome: things can only get bitter.

Friday 15 March 2013,
Home:
Leanne has finally announced where she is going to stand in 2016: Rhondda. She decided a while ago to demonstrate her faith in an imminent Plaid government by abandoning the safety net of the regional list, and to stand in a constituency instead. The idea – leading from the front, she's called it – has been rather obsessing her lately, so I'm glad it's finally decided, though as I've said quite plainly to her, I think it's daft, and for several reasons.

Most regrettably, I think she is inadvertently rubbishing the status of regional AMs. They're already perceived as second class; this only reinforces it. The system of electing AMs unquestionably needs a radical overhaul, but this doesn't tackle the issue. I worry too that it will mean a concentration of resources, energy and time in one place, which could be damaging for party morale.

Ironically, this sweat and confected media kerfuffle will almost certainly come to nothing anyway. Labour only introduced the rule outlawing dual candidacy in both a constituency and regional list out of sheer spite. Now that they're out of government, it is nigh on inevitable that the rule will be changed back, in which case, she'll have a fall-back position on the list anyway.

Wednesday 10 April 2013,
Home:
Leanne stays at ours on her way up to Anglesey, where there are council elections taking place in a few weeks time. I'm going up there with her tomorrow. Just before we all retire for the night, she says quietly to me, "Why don't you put your name forward to be the Westminster candidate in Ceredigion?"

Like most people, I've only experienced a handful of real "eureka moments", when a perfect idea has blasted out of nowhere straight into fully-formed reality. This is one of them, and it makes my heart race with exhilaration. I go to bed, and lie there with my synapses exploding with connections and possibilities. Of course! Why had I never thought of it before?

Ceredigion is only five miles down the road. It's where I first lived when I moved to Wales; I'd still be there had I been able to afford it. Aberystwyth is my town in a way that Welshpool or Newtown, Montgomeryshire's largest, will never be. And, as Leanne points out, I've been quite rude in print and on telly about Newtown, which would undoubtedly resurface if I stood here. Aside from a faint sneer at Borth in the first couple of editions of the *Rough Guide,* I have never had much of a downer on anywhere in Ceredigion. Quite the opposite in fact; I've always raved about it.

Then there's the Westminster factor. I'd presumed that if I was going to stand for anything, it would be for the Assembly, but as a textbook Middle Englander, I could be far more useful as an ambassador for Plaid in London. It is much needed: with the Scottish referendum next year and the ongoing ructions over our membership of the EU, the constitution of our country is facing fundamental changes. I would love to play my part and help break the stubborn taboo that to be an advocate of Wales, or of a different constitutional settlement, you have therefore to be inherently "anti-English" in some way. My life and my writing both give lie to that. It is perfectly possible to love both England and Wales, love them with a passion, but not to believe that an eighteenth-century structure, one created explicitly for imperial gung-ho and rapid industrialisation, is the best way of running either.

The crunch though is that Ceredigion is very, very winnable. The LibDems benefited from a perfect storm last time when their majority soared to well over eight thousand, but Plaid held the Westminster seat ten years ago and they've kept it throughout at Assembly level. And there would the exquisite irony in taking on the party that was my first true love in politics.

From being a Liberal member at fourteen, I've long known that their noble words rarely match the grubby reality of their deeds; that they'll do anything and say anything to win, for they are universally heralded as the filthiest fighters in politics. Their first stint in government for eighty years has demonstrated this truth to all. Long-cherished principles were swiftly hurled overboard in their hunger for the trappings of power, from the cars and grace-and-favour country houses to the upsurge of new Lords, knights and MBEs among their ranks.

While busily filling their own boots, the LibDems have helped create and sustain one of the most punitive right-wing governments we have ever seen, and like the weedy kid egging on the playground bully, they've even thrown in some contributions of their own to the Tories' ideological war: privatisation of the Royal Mail for instance, the brainchild of Vince Cable and something supported by every single LibDem MP. I would relish taking them on.

I fall into a contented but excited sleep. This is going to happen.

Thursday 11 April 2013,

Aberffraw, Ynys Môn:

Leanne drives us both up to Ynys Môn, where there are local elections in a few weeks. Everywhere else in Wales held their council elections last year, but true to form for this obdurate island, the administration of Ynys Môn council had collapsed by then and was being run by Welsh Government commissioners. Famously having elected MPs from all four main Welsh parties since the war, Anglesey is the island that will not be told by anyone. Only Ceredigion comes close in the bloody-mindedness stakes. The two constituencies have a lot in common.

Some good canvassing in villages on the west of the island, and we round off the day with local Pleidwyr[16] in a pub in Llangefni, before heading over the bridge to stay with friends in Llanrug. There is a palpable sense of excitement among Plaid members at the moment. A year on, Leanne is unquestionably getting into her stride, and the further she is away from the spin doctors and image makers, the better she gets. All afternoon, canvassing in Aberffraw, she engages honestly and thoroughly with everyone she meets, from young mums taking a walk in the spring sunshine to a couple of toothless old farm boys straight out of a Kyffin painting.

In the car, we talk about Ceredigion. I've not had much chance yet to discuss it with Preds, but I know that he is up for it if I am. And I most definitely am. Occasionally, all the signs line up and point in the same direction. This looks like one of those times. Adam Price's words, from when I was contemplating becoming a candidate a few months ago, echo in my head: "If not now, when?"

---

16 Members of Plaid Cymru.

Friday 12 April 2013,
Bishop's Castle, Shropshire:
After another day's canvassing on Anglesey, Mabon ap Gwynfor[17] gives me a lift to the station in Bangor. He very nearly won the Ceredigion nomination last time round, for the 2010 election. It was a much hotter ticket then, aiming to overturn a LibDem majority of 219, rather than the more precipitous 8,324 this time round. There were three of them up for it: Mabon, Siôn Jobbins and the eventual winner, Penri James. At the time, most people I knew thought that Mabon should, and would, win it. I ask him what went wrong, and he says that the majority of the party faithful in Ceredigion are quite conservative in their outlook, and that he was regarded as just too young and fiery for the job. Penri, a long-standing councillor and rock solid Cardi, was thought to be a far safer pair of hands.

Train from Bangor to Craven Arms, where Preds meets me and we head off for a night in Bishop's Castle. He tells me to go for Ceredigion, if that's what I want, and that he'll keep the home fires burning, but won't be out there being a political spouse, pulling raffles and smiling for photos. In the two years since we moved, he has made our new house such a fabulous home, and I ache with love and gratitude for his quiet, dazzling talent. If I do go for it, a secure home, with him at its heart, will be the most important thing of all.

He suggests too that I should think about the impact this might have on my writing. Standing for Westminster in Ceredigion will be far higher profile, and much more of a commitment, than making up the numbers in Montgomeryshire; there will be precious little space left in my head for anything creative and it will, he's sure, mean that I have to put my work aside for the duration. Perhaps he's right, but I feel that it is something I can manage, and with a small

---

17   Oftentime candidate for Westminster and Assembly elections, and grandson of Gwynfor Evans, Plaid Cymru's first MP (and party leader 1945–81).

cushion of savings, this may well be the only time in my life that I can afford to go for it.

We book in to our B&B in Bishop's Castle and head out to the pub to meet my big sister Sue and her boyfriend Andy. It's our regular rendezvous, and our usual evening of good beer, food and laughter. They all think that I should try. Sue almost gets tearful and starts talking about my "destiny". I get another round in.

Tuesday 23 April 2013,
Home:
Nominations to be the Plaid candidate in Ceredigion close. I hear that there are two others in for it, though cannot yet discover any more details. Word is evidently out among Plaid people, though, as I've suddenly gained a whole load of new followers on Twitter. That's where the political action is, it seems. Barely a day goes by without a round robin email from Plaid HQ, encouraging us all to tweet positively about the message of the day, or any media appearance by the leadership.

Tuesday 30 April 2013,
Aberystwyth Arts Centre:
I meet an old Plaid Ceredigion mate for a *paned* in Aberystwyth. He is very encouraging, though far less optimistic than me that we can recapture the seat in one go. I ask him what went so badly wrong last time round, and he immediately says, "sorry to say, but it was the choice of candidate. Penri is a good guy, but he just doesn't come across too well on the doorstep. He didn't have much chit-chat, and though that shouldn't matter, it does for many people. It made a hell of a difference unfortunately."

Tuesday 14 May 2013,
Home:
I finally put a public statement out on my blog that I am running for Ceredigion. Entitled *MP MP?*, it gets a fair bit of attention and throughout the day, I receive loads of encouraging tweets,

texts and emails. It's very heartening, and there's no going back now.

Most of the people who know me conclude that I am probably having a mid-life crisis. On balance though, they seem to think that trying to become a Plaid Cymru MP is preferable to buying a Harley Davidson. Though there is one phrase that keeps coming at me, from almost all of the people who know me best: "that's great, but... but, you really are going to have to develop a thicker skin for this, you know." I do know. Like most writers, my hide is gossamer thin and bruises far too readily. That won't do in politics.

Wednesday 15 May 2013,
Y Plas, Machynlleth:
I've finally found out who I'm up against for the nomination: Owain Davies and Doug Jones. They're both new members who have come to Plaid through the Ceredigion Against the Cuts campaign. "It's a choice between two Trots and an Englishman," sneers a local LibDem online.

Evening at the Dyfi Biosphere AGM, where there are numerous local bigwigs, including many from Ceredigion. A few quietly wish me well. There are a lot of buzzwords – facilitation, empowerment, community, partnership, stakeholders and so on – but it all seems very woolly. I've managed to steer clear of these sort of meetings for years, but perhaps not for much longer.

Friday 17 May 2013,
Morlan Centre, Aberystwyth:
I've arranged to see Cynog Dafis at his home in Llandre, on my way into Aberystwyth. He's extremely helpful, although not prepared to make any public endorsement, which is fair enough. In any case, he tells me, he's pretty semi-detached from the action these days. He says that he didn't much enjoy his eight years in Westminster, though he is proud of a few achievements, particularly in environmental matters.

Into Aberystwyth, and a meet up at Baravin with the inner circle of today's Plaid Ceredigion: AM Elin Jones, Simon Thomas, Cynog's successor as MP and now a regional AM, and Owen Roberts, Elin's communications chief in the party's Aberystwyth office. They are keen to impress on me that the party machine in Ceredigion is sleek, streamlined and ready for action, and will be there for me all the way. Simon is happy to declare his support publicly, but obviously neither Elin nor Owen can do so, although they will help steer me in the right direction. Their support is purely pragmatic, from the belief that I'm the likeliest of the three potential candidates to win the seat back.

Owen has only lately jumped from being a history lecturer at Aberyswtyth University to working for Plaid, though he's been involved with the party for years, and was part of Penri's campaign in 2010. He winces at the memory of the eve-of-poll rally held on a busy Saturday morning in the centre of Aberystwyth, addressed by Penri, Elin, Dafydd Iwan, Ieuan Wyn Jones, Jill Evans, Elfyn Llwyd and, in what was supposed to be something of a coup, Ron Davies. "A big crowd all turned inwards, all those shouty speeches, and folk chanting *Pen-ri! Pen-ri! Pen-ri!* – it looked like a bloody Nazi rally. I dread to think what people trying to do their shopping must have made of it" he sniffs. I like him.

We talk about John O'Farrell's doomed candidature in the Eastleigh by-election, something that has slightly spooked me. I remind them that I've got more than twenty years worth of writing, literally millions of words, out there, covering the full gamut of sex, drugs, rock 'n' roll – and politics. "That might be a problem if this were a by-election," says Simon, "but honestly, in a general election, I can't imagine that anyone will bother digging that hard."

I stay in Aberystwyth for the European election hustings that evening at the Morlan. There are five candidates, though it really doesn't matter who comes anything other than top, as Wales is now down to four MEPs. We have no chance of winning more than one, and even that might be a struggle. Jill Evans, who's been our MEP since 1999, is almost certain to win top place on our slate, though I put her as number 2, behind Marc Jones of Wrexham. He is an excellent man with rock solid politics, a real community champion and very hard grafter.

Friday 24 May 2013,
Y Talbot, Tregaron:
Fundraising auction for the local Plaid branch, at which Leanne is the guest of honour. She invited me along as her plus one, a chance to be seen and shake a few useful hands. Dai Jones Llanilar does the auction, and brilliantly. He is hilarious, and I particularly love how in between lots he rests the gavel on top of his belly, as if it were a shelf.

Leanne is sat one side of me, and on the other Meredydd Evans and his American-born wife, Phyllis Kinney. One of the most legendary of Welsh musical couples, now both well into their nineties, they are the sweetest and most stimulating company. There are some other fascinating people there, too, and most unexpectedly, I really enjoy the evening.

The only note of discord comes from Tregaron's Plaid councillor, Catherine Hughes, a powerhouse of a woman who tells me how deeply unhappy they are locally about the actions of the Plaid-run Ceredigion council, who are cutting services here to the bone. A few party members have resigned, and there's a very sour mood out there towards us, she says. Pinning the blame where it really lies, on the cuts from central government that are then disproportionately walloped on to rural councils by the Labour Assembly administration, is so difficult. I know that if I do win the nomination, it's a theme that will dominate the next two years.

Wednesday 29 May 2013,
Hay Literature Festival:
I'm speaking at Hay in an event about community activism,

and one of my fellow panelists runs a growing tourism business in south Ceredigion. He's a dynamic and bright bloke who moved to the area from London a few years ago. We agree on very many things, and have pretty similar backgrounds and experience, but he is distinctly unimpressed with Plaid. To him, in his part of the county, the party seems clannish and exclusive, and highly suspicious of tourism. Some of that, I suspect, is his projection, but I'm sure there's some truth in there too.

Thursday 6 June 2013,
Llety Parc Hotel, Aberystwyth:
First hustings for the nomination at the end of a glorious summer's day. I am terrified, but strangely calm. There are about eighty party members in the hotel's function room, including some familiar faces. This is the first time I've met my two fellow candidates. Both have come to Plaid relatively recently through their union work, Owain at the county council, and Doug at the National Library. None of us has ever done this before, so we're a little shrill and nervous, and keen to get on with it.

It seems to go well enough. My pitch is that we need to win the seat back, and nothing less, if we are to generate momentum towards the Assembly elections in 2016. In order to have any chance of winning, we need to build new alliances, something I believe I'm ideally placed to do. I make it clear that this not just about electoral expediency; too many of our communities are strained and anxious, and I want to help invite incomers in to the Welsh way of life, to stimulate their curiosity and sense of belonging.

I do about a quarter of my speech in Welsh. Owain, who grew up near Cardiff, is a Welsh learner too, though he is less confident than me in using it publically. His speech is thoughtful and interesting, if a little hesitant. Doug, a native of Ceredigion, does most of his speech in Welsh, but tries to pack way too much into it and ends up rattling it out at a hundred miles an hour. It's a shame, because there is some excellent stuff in it.

There are stacks of questions, on the economy, education, health, Cymraeg, broadband, Plaid's future strategy. After two hours of sweaty speechifying, the chair says that we'll take one more question, and is that alright with the three of us? Yes, yes, of course, we say, and for some stupid reason I expect a light-hearted finale to the evening, the kind you sometimes get on *Question Time*, something like "what historical figures would you most like to go for a picnic with?" or "which book would you save from a burning building?" Sadly, instead it's a question about badgers, and our attitude to their mass extermination. We all mumble fairly unconvinced and unconvincing replies, and the evening peters out like a sagging balloon. The relief of having got through it without saying anything too stupid is immense.

Hard to gauge how people are voting. I get a few sly smiles and thumbs-up from people, but Cardis are a famously inscrutable bunch, and I really have no idea.

Friday 14 June 2013,
Ysgol Bro Siôn Cwilt, near New Quay, Ceredigion:
The second and final hustings meeting, in a shiny new primary school. It's a smaller turnout this time, twenty or so, mostly grey-haired men with their arms folded firmly towards us. This is going to be a tougher gig than last week's in comparatively cosmopolitan Aberystwyth.

One questioner asks if we will commit ourselves to fighting two elections, because that's what it will take to win the seat back. My response is that for perhaps the first time, the conditions look to be in Plaid's favour for a Westminster election, so of course we can succeed in one go, and I don't want to hear any nay-saying on the matter. I sound like Mary Poppins, and no-one looks very convinced. After the questions, we are bundled into the primary school's library to see the votes being counted. The walls are covered in cheery colours and enthusiastic slogans; the chairs are dolls' house tiny.

It quickly becomes clear that I have won the nomination, with nearly three quarters of the first preference votes. Elin Jones turns to me. "Are you quite sure you know what you've let yourself in for?" she asks. Well no, I don't. However, as something of a political anorak who'd observed every election since 1979 from the sidelines, I thought that was probably training enough.

Back into the hall, where most people have stayed for the denouement. Geraint, the election organiser, announces the result and I say a few words of thanks, some in Welsh, but mainly in English. There are big smiles all round, and people line up to shake my hand. As Llinos Dafis, Cynog's wife, does so, she looks me straight in the eye and says, "Llongyfarchiadau – ond nawr, rhaid i ti ddysgu sut i wneud dy wleidyddiaeth yn y Gymraeg."[18] I nod and smile, slightly frozen. This is one towering responsibility.

Leaving the school, I am in a daze and sit in the car to tug deeply on a fag and call home. Preds has already seen the news on Twitter. "Llongyfarchiadau," he says on picking up the phone, and then, without pausing for breath, "what the fuck have you done this time?"

---

18   "Congratulations – but now, you must learn how to do your politics in Welsh."

ALL EARS

June – December 2013

Saturday 15 June 2013,
Penarth, Vale of Glamorgan:
Quick stop in Aberystwyth, en route to Penarth and a friend's fortieth birthday party. Plaid Cymru National Council is meeting at the Morlan Centre, so I call by and am enthusiastically greeted by all. It's a wonderful feeling. I've had texts, tweets and emails by the score too. All seem to be expecting great things from me. I hope I can do them justice.

We arrive at the party, and everyone is out in the back garden. There's a table of mates from Machynlleth, who break into cheery cat-calling when they see me. To mask my faint embarrassment, I plaster on a grin and go round pumping the hands of all the lads.

"Blimey," my friend Liz breathes into my ear, "you worked that table just like a proper politician. God help us."

Monday 17 June 2013,
Home:
A blizzard of emails to sort through, all very positive. Owen Roberts in the Plaid office in Aberystwyth wants me to hit the ground running, as do I. He's trying to slot me in to various meetings and photo opportunities. I think we'll work together well; from what I can gather, our political outlook is similar, and we both have a nerdy fascination with the nuts and bolts of it all too. On top of that, he's good company.

It looks like I'm not the only new Plaid candidate entering from left field. Ieuan Wyn Jones has announced that he is quitting the Assembly, in order to head up the Menai Science Park. It's all very sudden. Of course, conspiracy theories are circling, that he couldn't bear staying under Leanne's leadership, but I think it's a wise move, for him and the party. Rhun ap Iorwerth, the BBC political correspondent, is in the frame to become the candidate for the ensuing by-election in Ynys Môn. I saw Leanne briefly in Aberystwyth on Saturday, and she is very excited about both of us. In April, she showed me her handwritten wish list of dream candidates for Westminster and the Assembly. It seems to be coming true.

Tuesday 18 June 2013,
Burry Port, Carmarthenshire:
A day's recording for the BBC around Ceredigion and northern Pembrokeshire. It's a series I'm presenting for Radio Wales, provisionally called *The New Welsh*, about incomers and their hopes, dreams and fears for their new life on this side of the border. When I decided to go for the Ceredigion nomination, I asked the Beeb whether that was likely to be a problem for them, or any kind of compromise to the series. No, they assured me. On winning it last week, the producer contacted them once more to double check. Again, no problem. And I guess not; there are plenty of politicians, past, present and doubtless future fronting BBC series.

I'm glad they're OK with it, because it's hugely interesting and is raising some important issues about identity and the modern movements of people – topics that rarely make it on air in anything but the most sensationalised of ways. Today we met some fascinating people, and got some thoughtful interviews from them. For so many of them – us – Wales has provided a deep, nourishing sense of home, and we are desperate to repay that, in whatever inadequate ways we can.

On the way back to stay at director Gaynor's place in Burry Port, we stop for food. The landlord of the rural pub we land in has a bee in his bonnet about a local windfarm application, and when Gaynor tells him that I have just been selected as Plaid candidate in neighbouring Ceredigion, there is no stopping him. Even as we try and eat, he pulls up a chair and harangues me about the windfarm, and then broadens it out into disdain for politics and politicians in general. This, I realise with a thud, is going to be my life for the foreseeable future.

Wednesday 19 June 2013,
Lampeter, Ceredigion:
Another day of recording for the BBC series. One of the interviews today was with an estate agent in Lampeter. He was disarmingly frank about how they market part of their housing stock squarely at incomers: most remote and/or period properties, and those houses whose winter damp or dark are not evident on the lovely May day when the new owners first clap excited eyes on it. Often, he said, the same place will be back on the market two or three years down the line, ripe and ready for the next couple of starry-eyed downshifters. Not great for the strength and continuity of the local community, he readily admits, but terrific for his business.

Wednesday 26 June 2013,
Marine Hotel, Aberystwyth:
An open meeting, organised by the Aberystwyth branch of Plaid, to introduce me as the new candidate. It's been a golden summer's day, and as the evening sun bakes the hotels along the prom, I wonder who on earth is going to bother coming out for a political meeting on a midsummer night like this? If I had any choice, I'd definitely be on the beach.

Over thirty people show up, and pack into the small and increasingly sweltering room. I speak, outlining a bit of my background and ideas, and try and answer why I'm entering politics. Essentially, it is my fury at growing inequality that propelled me into standing, and very much linked to that, a certainty that the UK as a nation-state has had its day. "In this room, there will be many different reasons for being Plaid: cultural, linguistic, family, community, even romantic," I say. "Mine is sadly unromantic. It's a cold, hard pebble of certainty that no Westminster government, of any colour, understands Wales, and it never will."

I talk of my respect for Leanne and Elin, and the mighty potential of our area. One of my topics is tourism, and how we cannot wish it away as a tool of oppression, as some say.

That is a principle you can afford only if you yourself never go and be a tourist elsewhere. Otherwise, it is just hypocrisy. On the other hand, those who argue that tourism is the only show in town are wrong too, for that is when it tips into cultural prostitution. We must strive to make it better, and as part of a mixed economy. I set Aberystwyth the challenge of becoming the Donostia/San Sebastián of Wales.

The organisers are cock-a-hoop, particularly because a fair proportion of those who came are new faces. People seem genuinely excited by me as a different kind of candidate; I just hope it translates into them getting properly stuck in. Complacency has been the Plaid Ceredigion downfall too many times before.

Thursday 27 June 2013,
Elin Jones's house, Aberaeron:
An afternoon with photographer Marian Delyth taking promotional pictures of me in various locations. We finish off at Elin Jones's new house in Aberaeron. She only moved in at the weekend, but you'd never know it – the place is immaculate and looks like she's been there forever. We've been in Rhiw Goch over two years, and there are still dozens of unpacked boxes.

In her garden, overlooking the town's handsome harbour, we pose together for the camera. As we stand there with fixed smiles, Elin whispers out of the corner of her mouth, "Here we are again. First it was Cynog. Then Simon. Then Penri. And now it's you. I've seen all you boys off!" We laugh – her slightly more than me.

Friday 28 June 2013,
Plaid Cymru office, Aberystwyth:
First campaign group meeting, and everyone is quietly excited. I've asked people to prepare what they think are the pros and cons of both me and my main opponent, the incumbent Liberal Democrat MP, Mark Williams. I'm

47

expecting a rigorous inquisition about my writing, and the million or more words I've put out there over the last twenty-plus years as a freelancer.

Instead, the only three drawbacks identified about me are:

- "the gay thing", as it is decorously put.
- that I live just over the county border. I have, of course, measured it on the map. It is 4.9 miles as the crow flies.
- my ear-ring, a stainless steel loop about a centimetre wide. Strangely enough, the only male MP ever to have sported one was Simon Thomas. The memory of his ear-ring still seems to haunt many in Ceredigion, as if it played a significant part in his downfall.

"What about my writing?" I ask. "It's not all been the *Rough Guide to Wales*, you know." "Oh, don't worry," I'm told, "it'll be fine."

Monday 1 July 2013,
Home:
Email from the BBC: "Sorry for this change but we are going to move *New Welsh* to the New Year. Steve wants to make something much bigger of it – 'a focus' or spotlight or even a season – and we feel we can't really do that for September. The line would be: 'In the year that Scotland goes to the polls etc'…" Exciting.

Wednesday 10 July 2013,
Home:
An ear infection has knocked out the hearing in my good ear, and I'm almost completely deaf. I can't even use the phone. Since losing an eardrum almost twenty years ago, I've got reasonably used to partial hearing, but the sudden disappearance of the remainder is terrifying. It's very odd timing: I become a politician and immediately go deaf.

Monday 15 July 2013,
Home:
Someone asks me what an MP earns, and I realise – with slightly perverse pride – that I don't know. I haven't looked. Now that the point has been raised though, I have to find out. A quick google later, and I discover that it is £67,000, plus an assortment of expenses. Even the basic rate is getting on for three times as much as I've ever earned in a single year.

Monday 22 July 2013,
Llangefni, Ynys Môn:
The Ynys Môn by-election campaign is going full throttle, with polling next week. It's all happened very quickly. In the space of just a couple of weeks, Rhun ap Iorwerth left his job as a BBC political correspondent, joined Plaid, was accepted on to the national register of candidates and then selected as the by-election candidate. It is quite a coup – he's a star, and he knows it. Next to someone so gleaming and confident, I feel such a lump.

Leanne, Rhuanedd and almost all of the Tŷ Gwynfor staff have decamped to Anglesey for the duration of the campaign, as witnessed by my Twitter timeline, full every day of photos of grinning, sunburned canvassers. I've promised to go up and help, but am still almost stone deaf, so all I can usefully do is a day's leafleting around Llangefni. It's very frustrating, and horribly isolating.

At campaign headquarters, I see Elin Jones who is grinning from ear to ear. "It's going brilliantly," she has to shout to me. "We're really playing the local card, that Rhun and his wife both grew up here and are bringing up their young family on the island. We're banging that home, local local local, time and again, and it's working a treat." Indeed, the leaflets, most of which look to be visually modelled on *Take a Break* magazine, are chock-full of pictures of Rhun and his photogenic progeny. "It's not a strategy that's going to work very well for my campaign," I say to Elin, a little sourly. She smiles and shrugs, and dashes back out to glad-hand some more voters.

Wednesday 24 July 2013,
Bronglais Hospital, Aberystwyth:
At last, the antibiotics have kicked in, and the hearing in my working ear has started to improve. My regular ENT consultant at Bronglais, Mr Morgan, cleans out the infected ear, and suddenly I'm back in a world of birdsong and music. Even the traffic sounds good. I almost weep with relief – how true is the old adage, that you don't know what you've got till it's gone?

Thursday 1 August 2013,
Home:
The Ynys Môn by-election today, and it's looking good. Many older campaigners have been saying that the feel-good atmosphere of the campaign, through a gloriously hot July, reminded them of Gwynfor Evans and the Carmarthen by-election of summer 1966.

Although not on that scale of historic results, it's a brilliant night for Plaid. Rhun takes nearly sixty percent of the vote, the highest anyone's managed on the island since 1931, and that in a straight two-way fight. Rhun had five opponents. It's a doubly thrilling result for me, because the LibDems slump to last place with 1.4 per cent, behind even the Socialist Labour Party. The LibDem eve of poll leaflet boasted what a great voice their man would be... at Westminster. In a by-election for the Assembly. Impressive.

Friday 2 August 2013,
Plaid Cymru office, Aberystwyth:
Second campaign group meeting. Elin suggests that as I still seem to be sporting an ear-ring, all photographs of me in campaign literature could be taken from the other side. Her fixation with it is fascinating. It's no problem to people of our generation, she says, "but I know that my parents, and

their friends, would find it very strange." Her parents, retired farmers from Llanwnnen, near Lampeter, loom large in Elin's politics. She often references them when thinking about what to say, or how to say it. I'm intrigued too by her habit of talking about herself in the third person, and using her full name. "That would be a good Elin Jones story", or "we'll have to come up with an Elin Jones angle on that", she'll often say. I can kind of understand it; the politician out there isn't quite the same as the real person, and perhaps this is her way of articulating that difference.

Jewellery aside, there are causes for optimism. The UK government has just announced that it is going ahead with individual voter registration, which could be a big factor in Ceredigion, for it will apply to students in halls of residence and university houses in both Aberystwyth and Lampeter. Many will probably choose to keep their votes at home, and many others just won't bother. Considering that we were hammered in the student vote in 2005 and 2010, this is good news.

We discuss what to put in the first newspaper of the campaign, out later next month. For the front page, I'm keen to go with a hard-hitting denunciation of the government's austerity agenda, and how it is driven by ideology, rather than fiscal necessity. It's a belief that I think a lot of people feel deep in their bones, and it is up to us to state it unambiguously, because the Labour party is never going to. Tŷ Gwynfor has been putting out some good stuff on this: strong, clear and principled.

Elin and Owen would like to tie that more clearly to a specific issue, to mitigate the danger of it being too theoretical. Our opposition to the privatisation of the Royal Mail is suggested as a way in, and I agree. It is rural and remote areas that will suffer as a result, for serving a county like ours is never going to make money. Even better, with Vince Cable as its mastermind, it's a measure we can nail firmly on to the LibDem side of the government.

I'm ordered to get on to Facebook, something I've happily

avoided thus far. No-one I know who uses it much enjoys it; everyone seems to think of it as a necessary evil, like VAT or hangovers. A couple of the younger committee members volunteer to help steer me into Mr Zuckerberg's arms.

Monday 5 August 2013,
Home:
Message from the producer of my series for BBC Radio Wales. They've pulled the plug on it, shortly after saying they were going to make more of it. After twice assuring us that my being a Plaid candidate wasn't a problem, they have now decided that it is.

So what's changed? Producer Dinah tells me that the decision was first conveyed to her on Friday. What else happened that day? Ah yes: a former BBC journalist trounced all comers in a by-election for Plaid Cymru.

As agreed at the campaign meeting, I email the editor of the *Cambrian News*, to ask if I can come and meet her and see the newspaper's operation.

Tuesday 6 August 2013,
National Eisteddfod, Denbigh:
A discussion session in the Eisteddfod learners' pavilion with Bethan Gwanas and Simon Thirsk, author of the gently provocative novel *Not Quite White*, the allegorical tale of an imaginary, and entirely bonkers, north Wales town. Bethan, Simon and I have done a few public *dysgwyr*[1] sessions before together, and they're always fun, but today, I'm in a foul mood. I'm indignant about the BBC series, but worse, it sounds as though Ulrike, my dear friend and old housemate in Birmingham, is at death's door from cancer that was diagnosed less than two months ago.

Bethan gives me a rousing introduction: at the mention of the fact that I've just become the Plaid Cymru candidate in

---

1   Welsh learners.

Ceredigion, the audience burst into rowdy applause, led by a very enthusiastic Dewi Pws. I wish I could say that I respond in kind, but I'm short tempered, my microphone keeps cutting out and at one point I go off on one about being fed up at switching on Radio Cymru, only to hear that the topic of debate – yet again – is the language itself. It is, I rant, the worst sort of introspective self-absorption, the action of a moody teenager, not a mature nation. It is not the way to win friends at the Eisteddfod.

After the session, I receive a message from Ulrike's husband, telling me to get to Brum sharpish. She doesn't have long. Distracted and upset, I charge my way through the crowds, and can find no words for the many people that reach out to shake my hand and wish me well.

Thursday 8 August 2013,
Home:
A brief turnaround at home, before heading back to Birmingham for the next week to help arrange poor Ulrike's funeral. I reached the hospital only hours before she died. She was plugged into a wall of machinery and could barely breathe, only managing to say two things to me: that she wanted me to conduct her funeral service, and that she loved me. I told her how much I loved her, and kissed her goodbye.

Although not in the mood, I'm booked in this evening for a phone conversation with Jeremy Grange, the Radio Wales executive producer who was overseeing my aborted series. He and I worked together a couple of years ago on a Radio 4 series[2]; he is a lovely man, a brilliant producer and we got on terrifically. Tonight's conversation is strained and painful for us both.

He weighs up his words with great care, but I get answers to my main questions. The decision to cancel *The New Welsh* was made by managers in London, it having been referred

2   *On the Map*, a ten-part series, first broadcast in spring 2011.

"upstairs" by those in Cardiff. They cancelled it, he tells me, without hearing one second of what we've recorded over the last few months.

The problem, he repeatedly says, is one of "perception", especially the perception that BBC Wales is a hotbed of Plaid sympathisers. This is something our opponents always love to stir, even when there is scant evidence to support the claim – most notably in the programming, which has in recent years become measurably more royalist, loyalist and draped in the Union Jack. The big BBC Wales TV series this year has been one fawning over Prince William's helicopter rescue career, and last year they blew an outrageous proportion of their programme budget on staggeringly tedious coverage of following the Olympic torch every inch of its way around Wales.

As soon as Rhun made public his choice to leave the BBC and become a Plaid candidate, there were snide insinuations on social media from the likes of Alun Davies[3] and other Labour luminaries about his past impartiality as an interviewer. It was unfounded bullying, but it has worked a treat and made the BBC even more paranoid about upsetting them.

Meanwhile, the revolving door between the big parties and the BBC, in Wales and beyond, continues to whirr ceaselessly. Labour, always the first to scream "Plaid bias!", are stuffed with former BBC high-fliers: Owen Smith, MP for Pontypridd and Shadow Welsh Secretary, used to produce political programmes for BBC Wales; Chris Bryant, MP for Rhondda, is the corporation's former Head of European Affairs; his Assembly counterpart Leighton Andrews their former Head of Public Affairs.

These, though, are largely from the BBC's bottomless pool of managers, and thus immune from standards applied to lesser mortals. It's far easier to pick off a lowly freelancer standing for a tiny party.

---

3   Labour AM for Blaenau Gwent.

Thursday 29 August 2013,
Home:
Recovering from a small operation on my ear two days ago, I watch the recalled Commons debate on bombing Syria. It is painfully self-congratulatory, full of Sir Bufton Tuftons – on both sides – declaiming that "this is the House of Commons at its finest" and so on. When Cameron is finally, narrowly, thankfully defeated, all hell breaks loose. The media can talk of nothing else, as has been the case for days. It is always the same: acres of newsprint and hours of airtime all dedicated not to teasing out difficult international issues, but obsessed only with the UK's response, and what it says about us. I'm sure the poor sods huddled in the rubble of Homs or Damascus are talking of little else.

The government loses the main vote, thanks to nine LibDems and thirty Tories rebelling. Mark Williams is not among them. He dutifully votes with the Tories against the opposition amendment, and then mysteriously disappears altogether when it comes to the substantive vote. Firmly on the fence again. I wonder how he'll spin it in the constituency?

Friday 30 August 2013,
Home:
A tweet from Mark Williams: "If there is a second vote to authorise direct military intervention in #Syria, I will be voting against that motion." Total cop-out. He had the chance to do just that last night, and he blew it. Not as weird though as a tweet this afternoon from his sidekick Elizabeth Evans, the LibDem councillor in Aberaeron and Assembly candidate against Elin: "Can anyone tell me please if President Assad has a #Twitter account – would quite like to speak to him. #Syria."

Thursday 5 September 2013,
Cenarth, Dyffryn Teifi, Ceredigion:
Sunny day canvassing the Teifi valley, including lunch at a café in Cardigan run by a Plaid town councillor. It was like a

lo-fi version of *The Godfather*: Elin Jones, me and two of the town's county councillors round a big table in the middle of the café, the owner and staff fussing around us. For better and for worse, Cardigan's politics has an old school tang of small-town skullduggery. Years of travel writing have sharpened my ability to smell it in the air, and it is a shock to find myself suddenly on the other side of the divide.

Out into the villages to the east, many of them scarred by shocking housing developments – new estates pushed through a bent planning system by landowners, who then filled their scrubby patches with jerry-built houses and pavements, laced together with malfunctioning drainage and lighting. They remind me of those half-built places you see in Spain – El Dorado, but in the soft drizzle of Ceredigion. They are a vicious headache for everyone. The council want developers to finish the job before they officially adopt the roads and become responsible for their upkeep, but the developers do all they can to avoid it. Stalemate ensues, sometimes for decades. Meanwhile, the houses and infrastructure continue to crumble.

On one such estate today, I am warned by a lady on the doorstep to avoid the builder, who lives in his caravan on wasteland at the top of the estate. "He gets very angry," she tells me nervously, and in those four words, I get a harsh glimpse of the misery that it has made of her life. Confronting vested interests, wherever they are, will be a huge part of this job, and it has to be done. There are too many in this sort of situation, and it poisons our communities.

Friday 6 September 2013,
Home:
Leanne and Helen Bradley[4] stay tonight; it is great to see them. Helen is as sharp as a tack, one of the impressive group of women at the head of Plaid. They talk through the party strategy for next year and how it is all looking thus far. Good, it

---

4   Plaid Cymru Head of Communications.

seems. Leanne wants Plaid to look like a government in waiting, bursting with ideas, policies and talent. It's fairly obvious stuff, but I'm genuinely impressed by how well considered it is and how comprehensive the plan. Whether it translates into reality is, of course, another matter entirely.

Leanne and I talk, too, about our shared difficulty with politicking in Welsh. Being learners was key to the selection of us both – longed-for proof to the wider world that Plaid isn't only about the language. The minute we were both in place however, the pressure started to do much more *yn Gymraeg*. It is a conundrum. Like me, she feels happy to use and improve her Welsh in social situations and so on, but is very apprehensive about employing it on the field of battle.

"It's difficult enough trying to perform at First Minister's Questions in English," she says, "but the idea of me, a not very confident learner, taking on Carwyn, a native speaker, in Welsh is just not going to happen. But I'm always getting people telling me that I should. It's quite tiring."

Monday 9 September 2013,
Plaid office, Aberystwyth:
Third campaign meeting, and no-one mentions my ear-ring. The biggest job at the moment is to fill the many holes in "the quilt", our network of leafleters throughout the county and the group of distributors who get the bundles to them. The quilt is looking distinctly threadbare in places, and I've done a few sessions of phone-bashing to try and persuade some new volunteers.

Otherwise, we finalise the stories for the newspaper, talk about postal votes, at which we are notoriously bad compared with the LibDems, and about various campaigns that we could and should be part of. From now on, I'll be out canvassing for two days a week, so there is much to organise to make that happen.

I never did get a reply from the editor of the *Cambrian News* to my request a month ago for an informal meeting.

Tuesday 10 September 2013,
Great Darkgate Street, Aberystwyth:
Street stall over lunchtime in central Aber, mainly focused on getting signatures for our petition against Royal Mail privatisation. People seem fairly aware of the issue, and almost unanimously against it. As we need to get a photo of us and the stall for the front of our newspaper, Owen has spent £26 on eBay on a life-size cardboard post box, which Gwen has decorated with signs saying *Achubwch ein Post!* and *Save our Post!* Unfortunately, the post box is as flimsy as a politician's promise; it keeps collapsing and at one point takes off on a sudden gust of wind, almost decapitating a few passing shoppers.

Wednesday 11 September 2013,
Penrhyn-coch Football Club:
A lacklustre afternoon's canvassing in Llannon and Llansantffraid, before grabbing a bite to eat and going to speak at a Plaid branch meeting. This is Owen's branch, and he gives me a lovely introduction, saying that they decided the ideal candidate would be an entertainer from Kidderminster, but as Robert Plant wasn't available, they had to make do with me.

I give more or less the same introductory spiel that I used at the branch meeting in Aberystwyth a couple of months ago, but it already sounds a bit stale, and is proof (something I remember from my stand-up days) that the same material can go down so differently in a new setting. This is a tougher, more traditional crowd. Llinos Dafis grills me on the issue of drones at Aberporth, a real hot potato for Plaid locally, and me too. Their warfare and surveillance capabilities are horrendous, but there are many positive civilian uses for them too. How, and where, do you draw the line? I feel sure that my equivocal response has pleased no-one.

The second the official meeting is over, it is like a different event. Everyone warms up, chats freely and there's plenty of laughter. I get on particularly well with Richard Owen, who will soon be retiring from the Welsh Books Council, and on my drive home, I wonder whether he might be dragooned into being my election agent, something that Owen and I have started to discuss.

Thursday 12 September 2013,
Portmeirion, Gwynedd:
We arrive and pitch tents for Festival Number 6. It's bigger than last year, but just as magical. Clough Williams-Ellis would have adored it. After such a crazy summer, I'm ready for a hedonistic weekend. My heart sinks on seeing Keith Morris, Aberystwyth's ubiquitous photographer, who immediately trains his camera on me and starts snapping. He's a good bloke, but this is my down time, and I don't want him sneaking a shot of me dancing like a loon or with a spliff hanging off my bottom lip. We have a little chat, and I think he gets the message.

Tuesday 24 September 2013,
Neuadd Pantycelyn, Aberystwyth:
After a bizarre interview on Radio Bronglais, I sit for a few hours on the Plaid stall at Ffair y Glas, the Welsh-language freshers' fair in Pantycelyn. There is quite a bit of interest, though I well recall that you sign up for way more than you ever actually do. We really need student power though; we lacked it last time, with severe consequences. Our campus commander Aled Morgan Hughes is quite brilliant, but he cannot do it as a one-man band.

I go and chat to people on the other stalls: the Welsh as Second Language group, an assortment of men's and women's rugby teams, the Urdd and *Golwg* magazine. Otherwise, it is mainly public sector organisations handing out glossy, if terrifying, bumf. There are leaflets and advice packs on problem drinking, drugs, quitting smoking, personal safety, consent issues, eating disorders, bullying, sexually transmitted diseases, academic pressure, mental health, being broke and online security; the cumulative effect is apocalyptic. Welcome to university.

Wednesday 25 September 2013,
Aberystwyth Arts Centre:
The main Freshers' Fair, in a packed and noisy marquee on the lawn behind the Arts Centre. On arrival, I'm told that I've just missed Mark Williams on the LibDem stall. The Plaid stall is wedged between the LibDems and the Conservatives, making us a kind of cordon sanitaire, or possibly the coalition's condom. Everyone gets along pretty well, with the noticeable exception of the nearby Labour students, who refuse to engage with any of us. I've long believed that Labour loyalists are the most blindly sectarian of any party. It evidently starts young.

Friday 27 September 2013,
White Horse Tavern, Machynlleth:
Vaughan Williams, who, along with his boyfriend, has been an enthusiastic member of my campaign team, has asked to meet for a chat. Originally from Holyhead, he's considering going for the Ynys Môn nomination for Westminster, to be decided upon in a fortnight. He needs no persuasion, as he's mustard keen to go for it. My only advice is to tone it down a little on Twitter, where he can get pretty fierce at times. I'd miss the two of them if he gets selected though. They've been a welcome splash of energy in the otherwise fairly placid waters of Plaid Ceredigion.

Wednesday 2 October 2013,
Penrhyn-coch:
Photo call with the irrepressible Llanbadarn councillor Paul James outside Aber's main police station; the latest addition to the candidate's photographic bingo card held in the office. They are gathering pictures for all occasions and for all possible press stories: me looking sad outside the hospital – and looking happy outside the hospital too, just in case; me

grimacing by a post box, as I contemplate its uncertain future under privatisation; me keeping an eye on the University and the National Library; me looking like a less fun version of the Green Cross Code man at difficult traffic junctions, and so on. I head to Penrhyn-coch to canvass with Richard Owen and a small team. Richard has agreed to be the election agent. I'm very pleased, for we will have to work closely together, and are, I think, very much on the same wavelength politically, despite coming from such different traditions. He is also a very cultured man, but evidently prepared to put in the donkey work too.

I drive home pondering an interesting conversation with Owen earlier. We were talking about Welsh Labour, and the enduring chasm between their pro-devolution wing and their loyal Brit brigade, who smell a nashy plot in everything. This split is ancient and still causes havoc today, for Wales as much as for the Labour Party. "It's ironic, isn't it," I said to Owen, "that the party which gave us devolution is the one which has adapted least successfully to it?" He shrugged and said quietly, "There are many who'd say that that was us." It's a thought I'd never entertained before. I think of the people I've met in Plaid far more comfortable in a pressure group than a serious political party. I think too of our electoral harvest. Since that dazzling first Assembly election in 1999, when we even outperformed the SNP, Plaid has been in a fairly steady decline. I chew on this all evening.

Thursday 3 October 2013,
Talgarreg:
An interview at Aberystwyth University with Harry Taylor, editor of the student paper, *The Courier*. We find a lot of common ground politically, and bizarrely, he is also from Kidderminster. The fact that a fellow Kiddy boy has become a Plaid candidate fascinates him, and he is very receptive to our ideas and policies. I think he'll give me a good write-up.

Then for an afternoon's canvassing with Llŷr Gruffudd[5] around Ffostrasol. We get some delightful reactions. He is excellent on the doorstep, and in meetings too. After a brief campaign committee in Talgarreg village hall, Llŷr hosts a public meeting there, largely in Welsh, about agriculture. It's less than ninety miles from Kidderminster to Talgarreg, but it feels like a million. I have such a lot to learn.

Friday 4 October 2013,
Capel Brondeifi, Lampeter:
Sweet, old-fashioned evening in Lampeter at a branch fundraiser. Entertainment comes from Meinir Gwilym and Gwenan Gibbard, who are both on top form. Elin tells me to do a little speech to introduce myself, and that it would go down well if I did it in Welsh. It's the first time I've done the whole thing *yn Gymraeg* at a Plaid Ceredigion event. It goes reasonably well, and as I come off the stage, Elin is beaming at me with the kind of pride you normally see on mums' faces at the school nativity play.

There's tea, some great cakes and interesting conversations with the members there. I've always had a soft spot for Lampeter. Having a university in what is essentially a large village, miles from anywhere, gives it a unique edge and a surprisingly cosmopolitan population, though rooted firmly in agricultural, Welsh Wales. It's a mad combination, but somehow it works.

Unfortunately, times are tough at the university, as they are in Aberystwyth, and for similar reasons. Money is tight, and that's the focus of most concern, but woeful management exacerbates both situations. It is the same right across the public sector. There's an entire breed of managers, who hop from a health board to a university to a government advisory post without breaking stride, and whose main skill seems

---

5   AM for North Wales from 2011; Plaid Cymru's spokesman on agriculture
     and rural affairs.

to be in securing their own position, on whacking great salaries, benefits, pensions and unbreakable contracts. They are brilliant at deploying the latest buzzwords, but have the empathy of cats. It's a growth industry ignited by Tony Blair; the fire rages on.

Saturday 5 October 2013,
Marine Hotel, Aberystwyth:
The gentle fundraising event in Lampeter last night turned into a hefty session in the Cwmann Tavern, so that this morning's street stall in the town is conducted with a pounding head. We get some good reactions, though, and it's always fun to be with Elin in her *milltir sgwâr*.[6]

Some listless canvassing follows, and then I head back north and to Ynyslas beach, hoping that a blast of sea air will shake away the cobwebs before I have to compère tonight's Pride on the Prom in Aberystwyth. I've been dreading it. The organisation has been chaotic and, with a couple of honourable exceptions, the programme is dire. They're relying on me to get the party started, which is tough in a half-empty hotel function room, and even tougher when they insist on kicking it off with a minute's rather awkward silence for poor little April Jones, through which the disco lights continue to flash. Microphones fail to work, acts take for ever to set up, and I'm left flailing, trying to fill the gaps. A friend describes the occasion as "*Father Ted* does Pride" which is perfect, though I have to remember not to call it that from behind the mike.

Tuesday 8 October 2013,
Bow Street:
A good canvass tonight. Two people tell me, "I think you've won me back to Plaid". Some others say how much they used to enjoy my TV programmes, which is lovely to hear but I doubt that it translates into votes. One bloke, a former policeman,

---

6   "Square mile", your home patch.

fixes me with a disconcertingly blank eyeball-to-eyeball stare, as if I were a suspect. Though being an aspiring politician, I suppose I am. Another starts off demanding an apology for two different occasions when he said that Plaid members had blanked him, though he then warms up with a good chat. He is interesting, and says twice at the end "Thanks so much for listening to me." I get the impression that not many do. This is such a strange, and strangely privileged, glimpse into so many different lives.

Thursday 10 October 2013,
Plaid office, Aberystwyth:
We've had dozens of responses to a survey of tourism businesses in the county, to gauge how things are for them. Most have had a better year, thanks mainly to the good summer. No-one seems to think that there's any discernible improvement in the economy. Responses from the south of the county all cast jealous eyes at Pembrokeshire. In answer to our question about the branding of Ceredigion as a tourist destination, a few – mainly in and around Aberporth – come out with the old chestnut that it is unpronounceable and that we should "bring back Cardiganshire". And 1961, I'm guessing.

Friday 11 October 2013,
Aberystwyth Arts Centre:
Plaid Cymru conference, and I'm on proud host duty. The day starts with a fact-finding trip to IBERS[7] at Penrhyn-coch, with Leanne and Llŷr Gruffudd. Timings are tight and Leanne is very late. She and her crew finally show up almost thirty minutes over time; I soon learn it is because they went to the village of Goginan, nearly ten miles away, rather than Gogerddan, the name of the old plas at the centre of IBERS' campus.

---

7   Institute of Biological, Environmental and Rural Sciences, the latest incarnation of Aberystwyth University's famous plant breeding station, founded in 1919.

It's an interesting tour, and inspiring to see such world-class R&D happening here, but we have to do it in the company of the Vice-Chancellor and her retinue. They use such impenetrable management speak that I have trouble even understanding what the hell they're talking about. Having been self-employed for over twenty years, I've not suffered much of this deathly corporate jargon, and my skills in it are useless. I realise with a shudder that if I win, I'll probably be talking like that myself before long.

Back into town and to the conference. There's a good turnout, and the atmosphere is buoyant. My only gripe is the slogan that's been picked: *Wales First / Cymru'n Gyntaf*. It looks naff enough on the podium lectern, from where it will be beamed all over the media, but even worse, it is the slogan Tŷ Gwynfor has chosen to take us through the European elections next year. In the context of an international poll across twenty-eight nation-states and numerous stateless nations, it's unforgiveable. Declaring that your corner must come first has been the slogan of Eurosceptic neo-fascists like the French Front National, Greece's Golden Dawn, Austria's Freedom Party and of course, Britain First, that ragbag of violent neo-Nazis. I think of how many times I've had the conversation with floating voters nervous of "nationalism", where I've had to assure them that Plaid are progressive and internationalist – as indeed, our record proudly demonstrates. In just two words, this undoes all of that.

Leanne gives a decent speech, with flesh on the bones of policies such as bringing health and social care provision together, a not-for-profit national energy company on similar lines to Dŵr Cymru, rent control in the private sector, opposition to fracking and a re-affirmation that we are pro-European, but want significant reform of the EU. She also conjures up memories of Cynog's win here in 1992, and calls me Ceredigion's next MP and "Wales' modern-day George Borrow". Hmm.

Saturday 12 October 2013,
Marine Hotel, Aberystwyth:
My speech goes down well, in front of a full house. I was terrified beforehand, dry-mouthed and shaking, but as soon as I walk out to the podium, I feel an ethereal calm descend on me. It gets lots of good reactions, and promises of help. Having the conference here is brilliant for the campaign. It's good that people can see we're really going for it.

A great LGBT fringe meeting to round off proceedings. Dafydd Êl is on wondrous and outrageous form: "Someone just switch me off," he sighs at one point, which would be music to Leanne's ears. I speak, reminiscing about the first Plaid event I'd ever attended, at Trinity College Carmarthen in 1989, when I was asked to come and lead a session on lesbian and gay rights, and then copped off with a visiting Scots Nat. Plaid has been firmly on the right side of the issue at all times, and I'm very proud of that.

The conference dinner tonight in the Marine is raucous. Everyone is so fired up and excited. Add booze and food, and the whole thing takes off like a rocket. Or like a plane from Terminal 5 perhaps: Heathrow airport, or rather their campaign for a third runway, is sponsoring the dinner, which buys them a short speech at the beginning. I'm sat with Cynog and Llinos Dafis, whose faces throughout this homage to air travel are a picture.

Dinner over, the party rocks on into the night. I catch Owen at one point, and he tells me that Elin is having a rare foray into the lands of public drunkenness. She is too, and it's so sweet. On seeing me, she grins and beckons me over, "Come here!" she says, "We've not had a proper cwtch yet – it's about time!" We do, and I couldn't be happier. For an habitual outsider, it is a joy to feel part of the tribe.

Thursday 17 October 2013,
Victoria Hall, Lampeter:
My first encounter tonight with my main opponent, the

incumbent LibDem MP Mark Williams. We are both speaking at the packed launch meeting of the campaign to rebuild a railway between Aberystwyth and Carmarthen. Of all the places en route, Lampeter is the one that stands to benefit the most. It is so isolated.

Mark is late for the meeting, and unfortunately I've already spoken by the time he scuttles in, chucking out smiles and apologies to all. He nods and grins at me as he sits down, before delivering a punchy speech promising his commitment to the cause.

As the meeting breaks up, he and I shake hands and talk for the first time. It's very good natured. He says we should go for a drink some time, for he's sure that we'd have a great deal politically in common. He is very practised at making you feel warmly towards him. In the hubbub, he mishears some comment I make about tonight's provision of cakes, and thinks that I have said "case". He looks momentarily flummoxed, but then manages to find something to say about my case, a leather satchel. "Oh yes, I've got one like that. It's quite essential," he says gesturing towards it. He can obviously pull some soft soap out about anything; no topic too tedious nor tangential. What a pro.

Friday 18 October 2013,
Neuadd Caerwedros, near New Quay:
A Plaid branch meeting in the tidy new centre at Caerwedros. There's only about a dozen of us sat in the middle of the large main hall, so that it is impossible to get any oomph going. It is not a good meeting. I get people's names wrong, waffle badly on elements of party policy, and mangle my mutations terribly.

Some nights, my Welsh is just dreadful; this is one of them. And if there's one part of the county where I need to prove that I can get by in the language, it's here. Before being selected, I'd have thought that the deepest Cymric heartland of Ceredigion would probably be around Tregaron. But it isn't, it's here in the hedge-banked lanes and muddy yards of central, not-quite-coastal Ceredigion, where you'd probably find more eisteddfod chairs lurking in dark parlours than anywhere else in Wales.

Like all political parties, Plaid is a precarious alliance between different traditions. There's the fiery, urban and left-wing republicanism, as personified by Leanne, and the more conservative cultural nationalism of rural Wales. In Ceredigion, uniquely to some extent, you get equal dollops of both, but here in Bro Siôn Cwilt[8], the latter is firmly on top. It shows itself not just in what people say, but how they say it. There is only one young woman here, and she makes some brilliant contributions. Almost every time she speaks though, she is interrupted by much older men. Afterwards, I ask her if she noticed. She shrugs. "It happens all the time – it's a real Ceredigion thing," is her resigned reply.

The rather antediluvian atmosphere makes me self-censor. In previous getting-to-know-me presentations in Aberystwyth and Penrhyn-coch, I'd told a cute little tale that illustrates both how laid back rural Wales can be, and how efficiently it disseminates the news. It concerned my move from Llangynfelyn to Ceinws in 2001, when knowledge of me as Gay Mike travelled in advance, thanks to someone in Borth having relatives in my new village. Consequently, I never had to come out there, and was accepted as gay from the outset. Here in Caerwedros, I cut that story out, as I do any mention of Preds. I figure that I'm already a leap into the dark for most of them, and underlining that I'm gay might prove too much. This is, I realise, a paranoid assumption about *their* assumptions, and I feel deeply ashamed of my cowardice.

After the meeting, the talk is nearly all of the language, and what they see as its calamitous collapse. When the 2011 census results appeared, the proportion of Welsh speakers in Ceredigion had dipped below fifty per cent for the first time,

---

8   The name given to the area around Synod Inn in mid Ceredigion.

sending a spasm of shock through the county. People are still reeling from it, and worry that we are now heading towards the endgame.

I can understand how it seems like that, when all you have to measure it against is a quantifiable, if subjective, sense of personal loss. To many people here, they look at a street of houses in their village and recall Welsh bursting spontaneously out of every one. There is almost nowhere left like that now. But to an outsider like me, Cymraeg remains a thing of immense strength and depth, not weakness. It is changing, as is every living language, and yes "thinning" as Gwyneth Lewis so aptly put it, but it will not die, I am sure of it. Unfortunately, I communicate this in appalling Welsh, which probably only confirms their worst fears.

Tuesday 22 October 2013,
Bow Street:
The weekly Tuesday evening canvass, with Cynog Dafis and others in Llandre and Bow Street. At one house, Cynog calls me over to a woman who wants to ask about energy policy. I explain that I'm against fracking, but not in favour of carpeting the hills with many more wind turbines, and that there are other forms of renewable energy, most notably tidal and solar, that we are ideally placed to exploit and need to expand. We also discuss greater community ownership of energy schemes, something that works well in other countries. She seems happy with this.

As we walk away, Cynog says "Dw i'n anghytuno gyda ti ar bron bopeth yna."[9] These are words to chill the soul, especially from Cynog. He tells me that he is in favour of fracking, and that exporting water to the rest of the UK for the process could be a good earner for Wales. He says too that he can't wait for the day when he climbs Pumlumon and sees forests of wind turbines stretching off in all directions. The idea horrifies me.

---

9   "I disagree with you on almost everything there."

To him, Plaid's current energy policy is trifling stuff, especially the talk of hyper-localism. "We want a robust national network in Wales, to be a powerhouse, with plenty for export," he says. Of all the issues, energy is the one where Plaid is most divided. There are staunch advocates of nuclear power in the party, mainly in Anglesey of course, and it's a strategy that has attracted some green thinkers such as George Monbiot.

To Cynog, our idealistic energy policy is yet another example of Plaid Cymru loitering in its historic comfort zone of easy opposition, and it's one we need to get out of. He has a point there.

Monday 4 November 2013,
Ffordd Caradog, Aberystwyth:
Another visit to help canvass in the town council by-election taking place this week amongst the grand terraces of Bronglais ward. It is a lovely part of Aber, and full of some fascinating and forthright characters.

One is a woman who chases me out on to the street, telling me that we have lost her vote because of Elin's policy as Agriculture Minister to implement a badger cull. Although the heat has largely gone out of the issue, for a few people – on both sides – it is still the clincher. It had been a massive factor in the last Assembly election in 2011, when the Plaid office in town was picketed regularly and received numerous threatening letters and calls.

She is still shouting at me on the pavement. I ask her who she can vote for then, if opposition to a badger cull is the deciding factor. After all, the coalition government in Westminster has started trial culls in England. "Labour then!" she shouts back. "But Elin's policy was as part of a Labour-Plaid coalition," I reply. She pauses. "Well, I dunno, UKIP then!" Voting UKIP to help save wildlife? Good luck with that, madam.

Friday 8 November 2013,
Plaid office, Aberystwyth:
Lucy Huws, our candidate in the Bronglais by-election for Aberystwyth town council, comfortably holds the seat with 58 per cent of a low turnout. The LibDems are spinning their 128 votes as a couple of percentage points swing to them. Mark Williams's staff had decided to use this as a training exercise for the general election campaign, and they threw everything at it: student canvass teams galore and eleven separate leaflets. That's one for every twelve votes.

Sunday 17 November 2013,
Cwm Einion:
The smooth operational machine that I was assured was in place back in May has proved to be rustier than advertised. You can barely get into the office for boxes of our *Ceredigion Post* newspaper; they have been sitting there for weeks. The distribution "quilt" has gone very mouldy.

I spent all of yesterday delivering bundles of newspapers to distributors around the north of the county, and today pushing individual copies through doors in numerous villages. Once I'd got over my frustration at the chaos, I made the determined effort to enjoy it. It wasn't difficult. Some of the places I've delivered to are magical, especially in the last of their autumn colours. I build in one of my favourite regular walks, along the valley behind the waterfall at Furnace, and drive all the way down to the far end of Cwm Einion, where the only sounds are the rush of water and the mewing of kites and buzzards.

Monday 18 November 2013,
On the A487:
Driving to an Institute of Welsh Affairs meeting in Aberystwyth, I hear Michael Ignatieff interviewed on Radio 4's *Front Row*. Ignatieff, an author and broadcaster, was a regular BBC presence in the 1990s, before being lured back to his native Canada and election there as a Liberal MP. Within three years,

he was leader of the party, taking it to disastrous defeat in 2011, when they lost well over half of their seats, Ignatieff's included, and their status as the official opposition. He bowed out of politics just as swiftly as he had jumped in.

"I'd been a spectator most of my life, up in the stands as a commentator, a journalist, a columnist, and suddenly the chance to be down in the arena seemed irresistible. I had absolutely no idea what I was letting myself in for," he says ruefully. He describes his brief sojourn in politics as "hubris" and "self-deception", before making the point that such a career should come with a siren warning to all writers and journalists, for they "quite literally have a paper trail" that will get them into trouble if they have ever chewed over difficult topics in print. "It's not what you say, it's what they hear," he says.

There's danger, he warns, even in comparatively innocuous past utterances, if your opponents are determined enough to twist their meaning. And, he assures me as I drive distractedly through Bow Street, they will be.

Tuesday 19 November 2013,
Llansantffraid, by Llannon:
A telling encounter this afternoon, while canvassing in Llannon. One door is opened by a woman in her sixties, who, it transpires, as it does so often, comes from near where I grew up in the Midlands. She's been in rural mid Wales for over twenty years, and her daughter and grandson live nearby.

She questions the policy of teaching primary school kids through the Welsh language. "What use is learning Welsh, in this day and age?" she says. "He should be learning Spanish, or Chinese, something at least he could use when he's older. Something useful, y'know. I mean, where on earth is he going to be able to use Welsh?"

The answer seems so obvious, I struggle momentarily to process it. "Well... *here*," I say. "He might want to stay where he's been brought up, make his life here. Wouldn't that be great?

Three generations putting down roots in such a wonderful part of the world. And how good would having Welsh be then?"

She looks nonplussed, and then a smile spreads gradually across her face. It is like seeing the penny drop in one of those RNLI collecting tins on pub bars. Slowly, she exhales and says "Oh, yes... I see what you mean." There is a long pause. "I'd never thought of that. It would be good, wouldn't it?"

We talk more, about the benefits of bilingualism, and how it makes other languages easier to acquire. I point out that a considerable majority, somewhere over two-thirds, of the world's kids are raised in at least two languages. Monoglots are the minority, and a poor minority at that. Her receptiveness to it thrills me, and I hope that I've helped plant a seed.

Saturday 23 November 2013,
Canolfan yr Urdd, Glan-llyn, near Bala:
At the Plaid Cymru winter school (the summer school postponed because of the Ynys Môn by-election), there is a training session for election candidates. We are shown leaflets, calling cards and other goodies that will be issued to us, a Plaid branded teabag included. This, we are told, is to offer to someone we have just successfully canvassed, in order that we can invite them to have a cuppa on us.

I close my eyes and imagine dangling a solitary teabag in the face of a suspicious farmer somewhere near Ffostrasol. It doesn't end well.

Saturday 7 December 2013,
Tafarn y Llew Du, Talybont, Ceredigion:
Plaid Ceredigion's Christmas dinner, with guest speaker Rhun ap Iorwerth. He gives a superbly polished speech, including an anecdote about being mistaken for Matt Damon when he was canvassing in the by-election. A woman on our table hisses, "I've heard that story three times. Matt bloody Damon!"

Her aside, it's fair to say that Rhun is the darling of the room. He has come out as a supporter of the Wylfa B nuclear plant on Anglesey and is generally seen as a more conservative standard bearer in Plaid, a position that I know appeals to many members in Ceredigion. Leanne does not get so much as a mention all night.

Friday 13 December 2013,
Kraków, Poland:
After a freezing day in the Nazi concentration camps at Auschwitz and Birkenau, Preds and I reel back into Kraków, shell-shocked and silent. Nothing can prepare you for the place, and the sheer numbers who died there. The scale of it is beyond comprehension.

In a bar back in the city, I pick up a copy of the local English-language newspaper. It tells me that Nick Griffin, leader of what's left of the BNP, had recently been in town and warned a rally that "powerful Zionists want to destroy us. We, the nationalists, must stand together to fight for a white, nationalist and radical Europe". Is it 2013 or 1933 outside?

EURO VISION
January – August 2014

Wednesday 1 January 2014,
Home:
After our trip to Poland, I've been reading voraciously about the 1930s, and am spooked by the many parallels with today. As a result, New Year optimism is a little thin on the ground. It is a horrible irony that 2014 is likely to be a year in which people soberly commemorate the centenary of the Great War, while simultaneously voting in droves for various shades of neo-fascism in May's European elections.

Thursday 9 January 2014,
Aberystwyth Boat Club:
A good campaign committee meeting, including a discussion about how to play the news of cuts to policing – Dyfed-Powys have just announced 118 job losses among civilian support staff. I'm keen that we conflate this with the rapidly growing costs of the constabulary's Police and Crime Commissioner, the Conservative Christopher Salmon. When these posts were first contested in 2012, Plaid refused to take part as a matter of principle. I was glad; it's a ridiculous idea, and it was the first election since having the vote that I sat out. Many did likewise; the turnout across England and Wales was 15 per cent, the lowest ever.

I wish we'd continued as refuseniks, but it's not to be. Plaid are contesting the next PCC election, for two reasons: one good, one not so. The reasonable one is that it will be held alongside the next Assembly election in 2016, and to have a ballot paper on the same day with no mention of Plaid is thought too risky. Less appealing is that the ballooning budgets and staff rosters of the Commissioners, the very thing that I want us to make a noise about, are being seen by some in Plaid as a big fat pie that they'd very much like a slice of.

To the Boat Club for a constituency meeting, where Cynog Dafis outlines his ideas on the future of devolution. There is much discussion about Scotland, now that we are in the year of the independence referendum. Cynog is typically pragmatic about the Welsh route to a parallel place, but for some members, the SNP have provided the blueprint, and our job is to follow it to the letter. While it's good to dream, that seems to me to be straying into pure fantasy.

Mind you, there's no shortage of that in Scotland either. After a recent episode of *Borgen*, the slick Danish political TV drama, I saw on Twitter one SNP activist state that *"Borgen* proves small countries can work well politically." Er, no. It proves that small countries can make good telly.

Talking of every Plaid member's favourite TV series, Leanne has had a makeover, courtesy of image guru Claire Howell. With her hair up, she looks the spitting image of the PM in *Borgen*. I sent her a jokey message to say so, to which she replied that she was glad I'd noticed, and that it was no coincidence.

Friday 10 January 2014,
Ysgol Penweddig, Aberystwyth:
An afternoon with Plaid MEP Jill Evans, who has hotfooted it to Aberystwyth prom, scene of last weekend's devastating storms. My Twitter timeline has been full all week of politicians doing the hashtag sadface thing against the backdrop of the collapsed shelter. I feel cheap and dirty to be following suit.

The same feeling overwhelms me this evening, in a packed public meeting about the future of Bronglais hospital. The lure of four hundred motivated voters is just too hard to resist for politicians. Every single one is here, from regional AMs to town councillors, and they all get up to speak, carefully reminding us who they are and then making it quite clear how important they think the hospital is, and how hard they'll keep fighting for it.

I dry up, cannot speak, do not want to. I see a few Plaid people in the crowd nodding at me to open my mouth and grab the microphone. I can't. I just can't. It's a bloody pantomime.

Monday 20 January 2014,
Home:

The news is full of the LibDems suspending the membership of Lord (Chris) Rennard. Their longtime chief executive did not go quietly when it was revealed he had foisted himself on a succession of young women activists. Instead, he unapologetically tried to bluff it out, insisting that he would take his place in the Lords as a LibDem, whereupon the party withdrew the whip from him. He's now threatening legal action against them.

Twitter is aflame with it, of course. I hold back from chucking anything too combustible into the mix, though I do retweet a comment by a *Guardian* journalist pointing out that the women who complained have all felt forced into leaving the party. Mark Williams's pugnacious office boy jumps in to demand that we "But [*sic*] the fuck out. It's a LibDem problem."

It certainly is. We've also learned this week that Chris Huhne gave his wife crabs that he'd caught from some bloke, and that Portsmouth MP Mike Hancock had seduced a mentally ill constituent who came to him for help. While all political parties have their dodgy perv quotient, it always seems to be that much riper with the LibDems.

I remember it all too well from my teenage Liberal activist years in the early 1980s. Following a school project that had involved contacting MPs, I struck up a correspondence with Cyril Smith, the late, disgraced Rochdale MP. In scrawling handwritten letters, he beseeched me to visit him in Westminster, telling me that I sounded just the kind of lad who should think about a career as a Liberal MP, and he'd do whatever he could to help me on my way. My ego was tickled to bursting point, and I was desperate to take him up on the invitation, but my dad refused a trip to London, so it never happened. At the time, I was incandescent with fury, though now it seems like a blessed escape. In any case, there were quite enough homegrown gropers amongst Kidderminster Liberals, mainly married men happy to rub up too closely or leave a hand too long or too high on a fourteen-year-old boy's leg.

Wednesday 12 February 2014,
Palace of Westminster, London SW1:
Down to London for a few days, including a visit to Westminster that's been choreographed by Plaid staff there. Having cleared the security checks, I stand and shiver in Westminster Hall, where I'm to be met at 9.30. Suddenly, I notice a frock-coated flunky bustling towards me. "Sir!" he barks as he gets closer, "Kindly remove your hat in the Palace!" I am wearing a cap, as it is freezing, but I don't argue.

One of the Plaid members of staff comes to find me. Rhian has been working here for over twenty years and loves it. She whisks me off on a breakneck tour, with a constant flow of commentary. We hurtle through committee rooms and the Central Lobby, see the Lords and the Commons, admire the portraits and sculptures and Tony Benn's plaque in a broom cupboard commemorating Emily Davison, the suffragette who hid there during the night of the 1911 census in order to give the House of Commons as her address on the form.

Rather less stirring is the sight, as we walk through one of the palace yards, of Speaker Bercow's allotted parking spaces, in which are sat two enormous Chelsea tractors crowned with matching his'n'hers personalised plates. If I do make it here, I hope I'll be more of a Benn than a Bercow.

It is fascinating to hear the depth of Rhian's affection for Westminster. She is proud of how well Plaid Cymru are regarded here, much more so she says than the SNP. I can believe it. For inevitable reasons of both geography and history, Plaid are much more ingrained at a UK level, and a far cosier piece of the Westminster furniture. It's not hard to imagine some of our elder statesmen hobnobbing here in the bars and restaurants, and loving every minute. It would be very hard to resist, so overwhelming is the clubbable ambience of Harrow-School-meets-Harry-Potter.

I make my way into the public gallery for Welsh Questions and then PMQs. As I arrive, Jonathan Edwards[1] is on his feet in the chamber questioning the Welsh Secretary. As he finishes, he sees me, and gives a thumbs up. It's quite evident though that Welsh Questions is a bag of peanuts to the lavish buffet of PMQs; barely anyone is paying attention. MPs drift in continuously, chattering and laughing together or twiddling with their phones and iPads. The government benches are below me, and craning my head over I can see the familiar layout of Twitter blinking at me from dozens of screens. Suddenly, as if by magic, the noise evaporates, and Cameron and Miliband are in place, ready and off.

David Cameron – who I'm sat above, all the better to admire the skillful combover crafted to cover a substantial bald patch – is at his Flashman best, cocky, smooth and patronising. Ed Miliband is wretched. Harriet Harman sits to one side of him, Ed Balls on the other, but not a word or look passes between them throughout. There is no chemistry there whatsoever, and it makes Miliband look hopelessly lonely. I actually feel quite sorry for him.

The main issue of the day is most fitting for the British parliament: the weather. Large parts of the country, the coast of Ceredigion included, have been battered and flooded for weeks. The rail line to Cornwall has gone, washed away at Dawlish. Somerset has been substantially under water since Christmas. Government action has been decidedly patchy, but this week, the Thames has flooded Berkshire, and suddenly it is being taken very seriously indeed. Cameron is doing his best to sound statesmanlike as he assures us that action is forthcoming. "Money is no object," he tells us four times, a quotation I know I'll soon be using.

To lunch over the road in Portcullis House, with Jonathan, Elfyn Llwyd[2] and a few Plaid staff. Mark Williams spots me

---

1   Plaid Cymru MP for Carmarthen East and Dinefwr, 2010–.
2   Plaid Cymru MP for Dwyfor Meirionnydd 1992–2015.

This was no Mickey Mouse campaign…

One of the first official portrait photos by Marian Delyth, the week after winning the nomination. The earring was later airbrushed out.

MIKE PARKER

for the Ceredigion nomination

Plaid

We MUST win this seat back at the next UK general election. Nothing less will do. With your help, I'm the man to do it.

My background:
- Grew up in Worcestershire
- Lived in mid Wales since 2000
- Plaid Cymru member since 2000
- Self-employed for 22 years
- Renowned author – *Neighbours From Hell?*, *Map Addict*, *Real Powys*, *The Wild Rover*, *Rough Guide to Wales* and others
- Popular TV/radio presenter – *Coast to Coast*, *Great Welsh Roads*, *On the Map* etc.
- Current affairs columnist in *Golwg*, *Planet: The Welsh Internationalist*, *Big Issue Cymru*
- Journalist for *The Guardian*, *Western Mail*, *Sunday Times*, *Daily Telegraph* and many others
- Respected commentator and passionate communicator in Welsh and UK media
- Experienced speaker and debater
- Speaker of English, Welsh & French

My promise:
- To meet all members and branches
- To spearhead canvassing sessions in the constituency every week between now and the election
- To hold public meetings around Ceredigion on the issues of the day
- To liaise closely with Elin Jones, Ellen ap Gwynn, our team of councillors and branch officials
- To develop the media profile of Plaid's work in Ceredigion and our ambition for Wales
- To challenge other parties to open debates in the run-up to the election
- To get involved with community groups and campaigns across the county
- To participate fully in developing Plaid's vision for a successful independent Wales
- To take on the LibDems' record as part of this disastrous government

See you at the hustings!
- ◆ Thursday 6 June 7pm at Llety Parc, Aberystwyth
- ◆ Friday 14 June 7pm at Ysgol Bro Sion Cwillt, Synod Inn

www.mikeparker.org.uk

My pitch to members before the hustings in June 2013.

At the National Eisteddfod in Denbigh, August 2013, celebrating Rhun ap Iorwerth's thumping victory in the Ynys Môn by-election the previous week.

Speaking at the Plaid Cymru conference in Aberystwyth, October 2013.

Barley Saturday in Cardigan, April 2014, including an encounter with my Liberal Democrat opponent, Mark Williams MP.

Bottom photograph: Iestyn Hughes

Summer 2014. The only candidate in the village; the Lampeter agricultural show; a well-earned canvassing break with Elin Jones AM in Llangrannog.

Addressing the rally in support of striking National Library workers, September 2014. Aberystwyth super-snappers Keith Morris and Iestyn Hughes on the right.

Iestyn's view of the event.

Photograph: Iestyn Hughes

Edinburgh, 18 September 2014, the day of the Scottish independence referendum. An early morning 'Yes' street stall staffed by campaigners from Wales, while for the 'No' camp, it's all getting a little *Father Ted*. Careful now…

Launch of Plaid's general election candidates at the party conference in Llangollen, October 2014.

Filming the Channel 4 political slot on Aberystwyth beach with novelist Niall Griffiths, January 2015.

A selection of campaign material, together with my dad's rather more homespun contribution.

The campaign begins in earnest. The National Farmers' Union hustings, held in an actual cowshed. All candidates are present, from L to R: Daniel Thompson (Green), blowing his nose; Huw Thomas (Labour); Gethin James (UKIP); Wyn Evans (NFU); Mike Parker, speaking (Plaid Cymru); Mark Williams (Lib Dem); Henrietta Hensher (Conservative).

The fence by the Llety Parc in Llanbadarn Fawr, advertising a cornucopia of candidates.

With Leanne Wood and Elin Jones in Aberystwyth, on the Saturday after the Nazigate storm first broke.

Photograph: Keith Morris

It was, as ever, wonderful to see Leanne whose support throughout was rock solid.

Photograph: Amelia Davies

The Mikemobile in Aberaeron.

The highly charged atmosphere of the May Day bank holiday rally at Aberystwyth University, three days before polling.

Photographs: Keith Morris

CEREDIGION

WALES · CYMRU
PAYS DE G...ES

Election night at the count in Aberaeron. Above, after the declaration, I suggest in my speech that Mark Williams may be leader of the LibDems by breakfast time. Below, rueful contemplation of where it went wrong in a radio interview.

Photographs: Keith Morris

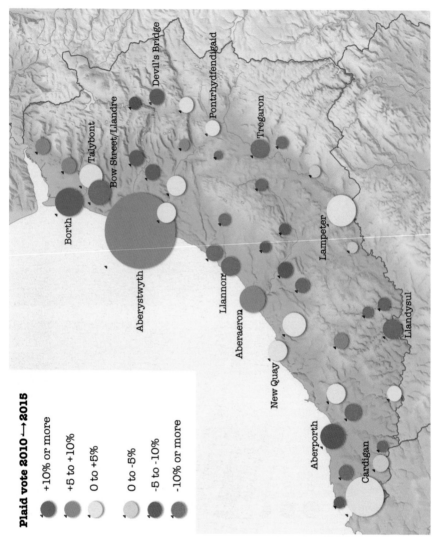

Plaid vote 2010→2015

- +10% or more
- +5 to +10%
- 0 to +5%
- 0 to -5%
- -5 to -10%
- -10% or more

Devil's Bridge
Pontrhydfendigaid
Tregaron
Talybont
Bow Street/Llandre
Lampeter
Borth
Llandysul
Aberystwyth
Llannon
Aberaeron
Llandysul
New Quay
Aberporth
Cardigan

See Appendix for an explanation of these maps.

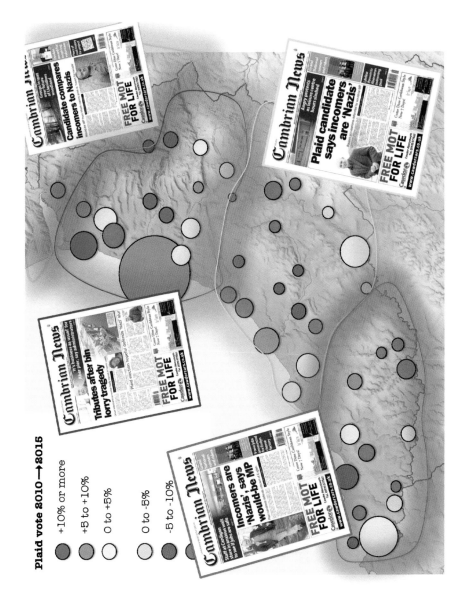

Plaid vote 2010→2015

- +10% or more
- +5 to +10%
- 0 to +5%
- 0 to -5%
- -5 to -10%

The core staff team: with Matthew Woolfall-Jones, Owen Roberts and Gwenllian Mair at a party to drown our collective sorrows on the weekend after the election. Below, less than a week earlier, the hope was intoxicating.

Photograph: Marian Delyth

and comes bouncing over to say hello. We share notes on the weather back home, and the battering that the coast is once again receiving. I bump into him another couple of times during the afternoon, and am love-bombed every time. Elin, Plaid's lively Westminster press officer, takes me around some more, and then back to the Portcullis House canteen to meet journalists from the *Western Mail* and Radio Cymru.

I leave about 5.30, and call Preds to meet me in a pub over the road. My day was like a gothic dream, the kind you have after eating too many ripe cheeses. I give him some of the gossip that I picked up, and we laugh at the absurdity of it all, and then go suddenly quiet at the true absurdity that in eighteen months time, I might be there for real.

Thursday 20 February 2014,
Yr Hen Llew Du pub, Aberystwyth:
Let this miserable winter end. Not once has it been properly crisp or snowy; instead, there's been endless drear, wet, wind and floods. Every morning the first things I see are grey skies, rain smacking the window and skeletal trees swaying in the gusts, so that the gloom sinks through my bones before I've even got out of bed. Our new American neighbour has been here since the first week of January, and she's only seen half a sunny day since arriving.

I've had a nasty cold too, and that has now mutated into my usual red raw sinuses and inflamed nasal polyps. It has all inevitably soured my enthusiasm. I drag myself to Aberystwyth to run a fundraising quiz night for Plaid. At times, I can barely get the questions out, so racked am I by coughs and wheezing. In a noisy pub, it is nearly impossible. I leave as soon as it's over, and head home, feeling woefully sorry for myself.

Thursday 27 February 2014,
Glasgow:
The end of a second whistlestop tour of Scotland for the Royal Scottish Geographical Society (RSGS), delivering my lecture

On the Map: Cartography and National Identity. Sixteen months ago, I gave the lecture in Aberdeen, Dundee, Dunfermline, Glasgow and Edinburgh. On this tour, I've spoken in Dumfries, Galashiels, Ayr and Helensburgh.

Both trips have been fascinating and fun. My lecture looks at mapping as an ingredient in fomenting nationhood and its uses in everything from the dark arts of propaganda to the lighter, but often no less political, uplands of art and pop culture. It focuses on Scotland, for there is so much source material here, but roves widely and includes cameo appearances by Wales, England, Denmark, Slovenia and the ghost nation of Pomerania on the Baltic Sea.

The independence referendum is now just six months away, and the change in atmosphere since my last tour is remarkable. As is obvious from the name, the RSGS is hardly the most radical of organisations, and their audiences tend to be older and more conservative than the population at large. Even so, many people quietly tell me that they have recently decided to vote Yes in September, or have moved from a firm No into the undecided camp. Something big is brewing.

Tuesday 4 March 2014,
Llanbadarn Fawr:
Off to see artist Mary Lloyd Jones this morning at her studio in the Old College, the Castle Gormenghast of the Aberystwyth skyline. She's eighty this year, but as fit as a flea, and gives me a whirlwind tour of the astonishing interior. She is such good company, and I end up staying for hours. Her pet project, to see the rejuvenation of the building as an international art venue, is very much supported by the University Vice Chancellor, she tells me. This is the first time I've heard anyone speak positively about the VC.

A few of us canvass Llanbadarn this evening. One man, late forties, tells me that he likes a lot of what he sees in Plaid, but that he cannot abide Leanne. Talking a little more with him, it transpires that actually it's female politicians as a whole that he hates. In the least surprising news of the day, he also tells me that he's divorced.

Saturday 8 March 2014,
Holland House Hotel, Cardiff:
Plaid spring conference in an airless Cardiff hotel that gives me a headache within minutes. It's not been the best couple of days, and I'm quite disheartened. It feels as if the air has been steadily leaking out of the balloon since Leanne's election two years ago.

Her speech at conference is good, in that she says some good things. With just two months to go to the European elections, it is great to hear her challenge UKIP, and the ugly politics they represent, in such clear terms: "And I say to UKIP today, your politics have no place in our country, not now, not ever." But she sounds painfully measured and scripted, and words like that need to be delivered with the passion I know she has in buckets.

Dafydd Êl then gives an interview to the BBC flatly disagreeing with her, and calls her comments on UKIP "facile". Cue a perfectly fabricated storm, lots of youngsters running around barking into mobiles and a few hours of artificial excitement pepping up a truly tedious atmosphere.

And that's my main problem with Plaid right now. It is so bland, so safe, so bleached of all colour, and I can't work out if this is inevitable. All parties sport the whalebone corset of Blairite stage management these days and we are no exception. But whereas Blair could get away with it twenty years ago, in the pre-internet era, people have become much more attuned to the hollow phrases of politicians. The more politics becomes just another branch of marketing, the more we drive people into the arms of Farage and his tedious "man of the people" drill.

I leave the conference depressed about more than this. There are some very dark forces at work in the world right now, and we need to tackle them with guts, imagination and honesty. I see very little of that here. Instead, the only moment of real passion in the whole conference erupts for the most pathetic of reasons.

Before the squabble with Dafydd Êl, yesterday's storm in a teacup had been a couple of tacky tweets from MP Jonathan Edwards. In a press conference for the forthcoming Britain and Ireland Lions tour, Welsh captain Sam Warburton, both of whose parents are English, had said that on a Lions tour, he is fine calling himself British. In response, Jonny tweeted: "I really find it difficult to understand how someone who does not consider themselves to be Welsh can be captain of the national rugby side," followed by a petulant "Justin Tipuric is a far better player anyway." It's a perfect Twitterstorm, with all of the right ingredients, including the inevitable graceless and unconvincing climb-down.

As a result, Jonny's been ordered to keep away from conference, so as to minimise the risk of the nonsense rumbling on any further. He does make a fleeting appearance on screen however, in the recent Plaid party political broadcast that's played to the hall as the warm-up to Leanne's speech. The second he appears, applause and cheering erupt in the hall. I despair. If we're going to pick fights, let them be better ones than this.

We like to kid ourselves that there is no crossover between Plaid and UKIP, but this is exactly the same sort of teary, beery, woe-is-me xenophobia that they do so well. I thought I was getting stuck into Plaid to help formulate something better: more positive, more inclusive, bigger and more hopeful. This last few days has left me wondering if that is even possible. God knows I hope it is, but I'm not sure.

Thursday 13 March 2014,
Capel Brondeifi, Lampeter:
Constituency meeting, with Hywel Williams[3] giving a thorough

---

3   Plaid Cymru MP for Arfon 2001–.

assessment of social policy under the coalition government. Welfare cuts and the bedroom tax are biting hard; I'm hearing it regularly on the doorstep. The LibDems have been entirely complicit in this, and it is my mission to have people join the dots.

On the way down to Lampeter, I listened to Leanne on Radio Wales. The interviewer kept banging on about the royals, and in exactly what circumstances she would be prepared to meet with them. It is such a sideshow, and should be shot down in flames as just that. Instead, Leanne says that she'll be at the next royal jamboree in the Assembly, and that she always said that she would when she stood for the leadership. It's the worst of both worlds, guaranteed to please or convince no-one.

Leanne is stumbling slightly, in truth. She has got into such a state about Dafydd Êl – late last night, a few of us received an email from her, to tell us that she'd sacked him as a Plaid spokesperson and Assembly committee chair, and for us to be her eyes and ears on social media. "I don't need to explain to you how dangerous this could be to our national project," she wrote.

I think she's in danger of missing the point about Dafydd Êl. She frets that his truculence is personal and aimed squarely at her, but I think it comes more from his perhaps understandable frustration at having been unceremoniously turfed out as Assembly Presiding Officer following the last election in 2011. He'd performed the role for twelve years, since the very beginning of the Assembly, and it was a job ideally suited to his temperament and grand style. More to the point, it took him out of the daily grind of party politics, for like the Commons Speaker, he had to be independent of all that. To go from those sort of ceremonial heights to the status of backbencher in the third largest party must have been tortuous for someone like Dafydd. It possibly explains too his surprise decision to contest the leadership when Ieuan Wyn stood down.

This stuff though bores and depresses me. It has been such a shock to see how much of a politician's firepower is trained not on his real opponents, but on his supposed comrades. Thank god for the canvassing. Being out there in the lanes and hills of Ceredigion, and talking with its residents, is the best bit of this whole experience. It is far more fulfilling than the tedious am dram of Plaid's internal battles.

Wednesday 19 March 2014,
Penparcau, Aberystwyth:
A visit to the food bank at St Anne's Church in Penparcau. It is a slick operation, and needs to be: applications for help have rocketed in the last couple of years. Malcolm Dye, one of the organisers, tells me some heartbreaking stories of desperation, here in one of the loveliest parts of one of the world's wealthiest countries. He says that they are just about coping with demand now, but is worried what will happen if – when – interest rates go back up, and the people barely keeping their heads above water go under.

Thursday 20 March 2014,
MGs café-bar, Aberystwyth:
A mostly brilliant night, a public meeting with Leanne and myself in conversation. Over forty people show up; many are complete newcomers to Plaid. After my grumpiness of the last few weeks, it is a relief to get back to what we both do best, namely talking ideas and ideals in, I hope, an open and entertaining way. We talk about a lot of other things too: our backgrounds, interests and enthusiasms. Our friendship too; it is nice to be reminded of it, for that's where all this began.

There is a great audience-wide discussion afterwards, broken only by the final question, which comes from Cynog Dafis. He is not happy. The evening had, quite deliberately, been advertised as being conducted in English, to allow it to flow uninterrupted and to attract people who probably wouldn't otherwise come. On both counts, it works a treat. Cynog makes an issue out of the lack of simultaneous translation facilities by complaining about it in Welsh, and then translating himself into English. The atmosphere nosedives in the room, and I'm grateful that town councillor Mererid Jones leaps in to pull the raffle.

UKIP tried to stir it about this too. The independent councillor in Aberporth, Gethin James, announced last week that he was joining them, whereupon he was promptly sacked from the Ceredigion council cabinet by Plaid leader Ellen ap Gwynn. He makes as much illiterate trouble as he can on Twitter: "I am the Un Welsh one because I've joined UKIP and their the ones who won't let me ask a question in Welsh", and, attempting to write his own headline: "Plaid Cymru's Mike Parker Say's I can't ask a question in Welsh at Plaid Cymru event in Aberystwyth this Thursday WTF."

Cynog is not alone either; I hear there are other Plaid supporters mortally offended by the words "Noson yn Saesneg"[4] on the event's advertising. God, it's depressing. Blanket bilingualism, while the thing to fight for thirty years ago, is sometimes so restrictive. It means that one section of the population can develop a fifty per cent deaf-blindness, while the other gets everything twice. It can also kill the rhythm and pace of an otherwise interesting discussion. Sometimes it's appropriate and works a treat, generally speaking in large meetings and conferences, but for smaller and more informal gatherings, it can be appropriate to have evenings solely in Welsh, such as the meeting with Hywel Williams in Lampeter last week, and sometimes in English, like tonight. When language – any language – becomes something that's calibrated rather than celebrated, we fillet it of all that makes it sing.

Friday 21 March 2014,
Home:
In a written parliamentary answer, Universities Minister David Willetts has confirmed that the Resource Accounting and Budgeting (RAB) charge on trebled tuition fees is now 45 per

---

4   "Evening in English."

cent. This is the amount that has to be written off, as graduates fail to earn enough or get lost from the system – after all, the period post-university is the one when people generally move around more than at any other time in their lives. It is hellish expensive to administer. The point at which the RAB charge becomes cost-neutral, i.e. when the Treasury is gaining nothing at all from it, is 48.6 per cent.

It's proof that this, like so much else of the austerity programme, is ideological. It's about making young people debt-slaves, and more acquiescent to a system that is screwing them. No amount of "I'm so sorry" from Nick Clegg can disguise the fact that it is his party that let this happen.

Saturday 22 March 2014,
Felinfach, Dyffryn Aeron:
We were supposed to be canvassing in Aberporth today, but decided to change plan, to let the dust settle after the local councillor's defection to UKIP. Accordingly, Gwen has arranged a session in Talsarn and Felinfach instead. As we near the end of the canvass, I receive a text from a volunteer asking if we are still in Aberporth. I reply to the effect that with the hoohah over UKIP, we are steering clear of it at the moment.

Seconds after sending it, I receive a tweet from Tomos Livingstone, a journalist at the *Western Mail*, saying "So you're avoiding Aberporth are you?" What I thought was a text was in fact the text notification of a Twitter direct message (DM), and replying as I had, made it a public message on my Twitter timeline. Whoops. A couple of other people quickly point it out to me, and in less than a minute, my phone rings. It is Owen, his first words "Are you sure you wanted to post that on Twitter?" I can hear Caryl[5] in the background, advising

---

5   Caryl Wyn Jones, former staff member of Plaid in Cardiff, now the CEO of the Ceredigion branch of the Farmers' Union of Wales. Engaged to Owen Roberts, they married in September 2015.

him on what I should do: delete it and then either send a ha-ha *mea culpa* joke DM to Tomos Livingstone or ignore it. I choose the latter. Time will tell if that was the right decision. But blimey, Twitter is a hand-grenade. Must be handled with care.

Tuesday 25 March 2014,
Plaid office, Aberystwyth:
Still some language fallout from the Leanne public meeting last week. Cynog and I have had an email exchange about it. I see his point – how to many people the appearance of an essentially monolingual English Plaid event sets a precedent that offends and scares them. But what was right in 1984 may well not be so in 2014. Earlier today, I asked Elin what to do about the simmering row. Her advice was to tell Cynog that someone else decided to hold it in English, thus meaning that I don't have to take responsibility for it. The choice was mine, though, and for what I still believe to have been the right reason. That I have to stand on.

I'm no Feng Shui expert, but the Plaid office is dreadful. The layout and lighting are terrible, and worse, there's nowhere to make a cup of tea. I don't know how Owen, Gwen and Mary work here; I'd never get anything done. It's unfortunate too that Owen and Gwen have to share the same room. They could not be more opposite: meticulous, methodical Owen, glowering across the room at scattergun Gwen, who gets it done but only in the nick of time and always in her own inimitable fashion. It can get very tense in there.

Thursday 27 March 2014,
Tafarn Dwynant, Ceinws, near Machynlleth:
Back at my old local for my monthly pub quiz. Tonight, one of the regulars tells me that this will be his last quiz, as he and his young family are moving to Scotland next week. He works for Dulas Engineering, and says that the renewables sector in Wales has all but collapsed since the Labour-Plaid

coalition came to an end three years ago. All the action is now in Scotland, and so must he be.

Yesterday, I bumped into another old friend in Machynlleth market, who also told me that he and his family were having to move, this time from Borth to Cardiff. He and his partner both depend on part-time and freelance jobs, and they have all become zero hours contracts of late. As a result, their already meagre income has plummeted. They are an enormously talented, hard-working couple, but cannot afford to scrape together enough of a living in Ceredigion. Both encounters work as a sobering reminder of what I'm fighting for in this election.

Tuesday 1 April 2014,
Penygraig, Aberystwyth:
This week's Tuesday evening canvass is in the Beverley Hills of Aberystwyth, the spacious avenues high above town. There are terrible smog problems in the south and east of England, but the effect here of the unnaturally still, clear air is to make everything seem sharper and closer than normal. As the sun goes down from my lofty viewpoint, I briefly see the Wicklow Mountains flare up on the horizon in the pink sunset. I'd heard this was possible from Aberystwyth, but had never seen it before, and it thrills me.

Mark Strong, the local town councillor, is with me tonight. With his rock star mane of hair, he doesn't look like the typical Plaid representative. We make a good canvassing team, though he's as chatty as me, and we spend far too long on some doorsteps. We have a tortuous discussion with a disillusioned ex-Plaid supporter. To him, the language is the main issue, way more important than any kind of self-government. "Mae'r iaith wedi marw yng Ngheredigion"[6], he says repeatedly, and there's no shaking him. We're too long on the neighbouring doorstep as well, talking with a spirited English woman who has lived here since the 1970s. She's pessimistic too, but for different

---

6   "The language has died in Ceredigion".

reasons. "It's our generation who have had it good, and yours who are going to have to pay for it", she says.

Thursday 3 April 2014,
International Politics Department, Aberystwyth University:
On my way to the university, I pop into the office to be given a slap on the wrist by Owen. The feedback from Mark after our canvass the other night mentioned how slow our progress had been. "If Mark Strong says you're talking too much, then believe me, you are," he says.

To the Arts Centre for a lecture by BBC Economics Editor Robert Peston. The great hall is packed, and he is excellent. He says that yes, there is a recovery starting, at least in the service sector and in the south-east of England, but that it is fragile, and in his estimation, will only last about two years, for there are far bigger dangers lurking not far ahead. He puts it into a political timescale, explaining that things will improve up to the general election next year, but probably not for very long afterwards.

I'm one of only a tiny number of Peston's audience to wander over the road to a European election hustings in the InterPol Building. Marc Jones, the second candidate on our list, is representing Plaid, and does so very well. Even so, it's an uphill struggle for him to make it of any great interest to us. Not that it much matters; I don't think there are any undecided voters here. It's just the hacks and anoraks.

Friday 11 April 2014,
Gregynog, near Newtown:
Driving to speak at the annual gathering of the Association of Welsh Writing in English, I hear Cameron on the news from the Welsh Conservative conference in Llangollen. Ramping up the rhetoric on the Welsh Government's custodianship of the NHS, he calls Offa's Dyke "the line between life and death". What irresponsible hogwash. The Tories are increasingly using the Welsh NHS to club the Labour Party; it's been faithfully

parroted on numerous front pages of the *Daily Mail*. As that is sadly the biggest-selling paper in Wales, it is working a treat. People are terrified. If they're prepared to be this filthy now, god knows what they'll throw as we get nearer the election.

Wednesday 16 April 2014,
Llandysul:
To the National Library to give a lunchtime lecture, *A Truly Fairy Place: Wales as the Eternal Picturesque*. It is such a pleasure to talk about politics and history in a more abstract, fluid way, as opposed to the staccato, often stale little gobbets that are my daily diet these days. A full house too, and lots of enthusiasm.

On a bit of a high, I drive down to Llandysul and meet a small but lively crew for some canvassing. It goes well, though I have trouble dissuading one of our volunteers out of his usual opening gambit, which is to holler "Ydych chi'n siarad Cymraeg?"[7] into the face of whoever opens the door.

Saturday 26 April 2014,
Cardigan:
It's Barley Saturday in Cardigan, the starting gun for the summer's events throughout the county. I came years ago when I was here on *Rough Guide* duty, and was awed to see the horses thundering up the main street, steaming in the chilly spring air. Today, it's just damp and miserable, but the atmosphere is terrific. Thousands line the streets, and it's not just horses in the parade these days, but vintage tractors and cars too.

I meet my Labour opponent, Huw Thomas, for the first time. I've heard lots about him, as he grew up in Aberystwyth before heading to Oxford and then Cardiff, where he is a city councillor and indeed a former member of the ruling Cabinet. All that, and he's only in his mid twenties; he is one ambitious young man. A couple of people who were his contemporaries

---

7   "Do you speak Welsh?"

at Penweddig school have told me that at the age of about fourteen, Huw used to strut around saying that he was going to be prime minister one day.

He's very personable, if prickly. Almost the first thing he says to me is a sarcastic "Hmmm, trying to rock the look of a gentleman farmer, I see," referring to the fact that I'm wearing a tweed jacket and flat cap. I've been wearing those for years; it's the most practical outfit for a middle-aged man in a Welsh winter. Huw is going to be a handful, I can see.

Before long, I bump into Mark Williams and his entourage. He greets me like an old friend, and it suddenly strikes me how bizarre it is that the two main contenders to be MP for Ceredigion hail from Hertfordshire and Worcestershire. We have a good-natured chat; he tells me that Jill Evans and I were spotted doing a photoshoot the other day on the headland in Borth, just up from his house. There are eyes everywhere in this game.

Wednesday 30 April 2014,
Tafarn Y Ffarmers, Llanfihangel-y-Creuddyn, Ceredigion:
A dinner rendezvous with Emyr and Diane, at their friend Rhodri's pub near Aberystwyth. I've never been before, and it's everything I had heard it was: a proper old village boozer, with good beer and sensational food.

At the end of the evening, and after a pint or two, Rhodri has something to tell me, and I can guess what it is immediately: "Many of my regulars, the fellers that prop up the bar here every Friday night, they'd love to hear what you've got to offer, and lots of them could vote for you, I'm sure. Except... you know what? They'd never be able to get past your ear-ring. That's all they'd remember, and I'm afraid to say it would probably be enough to put a fair few of them off."

I am fed up of talking about the ear-ring, but for the first time, I see the point. If there's one thing recent canvassing for the Euro elections has shown me, it's how random some people's voting intentions are, their decision made on the most oblique of factors. More often than not, the clincher will not be what I say or write, or the policies that the party has so carefully crafted, but on fleeting impressions, an inadvertently-hit prejudice here, a moment of connection there. My identity is not bound up in the ear-ring, but it is an issue. And the only way to make it a non-issue, sadly, is to get shot of it.

Thursday 1 May 2014,
Home:
Beltane, May Day, Calan Haf, one of the great pagan hotspots in the calendar. I've had some wild and crazy May Days over the years, but this is not one of them. Instead, I remember the tradition of the Beltane sacrifice, and take out my ear-ring. They're going to be thrilled in Pier Street.[8]

I'm less bothered about my new appearance than I thought I would be. Life is all about finding the right drag for the right occasion. It was one of the ANC leaders in South Africa who said that to be a real radical in politics, you had to dress like a conservative. That said, there's an uneasy voice deep within, whispering that the removal of my ear-ring is all about looking less gay, and is that something to be proud of?

Tuesday 13 May 2014,
Llandysul:
Out for a day's door-knocking with Jill Evans for the European elections next week. I've been out a few times too with Stephen Cornelius, who works for Jill in Brussels, and is third on the list of Plaid candidates for the election. For both of them, this is all just a blip of inconvenience in their lives, a momentary interruption to the smooth flow of life as a Eurocrat. They must hate it, having to go and effectively beg for their jobs from people who know absolutely sod all about it and care even less.

Canvassing for the Euro elections is such a tedious grind,

---

8   Plaid Cymru's Ceredigion office in Aberystwyth.

a daily diet of half-formed opinions and prejudices. I fear that UKIP are going to do very well. They've been built up relentlessly in the media over the last few years. Since the last election, Farage has been on the BBC's *Question Time* more than anyone except Labour's Caroline Flint, and that without having a single MP to his name. On the doorstep, if we get anything, it's reheated versions of his glib rhetoric, curdled into an unspecific hatred of "Europe" or "Brussels".

Plaid are far from immune to this either. Instead of banging the drum for continental co-operation and greater understanding, our entire campaign has revolved around arguing about how much we get back from the EU in hard cash. It's not very inspiring, and it is playing the game whose rules have been set by UKIP and the far right. People we have marked down as our firm supporters are proving to be anything but this time. There's a lot of dropped eye contact and awkward shuffling.

Thursday 22 May 2014,
Cardigan:
Owen and I came down to Cardigan yesterday to test out our polling day operation for next year. The whole town votes in the same polling station, so it is relatively easy to draw up a rota of people to cover a day of taking voters' numbers as they arrive. Backing them up is a crew going out to knock up. It's a fun day, but hard. The rain pounds down throughout, only finally petering out about seven this evening.

I've done a few sessions of number taking at the polling station. It is slow going, especially during the day. It's noticeable how many of those who do come and vote tell us that they haven't done so in years. I can guess who's getting their X, and it's not us. At one point this evening, there are ten or more Plaid people gathered outside the polling station entrance, rosettes akimbo, guffawing happily. It makes me terribly nervous. Not only is it firmly against the rules, it looks awful, like a knock-off Mafiosi.

We stop on the way home in Aberaeron, for the verification of the ballot papers as they come in from across the county. The count isn't taking place until Sunday, to co-ordinate with all of the other countries, so Owen is keen to glean as much information as possible from brief glimpses of the ballots being put into unsifted piles. There's about ten of our helpers busily scanning, a similarly sized gang of LibDems, and Gethin James, the UKIP councillor, who is strutting around knowing that this is their moment. He's a strange bloke. Quite pally, even when I'd really rather he wasn't, and then – bash – a sly or sarcastic dig. He tries to wind me up by saying that he'd heard we were making rather too much of ourselves at the polling station in Cardigan, but I don't take the bait.

From the little we can see of the ballot papers, it seems that we have done pretty well, and probably topped the poll in Ceredigion. The LibDems have tanked, and that is enough to put a spring in Owen's step. We head north, tired but overjoyed to have got this lifeless election behind us. Next stop May.

Monday 26 May 2014,
Home:
That was a close one. Jill was re-elected in the fourth and final seat. Seven thousand fewer votes, and Labour would have had a second at our expense. UKIP came horribly close to winning in Wales, and did so substantially in England, enough to make them the overall victors across Britain. This is the first UK-wide election since 1906 not won by one of the main two parties.

Good news in Ceredigion, though. We won comfortably with 35 per cent, trailed by UKIP on 20 per cent, and then the Conservatives (13 per cent), LibDems (11 per cent), Labour (10 per cent) the Greens (8 per cent) and assorted tiny parties. The headline there is the collapse of the LibDems, but we shouldn't read too much into it, however tempting it is to do so. In Ceredigion, we easily won the European election in 2009, the year before losing the Westminster seat by eight thousand votes.

Across the UK, it was a truly shocking night for the LibDems. They looked like they were going to lose every one of their eleven MEPs until they scraped the last of the ten places in the south-east of England. On one level, it's a shame, for we have precious few pro-European voices left, and they could at least be relied on for that. On another, I'm delirious with *schadenfreude*.

Thursday 29 May 2014,
Home:
A phone-in this morning on Radio Wales about the LibDems after their disastrous European election. A few of their MPs are agitating for a swift decapitation of Nick Clegg, which is picking up support. Paul Hinge, their councillor in Bow Street, has said the same on Facebook. Owen is going to dangle it in front of the *Cambrian News*. Neither Hinge nor any other Welsh LibDem was prepared to go on the phone-in, though; both the particpants, one pro-Clegg, one anti, were from across the border. It was pathetic. The woman calling for him to go was nearly in tears about how they are only trying to do their best, and why oh why had the electorate been so beastly to them for that? It's the LibDems in a nutshell: sanctimonious, narcissistic and incapable of taking responsibility.

Sunday 8 June 2014,
Home:
In today's *Observer*, the "This much I know" column, from Paddy Ashdown: "The best time in politics is before you get elected. In the eight years fighting to become an MP I had no money and two periods of unemployment, but everything was clear and black and white. Then I got elected and nothing was ever simple again."

Wednesday 11 June 2014,

Home:

The *Cambrian News* has ignored Hinge and the splits in the local LibDems, instead giving Mark Williams a full page to spin it his way. He insists there is no need for a leadership challenge to Nick Clegg, and allays any fears among his Ceredigion faithful that he will be pulled from them to address a higher calling.

"I don't want to be leader," he states firmly in the article. To emphasise the point, it is the quote pulled out as a subhead. As if anyone, anywhere has ever suggested that he was in the frame! "Ceredigion is such a huge area that it needs an MP specifically focused on it," he continues. "Besides that, if I went for it my wife would kill me."

What disingenuous guff. Any minister or party leader has a constituency to attend to, and they all do so quite adequately. Although Ceredigion is a big patch, you can still go from one end to the other in ninety minutes, and it has way below the average national number of constituents; it is 625th out of 650 in the population rankings. On top of that, devolution has meant that the policy area workload of a Welsh MP has diminished considerably in the last decade.

There's more chest-beating about how beastly the Tories are, and how he isn't "the favourite person in the Government Whip's Office". He's only voted against the government a couple of dozen times in four years – there are loads of LibDems (and even more Tories) who have rebelled far more often. But still he persists with his own myth: rebel without a cause.

Friday 13 June 2014,

Llanddewi Brefi:

It's been decided that Elin and I will do Fridays out and about together in the constituency through the summer. Last week it was a riotous outing to the Gŵyl Nôl a Mla'n[9] in Llangrannog.

---

9   The "To and Fro Festival", so called because there are two stages by the beach, which the crowds shuttle between.

Next week we'll be following Ras yr Iaith[10] across the county. This week it's some comparatively gentle canvassing with Mary and Gwen from the office around Llanddewi Brefi. It is a beautiful high summer day, and we have a fine time.

Elin and I are getting on well, as I felt sure we would. She is great company, never misses a trick and can instantly see the bigger picture in almost any circumstance. In another time, she would have been a superb Plaid leader, though I'm not sure how successful the image consultants would have been with her. Losing that election, having been the red-hot favourite, must have been so difficult, but I've never once seen an ounce of self-pity or recrimination from her. She's unstintingly loyal to Leanne, and has welcomed me in with open arms.

The reaction to her is positive right across Ceredigion. I can count on my fingers the number of people who've spoken negatively about her in a year of canvassing. But then, Mark Williams seems to be equally well regarded as the MP. It's a typically Ceredigion thing. After all, strip away the fierce local rivalry between the parties, and it's clear that there is much ideological common ground between Plaid Cymru and the Liberal Democrats. The animosity between us here is largely personal and tribal, and to voters uninterested in all that, it seems perfectly logical to support Elin for the Assembly and Mark for Westminster. There are very many who do just that.

We pop in to the village shop and see the owner. I interviewed him years ago on *Great Welsh Roads*, as he was then doing a roaring trade in T-shirts, in both Welsh and English, declaring *I am the Only Gay in the Village*. This was the catchphrase of Dafydd, a character in TV sketch show *Little Britain*, who supposedly lived in Llanddewi Brefi. Fans of the show even stole the village signs. I remember doing a piece to camera about that, standing by one of them. The director's idea had

---

10   "The Race of the Language", a run from Machynlleth to Cardigan, to
      celebrate Welsh. Inspired by a comparable event in the Basque Country.

been for me to do it with my upper half framed, before pulling away to reveal me in skin-tight rubber shorts, à la Matt Lucas as Dafydd. I'm very glad that I refused. I wouldn't fancy that footage resurfacing now.

Saturday 14 June 2014,
Lovesgrove, near Aberystwyth:
Blazing sunshine at the Aberystwyth and Ceredigion County Show, the largest in the area. It's a wonderful atmosphere. The animals are buffed to perfection, the vintage vehicles gleam, and the place teems with some incredible characters. It does seem mad that I could possibly hope to represent these people in parliament. Best not think about it too much, perhaps, as more and more people are telling me that we can win.

Tuesday 24 June 2014,
Neaudd y Paith, Capel Seion:
I'm doing some joint meetings in a couple of weeks with Andy Chyba of the Green Party, and have knocked together an e-flyer to advertise them. On sending it to Owen, his immediate response was that he liked the font I'd used, as it was a cheeky retro nod to the one used by the SDP in the 1980s. He is such a trainspotter. Which is exactly why we get on so well.

To a Plaid branch meeting tonight out in Capel Seion on the road from Aberystwyth to Devil's Bridge. This is the proper Ceredigion boondocks, *Hinterland* country. Even the name of the venue, Neuadd y Paith, hints at that. Paith, the name of the small stream below the village, means plain or prairie, and conjures up images of stubbly gauchos on horseback.

The small gathering is enthusiastic, though there is a strong element, as there often is with people whose activist days were in the Sixties and Seventies, of slight bewilderment at how sober-suited today's Plaid Cymru seems. Climbing TV masts, sit-ins and daubing road signs were the stuff of their youth, which surely makes the blood flow a lot quicker than the latest wrangle over the Silk Commission. I suspect that there are still a few cowboy hats hanging up in local porches, here on the Ceredigion *paith*.

Saturday 5 July 2014,
Castle Green Inn, Lampeter:
This year's summer school, at Lampeter University, has been rebranded as "Candidates' Academy", boot camp for those of us facing the electorate in ten months time. It is very upbeat, positively cultish at times. Despite the fact that our most recent electoral test, when real people cast real votes, had us scrape just enough to re-elect Jill Evans, we remain blithely sure that the triumphant uplands are just over the horizon. Everyone is certain that Ceredigion and Ynys Môn are in the bag, and now that Vaughan Williams has been selected for Llanelli, that too is coming our way.

I've volunteered to run a pub quiz for the evening, which is packed. A picture round of naming European prime ministers and their countries turns into a hilarious game of Spot the National Stereotype. As I know all too well from games of Scrabble at our kitchen table, Leanne is ferociously competitive, and I'm relieved that her team wins.

Monday 7 July 2014,
Home:
Ladbrokes have cut the odds on my winning, from 2/1 to 7/4. This is more than twice as favourable as the odds on John Rowlands regaining Ynys Môn, despite the fact that the majority he has to overcome there is less than 2,500.

Wednesday 9 July 2014,
Fachongle, Pembrokeshire:
A day of joint open meetings with Andy Chyba of the Green Party. The first one was at Fachongle Isaf, the farm in the Preseli Mountains of Pembrokeshire that was green guru John Seymour's home from 1964. Seymour was the original good lifer in Wales – almost literally, for it was the success of

1970s sitcom *The Good Life* that boosted sales of his books *The Fat of the Land* and the *Complete Guide to Self-Sufficiency*. He left Wales in the late 1980s, declaring that it was by then "insufficiently authentic", but returned to Fachongle, where one of his daughters still lived, for the last few years of his life. He is buried in an orchard.

Originally, Andy Chyba was the Greens' lead candidate in Wales for the European election, but he stood down last November, saying that the Greens should do likewise as a party, and concentrate instead on getting Jill Evans re-elected. He's long been an advocate of closer co-operation with Plaid Cymru, something seen with deep suspicion by many in his party, and ours too. Later this year, he's challenging Pippa Bartolotti for the leadership of the Welsh Greens, on a platform of closer co-operation with Plaid, something he has discussed favourably with Caroline Lucas MP. She does, after all, already work very closely with the Plaid team in Westminster. It's very unlikely though that there'll be a repeat of the formal pact between the two parties that got Cynog elected in 1992.

There are about a dozen of us sat in a circle in Fachongle's serene meeting room, and a good debate ensues. Remarkably, no-one mentions badgers, although there remains considerable nervousness towards Plaid. It's the old sticking point again of "nationalism", a word so toxic to people whose easy provenance in a comfortable majority culture means that they've never had to consider it much before, but who long ago, and far away, came to the conclusion that it is always A Bad Thing.

Thursday 10 July 2014,
Caerwedros village hall:
The constituency AGM, followed by a Q&A panel discussion about farming, with panelists from both farming unions, Ceredigion YFC and an HSBC agricultural adviser. Elin chairs the evening brilliantly. She'd been terrified that no-one would turn up on a lovely summer's evening, but there are a

good forty plus here, and she is in her element, amongst her people.

Inevitably, Alun Davies's sacking as Agriculture Minister this week provokes much comment. He had been forced out after trying to coerce his civil servants into finding out how much agricultural subsidy is paid to five opposition AMs who also farm. Elin's first question to the panel refers to the case: "Should the amount of subsidy taken by politician-farmers be in the public domain?" Wyn Evans of the NFU says that yes, there was an argument to be made for that, but then any subsidies from the public purse to anyone should also therefore be made known. He's right. The taxpayer funds a crazy range of employment, much of it utterly useless. No-one is going to miss another blue sky thinking consultant or PR slimeball, but we'd soon notice if the farmers vanished.

While there is much to be critical of in agriculture, it alarms me that farmers are increasingly being singled out for condemnation. I'm hearing it all the time, especially from fellow green incomer types in the pubs and parties of Machynlleth, and often in spectacularly vituperative ways. Many cite George Monbiot's new book *Feral*, a manifesto for the re-wilding of the countryside, as "proof" that farmers are hell-bent on poisoning the landscape, while being subsidised handsomely to do so. It's a highly selective interpretation of his book.

That said, I do think that George's usually impeccable standards of research and nuance take a bit of a hit in *Feral*. One of the strangest passages concerns his visit to interview Elin Jones, then the One Wales coalition government's Agriculture Minister. They do not get on. The tortuous situation with the badger cull is at its height, but the devil is in the detail. At one point, Elin pulls out a pen, which is branded with the logo of the Farmers' Union of Wales. To George, this confirms all his worst suspicions about their mutual cosiness. I see his point, and I'd probably be tempted to make it too in the same situation, but if that logic is applied equally, then, looking at the pens in my bag, you can call me a patsy for Barclays Bank, a Danish GPS company and Marriott hotels.

There is much in *Feral* that made me nod in furious agreement, but I think that he overstates the case and is too harsh on the hill farmers of Wales. There is little recognition in the book of the cultural landscape, and how farming has been the glue that keeps it together. I wish that George could be here tonight, and witness the thoughtful and honest discussion from people of all ages at the front line of farming. Their resourcefulness, and overarching urge to manage their patch in as sustainable a way as possible, rings out all evening.

I wish too that he could witness that the entire discussion takes place in Welsh. Translation facilities were available, but not needed. It is lovely to have an evening held quite naturally in Welsh, but without the language itself as its anguished focus. This is continuity against considerable odds, and should be something that excites green thinkers. Cultural sustainability is right up there with every other kind; you cannot have one without the other.

Friday 11 July 2014,
Aberaeron:
A difficult day's canvassing in and around Aberaeron, with a lot of strange and quite hostile reactions. On Wednesday, Andy Chyba said to me that some people's attitude to him had really changed since he started trying his hand at mainstream politics. I know exactly what he means. And though their reactions can be tough, it's not just friends and acquaintances. In the cosseted life of a writer and occasional stand-up, most of the audiences I encountered had chosen to be there and sometimes even paid to hear me. Now people look at me as if I am shit on their shoe.

One village is especially difficult. There a brooding atmosphere and a lot of eyes following our every move. I try and talk with a gang of beefy blokes drinking beers in the sunshine, but they just scowl and grunt at me. A woman answers one door, and begins to tell me of feeling bullied here, before suddenly starting to cry. It is quite disturbing.

Friday 18 July 2014,
Aberporth, Ceredigion:
A half-decent canvass in Aberporth, though one encounter leaves me rattled. It comes from a bloke, sixtyish, in a new-build house on the village edge. Detecting a London accent, I ask him what had brought him to the area. "Because it's white," he says flatly, before ploughing on, "I grew up in north London, and had to leave once they'd taken over [he pronounces "they" with an unambiguous capital T]. We went to Northamptonshire, and had to go when they took over there too. I can't go any further west now, unless it's into the sea."

This is what people are prepared to say to complete strangers on the doorstep. God only knows what they're saying behind closed doors.

Sunday 20 July 2014,
Clwb y Dre, Caernarfon:
A performance of my stand-up show, *The (Very) Rough Guide to Welsh*, at Gŵyl Arall. If there is a message to the piece, it's let's lighten up: the Welsh language is robust and deep and is not going to vanish any time soon. In it, I pick through some of the storms that blow up most weeks after some slight on Welsh occurs, whereupon it all kicks off on social media, before seeping into the papers and TV news agenda. It doesn't need much tweaking to find the humour.

Much to my relief, the reaction in Caernarfon, the Welshest of all towns, is stupendous. People love it, and only when it's done, and the audience is filing out, do I see that some Plaid royalty – Dafydd Wigley and his wife Elinor Bennett, Siân Gwenllian and Dafydd Iwan – are here. I am very glad that I hadn't realised that beforehand. Wigley comes up to congratulate me, and booms in his splendid baritone, "Well, my goodness, you're certainly going to liven up parliament!"

Saturday 2 August 2014,
Home:
Richard Owen, my agent, forwards me an email from the editor of the *Cambrian News*. He knows her from his days in the Books Council, and had written to see if we could arrange a meeting between us. I tried asking last year, but she never replied.

At least he gets a response, though she will not meet me. "My diary is pretty full at the moment," she writes. So the editor of the local paper is not prepared to even meet someone who may well be the area's MP in a year's time. Not just bad manners, but lousy journalism.

Monday 4 August 2014,
Aberystwyth University:
I've enrolled for a fortnight's refresher on the intensive Welsh course at the university. This is where I first learned the language fourteen years ago, and although everything is a little more hi-tech these days, it's the same atmosphere, many of the same teachers and the same unexpectedly diverse crowd of students. In my group of ten, I am the only one who actually lives in Wales; the others come from Brittany, England, Ireland, the US, Germany and Japan. In other groups, there are people from Australia, China, Finland, Palestine, Romania, the Netherlands, Canada and South Africa. It is so inspiring to see Welsh in such an expansive context. One of the longstanding tutors is Dwynwen Teifi, a *cymeriad a hanner*[11] from Llandysul. Every time she sees me in the corridor or canteen, she shouts "Esgusodwch! Mae'r Aelod Seneddol nesa yn dod trwodd!"[12] and suchlike. It is very embarrassing.

---

11 "A character and a half".
12 "Out of the way! The next Member of Parliament is coming through!"

Wednesday 6 August 2014,
National Eisteddfod, Llanelli:
The *maes* of this year's Eisteddfod is massive and exhausting
to navigate around, especially with the wind howling across it
from the Bristol Channel, just a few yards away. I'm speaking,
along with a few other candidates, at the Plaid stall, to a
sizeable and friendly crowd, and manage to do it without
murdering too many mutations. Rhodri Glyn Thomas[13]
introduces me as "un o'n hymgeiswyr mwya lliwgar"[14], and
makes some reference to my ear-ring before looking at me
and realising that it is no longer there. Even in its absence, it's
still getting attention.

Friday 8 August 2014,
Dà Mhìle distillery, near Ffostrasol:
Another day off school to go with Owen to the south of the
county. First stop was a sun-soaked Lampeter Show, which
was terrific and full of warm, weatherbeaten Cardi faces. Elin,
on her home turf, was on great form, and worked the field
with cheerful efficiency, throwing me at everyone in her path.
As ever, my favourite part of the show is the produce tent. It's
always a treat to eavesdrop on ribald opinions of other people's
onions, cakes or craftwork.

From there, we head to visit Longwood on the other side of
Lampeter. It's an impressive social enterprise, a commercial
timber operation in a community woodland. A new wooden
visitor centre is nearing completion; it is staggeringly beautiful.
One of the builders is an evangelist for this sort of low impact
building, and how this area is ripe with expertise and materials,
though hampered by suspicious planning authorities. He's
right, especially when you consider the half-built estates and
brick boxes on flood plains that have sailed through planning.

Final call was to the Dà Mhìle distillery to launch this year's

---

13 AM for Carmarthen East & Dinefwr 1999–2016
14 "One of our more colourful candidates".

Ceredigion Art Trail. Through August, scores of local artists open their studios to the public; it is a superb showcase for the area and all done on a perilous shoestring. My speech goes down well, and there are some great conversations afterwards. My fellow freelancers are exactly the sort of people I want to reach, for rarely do we get our voice heard. None of us are ever going to earn very much, but we're an important part of the life and economy of the area, never more so than in these straitened times. Creativity is often seen as an expendable extra, a luxury to be cast aside when the going gets tough. I'd say that it is precisely at such times that it's needed more than ever.

On the way back I say to Owen that I can really feel a shift towards us, and that we are reaching new voters. I am increasingly convinced that we can win. Owen agrees. Though, he tells me, many others – including some at the heart of the campaign – do not. They really don't believe that we can do it. I'm shocked to hear this.

Friday 15 August 2014,
Aberystwyth University:
My last day on the Welsh course. It has been great, though I'm sad to see one significant change between the course in 2000 and 2014. One of the things I loved about Welsh back then was it seemed relatively immune to the Blairite Newspeak that was then ripping the guts out of English, especially in the public realm. This last fortnight, we've studied things like PR releases, Assembly statements, journalism and numerous websites, and sadly, the cancer of gobbledegook seems to be infecting Welsh now in just the same way.

I can't shake off Owen's words that there are some involved with the campaign who don't believe it can succeed. I've been working on writing an upbeat progress report to send round to everyone, and it has only made me more certain that we can do it. Usually in Westminster elections, Plaid is inherently disadvantaged before a single door has been knocked. Not this time.

There is a swirl of factors that should work in our favour: the meltdown in the LibDem vote from the giddy heights of Cleggmania; that the very specific factors which boosted them in 2005 and 2010 (Iraq and tuition fees) are long spent; the traditional anti-Tory sentiment so strong in Ceredigion; the far lower profile of the badger cull; the new individual registration rules, especially in the universities; the probability that Plaid will be in the TV debates; the trend of giving an incumbent who has scraped in the benefit of the doubt, but once only; and finally, the positive doorstep response I seem to be getting. You could add to that the strength and success of the SNP in government, though how the referendum might play out is anyone's guess.

Saturday 16 August 2014,
Pontcanna Fields, Cardiff:
I've always joked that Cardiff Mardi Gras, the annual LGBT knees-up, should rename itself Pride Cymru, and they've only gone and done just that. Tŷ Gwynfor have asked me to represent Plaid with a short speech on the main stage, and I'm happy to do it. It's years since I've been to any Pride event, and Preds has never managed one. We opt to make a weekend in the capital out of it, and head off in high spirits.

Somewhere near Brecon, I receive a text saying that, sorry, but they've decided not to have any speeches from political parties after all. I'm annoyed, but quietly relieved too, as I know from the experience of regularly compèring Birmingham Pride how much the crowd hate those sort of incursions into their afternoon of entertainment from long-forgotten *X Factor* competitors.

Pride festivals have been thoroughly depoliticised since my first one in London in 1987. The backdrop to that was the Thatcher government's infamous Clause 28 of the Local Government Bill, which proposed outlawing the "promotion of homosexuality" and its "acceptability... as a pretended family relationship" by local authorities. It was legal nonsense, so unspecific as to be practically unenforceable, but it worked well as the intended dog whistle. It worked even better, though in precisely the opposite way to that intended by the Tories, as it galvanised gay people and social liberals against its undiluted spite. One of my favourite statistics is that the year before Clause 28 (1986), the annual Pride march in London had some six thousand participants. A year later, there were sixty thousand, me included. Many of us burst out of the closet roaring in fury.

Better still, in years to come, the clause came to be a massive millstone around the collective neck of the Conservative Party. To Tory fundamentalists, it became a totem they fought long and loud to preserve. To modernisers, it was a suppurating embarrassment, one that they knew alienated them from a sizeable constituency that they should be mopping up. The argument raged for years, wreaking untold self-inflicted damage, in a way that gives me great faith that eventually bigotry backfires. It's a thought to cling to now, when so much seems to be galloping in the wrong direction.

Pride Cymru 2014 could not be further from those heady, angry, idealistic times. Held in a fenced-off compound patrolled by surly security, it cost a tenner to get in or twenty if we wanted to go out and return. After half an hour in there, we've run out of things to do. I try and salvage something from the day by helping out on the Plaid stall. Adam Price shows up, which is almost worth the tenner. I tell him how much I'm disliking Pride, and, for that matter, the commercial gay scene these days. "Dear me Mike," he says, "don't tell me you've hung up your dancing shoes?" I have to admit that yes, I think I probably have.

Wednesday 20 August 2014,
Tregaron:
In a field outside Tregaron for the latest in the long line of village summer shows all over the county. Some are brilliant,

but this one is a little moth-eaten. Damp grey skies and a chill wind aren't helping either.

We're standing in the muddy field when the LibDem mobile rolls in. With so few people here, there is no avoiding them. In the produce tent, I bump into Mark, who beams and introduces me to someone as "Mike, my Plaid opponent – we're great friends aside from the politics!" I'd previously passed Elizabeth Evans, and asked her how she was. Rather unexpectedly, she glared at me and said that she had a migraine, "so don't be surprised if I puke all over you".

Catherine Hughes, the Plaid councillor in Tregaron, is brilliant at throwing me towards people, though I fail miserably to connect with a big group of farmers. "Oes yna rwbeth y'ch chi ise gofyn iddo?"[15] says Catherine, which is met by a tumbleweed silence, broken eventually by "O le y'ch chi'n dod, 'te?"[16] I gabble a reply in terrible Welsh, and everyone looks at their shoes.

Called in at the office on the way down to Tregaron. Owen was tamping about various things, including a letter we both received yesterday from Tŷ Gwynfor, outlining our campaign responsibilities over the next year. This was obviously something spat out by computer algorithm, as it told us quite baldly "We believe that in 2015 you could aim to increase your share of the vote since 2010 by 5 [per cent presumably, it isn't said] and achieve at least 12,728 votes." It's such tosh, designed to sound specific, as if part of some powerful psephological formula only available to the pointy heads in HQ, whereas in truth it's probably just an unpaid intern banging the figures into some cheap software.

I sent poor Owen's blood pressure even higher by spotting a piece in today's *Cambrian News* that had escaped him. No surprise that it had, for it was unrecognisable from his press release which formed its basis. That had highlighted figures he'd

---

15   "Is there anything you want to ask him?"
16   "So where do you come from then?"

found buried in an Assembly document, showing that Ceredigion house prices are now over seven times the average wage in the area. Fifteen years ago, the differential was 4.6. The paper went straight to Mark Williams, and made his anguished response the story. They even gave him opportunity to wax wondrous about some scheme run by "the previous administration", i.e. the LibDems, on the county council. The extensive quotation from me that Owen had included was watered down to a vague line at the very end. As if to underline what we're up against, the next page of the paper has a picture of a big posse of LibDems, Mark and Elizabeth included, behind SAVE BRONGLAIS placards. It is probably the most outrageous issue of the paper yet, and that is really saying something.

Friday 22 August 2014,
Plaid office, Aberystwyth:
On the interview panel today for a communications officer for the campaign. There are four excellent candidates, all prepared to work ridiculous hours for a pittance – it's a real sign of how poor the job market is for graduates who want to stay in the area. It was a tough decision, but a unanimous one: a lad in his mid-twenties called Matthew Woolfall-Jones, originally from Pontypool and now a postgrad and warden of Pantycelyn. He had the extra spark, and that's what we need.

There's some good-natured ribbing of Owen about a press release he sent out yesterday. It concerned maternity services, and was headlined COCK-UP OR CONSPIRACY? With my *Carry On* sense of humour, I'd found it hilarious, but Elin cuts me dead with a withering look, and says "Well, it takes a certain kind of mind to see that."

Owen has heard that Gethin James, the independent-turned-UKIP councillor in Aberporth, is almost definitely going to stand against me. I do hope there is a UKIP candidate, because I am itching to take the bastards on.

Wednesday 27 August 2014,
Roses Bar, Kreuzberg, Berlin:
Having a short break in our favourite city. It's an ever-dependable boost of energy, like plugging into a power source. As usual, we finish our night out by beating a drunken path to Roses Bar, a cathedral of kitsch on the city's southside. We get there about one o'clock, and it's heaving. Seconds after walking in, someone leans towards me and shouts over the noise, "You're Mike Parker, and you're going to be my MP".

It turns out to be composer Richard Baker and his boyfriend Gareth Evans, who live near Tregaron. We've never actually met before, but we all follow each other on Twitter, so it's like meeting friends of a sort. But I do find myself sliding into campaigning politico mode, even pissed, even at one in the morning, and even in Berlin's campest bar.

At one point, we talk about the phenomenon that is Roses Bar, and Richard mentions the fierce proprietress who runs the place with an iron rod. Had we met her? he asks. I was about to say that she once hollered across the bar, as I toked on a joint in the corner, "WHO is smoking dope in here?", but something stops me saying it. Maybe I will yet make a politician.

CALEDONIA DREAMING
September – December 2014

Thursday 4 September 2014,
Plaid office, Aberystwyth:
It's hotting up in Scotland. A YouGov poll came out the night before last, showing No on 53 per cent and Yes on 47 per cent. They traditionally place Yes lower than other pollsters, so this is significant. With just a fortnight to go, it has forced the British media to take the possibility of a Yes vote seriously for the first time.

This referendum will be studied for decades, whichever way it goes. It has been so absorbing. The No campaign has been shocking, and has reminded me of the election campaigns run by Welsh Labour, where sabre rattling and scaremongering become the substitutes for debate, smug in the knowledge that it will probably be enough. For Welsh Labour, it always has been enough thus far, but I'm not so sure it will be this time for the No campaign. There is a real chance that the tectonic plates of the UK and Europe will, a fortnight today, shift irrevocably.

This is not to say that the Yes campaign has been all sunshine and lollipops. Too often, it's been thin-skinned, aggressive and snappy, especially on Twitter. But then, discussions about knitting or kittens quickly turn rancid on Twitter, so what chance this? The much-vaunted phenomenon of the "cybernat", spraying online vitriol from a dingy bedroom, does indubitably exist, but so does its exact equivalent on the opposite side. The No campaign has been doing its utmost to taunt the idiots into action, and then screaming blue murder when it succeeds. Jim Murphy's narcissistic tour around a hundred towns atop an Irn-Bru crate is the perfect example. Inevitably, some ned lobbed an egg at him, and he fancied he was Joan of Arc.

Listening to the London media trying to digest it all, and the fact that the polls are rapidly narrowing, is so interesting. The BBC has been shockingly one-sided; Jim Murphy and his egg were their main headline for days. I've long been a passionate supporter of the Beeb and it grieves me to say so, but I am rapidly losing faith in it and can, for the first time in my life, imagine a far healthier cultural landscape without its ponderous paternalism. I worry that it flattens more talent and originality than it enables, and without doubt, it is increasingly fostering a smug and saccharine version of Britain that can be quite nauseating.

BBC Wales is one of the worst culprits. The NATO summit is on in Newport; it looks gruesome. There are tanks on the golf course at Celtic Manor, a fighter jet parked at its front door, battleships moored in the bay, massive security fences around Cardiff and Newport, public roads, paths and land closed off, helicopters whirring endlessly overhead and armed troops on the streets. Where is BBC Wales in all this? Not a word of inquiry or investigation, just breathless cant about how marvellous it is for Wales, how it has "put us on the map".

On the way down to Carmarthen for an ear appointment the other morning, I caught Radio Wales's phone-in. One old guy rang in to say that he wasn't that excited by the summit, that it was all a bit of an inconvenience and couldn't they meet somewhere more suitable? He was repeatedly berated by the DJ who shouted at him "But aren't you PROUD of us being the host of this huge global event?" As if anyone notices who the host city of a NATO summit is, or books a holiday there because of it.

A depleted campaign committee meeting this evening, but a good one. Our new communications officer, Matthew, is there. He has leapt in at the deep end, which is the only way to cope in this office. I'm really impressed by how much he has already absorbed, and he's coming up with some great ideas.

Monday 8 September 2014,
Home:
The Yes campaign in Scotland has taken the lead in a poll for the first time, and the hounds of hell have been unleashed. Large sections of the UK press, having condescended to treat the whole thing as little more than an amusing sideshow, have suddenly sat bolt upright and gone *"Jeeeeesuss!* It might happen!"

The next ten days are going to be a rollercoaster. Already we've seen the Queen's displeasure invoked, the upping of the terrorist threat, Miliband talking of border posts and guards, banks threatening to relocate their brass plaque HQs, supermarkets hinting at price rises and, on a daily basis, new Better Together promises being dreamt up on the hoof, despite this being illegal as we are now in the official period of electoral purdah. There is the sulphurous whiff of blind, thrashing panic.

Email from Owen: Elin wants to challenge Mark Williams to refuse the recommended MP's pay rise of 9 per cent. Will I say that I won't take it? If I must, I reply, but I'm not keen on this kind of gesture politics. Neither is she, he assures me, but the election is coming, it'll get me in the paper, and so on and so on.

Similarly, in last week's campaign committee meeting, we talked about our response to the Welsh government's plan to blow £1 billion plus on an M4 relief road. This would be the full amount available for the Assembly to borrow under new rules. There are many environmental, economic and pragmatic arguments against this idiotic idea, but Elin said that the focus of our complaint should be the "spending it all in the south-east corner of Wales" card. I said I didn't like playing one corner of Wales off against another, and that my hackles rose when I heard Plaid spokespeople doing just that. Elin's answer was that she didn't like it either, but that it really, really works.

Tuesday 9 September 2014,
Eisteddfa Gurig:
Matthew, our new communications officer, and I head out for an afternoon's filming. The idea is to produce a short introductory video that we can use in the adoption meeting later this month, and also stick it out there on social media. We're not the slickest camera crew – as batteries keep dying on us, we have to record on Matthew's camcorder, my camera and both our phones.

We grab footage in Aberystwyth, along the coast road to Aberaeron, then to Tregaron, Pontrhydfendigaid, Pontrhydygroes, Devil's Bridge and the peaty flanks of Pumlumon at Eisteddfa Gurig, to get footage of me passing the Ceredigion county sign on the A44. It's a beautiful late summer's day, and a joy to amble around the countryside looking for impressive things to film. There are so very many.

Wednesday 10 September 2014,
Plaid office, Aberystwyth:
Manic day. It kicks off with an interview from the Aberystwyth studio for the BBC World Service, for a programme looking at shifting patterns of national identity in the light of the Scottish referendum. London journalists cannot get their heads around a Plaid Cymru candidate with a mild Brummie accent.

From there to join the picket line at the National Library for their one-day strike. Most staff there have had no pay rise for five years, and almost a quarter of them are now earning below the living wage. Morale, unsurprisingly, is at rock bottom. It's very encouraging to see the level of support for the picket from passing motorists on Penglais Hill. People are really feeling the squeeze.

From there, we all process down into town for a rally outside Siop y Pethe. There is lots of support there too, including for me when I speak. Then a quick dash to Bronglais for an ear appointment, and to visit a friend there. Back to the office, a few hours of leafleting around Trefechan and then an Aberystwyth branch meeting, which is well attended and full of ideas. With Scotland so much in everyone's thoughts, and the back-to-school feeling of September, things have definitely gone up a gear. I'm tired, but wired and excited too.

Thursday 11 September 2014,
Home:
A week to go, and it's getting crazier by the minute in Scotland. Ed Miliband decided to cart a hundred of his MPs up for a

day's pressing the flesh in Glasgow. Striding down Buchanan Street, they were followed by a guy in a rickshaw, blaring out a recording of 'The Imperial Death March' from *Star Wars*, and booming through a loudhailer "People of Glasgow! Our imperial masters have arrived! Say hello to your imperial masters!" Bugger pointless screaming on Twitter – *that's* how to make your point.

Cameron and Clegg have been up there too in desperate last-minute pitches. It is telling how the tone of the No campaign has changed since the weekend's shock poll. For months, their strongest card was the pound, and their entirely unknowable assertion that in the event of independence, Scotland could neither keep it, nor enter into any kind of currency union. Now it is time for the lachrymose love-bombing. Cameron repeatedly tells us how "heartbroken" he'd be if "our family of nations was torn apart".

They sound like an abusive husband. He's tried the threats to cut off her cash supply, and when that didn't work, he went off, got drunk and returned with a bunch of wilting carnations from the all-night garage, and proceeded to shout through the letterbox how much he loves her and would do anything to keep her.

Friday 12 September 2014,
Richmond Hotel, Aberystwyth:
I'm guest speaker at Clwb Cinio, an all-male dining club in Welsh, with plenty of familiar faces in attendance. It's another strictly non-political night, so I give a map talk, and get plenty of nods of support. It's a lovely, old-fashioned evening, a fine ensemble of gentlemen and ageing rascals, and is what I imagine those famous gastronomic clubs of the Basque Country to be like. Albeit with rather fewer Michelin stars.

Sunday 14 September 2014,
Home:
A fascinating edition of Radio 4's *The Reunion* this morning,

bringing together some of the architects of New Labour. We're treated to a repeat hearing of Neil Kinnock at the 1992 eve-of-poll rally in Sheffield. I was a Labour activist at the time, and remember watching with mounting horror his vainglorious air-punching and *We're all-riiiiight!*s. Was it that which sank the campaign? Or were there darker forces at work?

In the 1992 election, I was out knocking doors most days for months, and saw something change in the final fortnight, a doorstep response that went viral: "I'm not voting Labour, because you lot will swamp the country with immigrants." It invariably came in the trim cul-de-sacs of south Birmingham, from grey blokes in cardigans, with a silent wife hovering behind in the shadows. The words "swamp with immigrants" were the same every time – a brutal chorus that had evidently been hawked door-to-door by last-minute Tory canvassers. They appeared on no leaflets, nor were uttered on the interminable TV and radio election broadcasts. They snuck in at the end under the radar, and were devastating in their effect.

I'm reminded of the concept of "snatching defeat from the jaws of victory" again a few hours later, watching coverage of a bad-tempered impromptu demonstration "against BBC bias" outside their Scottish HQ in Glasgow. It's not an official Yes campaign event, but there are so many Saltires and Yes banners that it looks like one. There's much to be critical of in the BBC's coverage, but this is awful. And anyway, with four days to go, shouldn't people be out there, pounding the streets and talking to voters? I'm pained to see, too, that there is a hardcore of Plaid people, some candidates included, furiously amplifying the nonsense on Twitter. Even if only guilty by association, this could well be the Yes campaign's Sheffield moment.

Monday 15 September 2014,
Home:
A depressing TV programme on BBC Wales about the Scottish referendum, and what our response should be. Leighton Andrews represented Labour, alongside the three opposition

leaders in the Assembly: Leanne, Kirsty Williams and Andrew R.T. Davies. It was very poor. They got bogged down in procedural wrangling about Silk 1, Silk 2, Barnett and so on, total bubble talk, of almost no interest to anyone normal. Leanne seemed nervous of saying the wrong thing.

Later the same evening, there was a *Sharp End* debate on ITV Wales, which featured Elin Jones in the studio in Cardiff and Adam Price in Edinburgh. Adam was OK, Elin so-so. We just don't sound as if we are energised or excited by this revolution happening under our noses; quite the opposite, in fact.

Tuesday 16 September 2014,
Cae Melyn, Aberystwyth:
An odd canvass up amongst the inter-war villas of Elysian Grove and Cae Melyn. The Scottish referendum is a topic on almost every doorstep. Some are captivated by it, others terrified. To the latter, it has hardened their resolve against Plaid, who they see as hailing from the same school of constitutional troublemakers. For a few, the possible break-up of the UK is their top issue, and they will vote for whatever Unionist party looks most likely to succeed. They are beyond reach.

Alarmingly though, for those keen to see Scotland go its own way, and there are many, there is a feeling that Plaid is too meek and mild in putting the case for Wales. One very articulate guy, who normally swings between Labour and the Greens, says that he is heartily sick of the three main parties, but feels that we sound far too much like them, in that we over-rely on bland, uncontentious statements that seem to have been sifted through a dozen focus groups. "Sometimes you lot sound like the ghost of Tony Blair and all that New Labour bollocks," he says. "Where's your passion?" It's very hard to disagree with him.

Today has been the day of "The Vow", the front page of the *Daily Record* that has already become the iconic image of the campaign. Signed by Cameron, Clegg and Miliband, it commits Westminster to enhanced devolution for Scotland, including the continuation of the Barnett Formula. While that may work in Scotland's favour, it is accepted by almost all in Wales that we are being seriously short-changed by it. There is not a peep about this from any of the Welsh branches of the big three parties.

Wednesday 17 September 2014,
Edinburgh:
A good train journey north, and as Preds and I get off at Waverley, we can feel a discernible throb in the air. Not at our hotel, though: the first thing we see as we arrive at the solid Georgian townhouse on the other side of Calton Hill is a "No Thanks" poster in the window. After a quick wash, we head out for food and to soak up the nervous excitement of the night before.

A car whooshes past with a replica of the Statue of Liberty strapped to its roof and people waving the Scottish flag through the windows. Passers-by cheer and snap photographs as it goes by. A caterwaul of bagpipes floats on the night air. Bright pools of light on street corners reveal camera crews beaming live reports all over the globe. Even in the urbane West End of this most solidly masonic of all British cities, Yes posters far outnumber No.

They've wheeled out Gordon Brown to make the eve-of-poll plea for No, and it's another rabble-rousing, fist-pounding performance. At one point he booms "The silent majority will be silent no more!" – an ironic turn of phrase for a man whose volume level is permanently cranked up to 11. It is remarkable how the No side has contrived to present itself as the browbeaten underdog, when it has the support of 635 out of 650 MPs, all but one of the thirty UK and Scottish newspapers, the entire mainstream broadcast media, the banks and big business. In what parallel universe does that constitute a "silent" majority?

Thursday 18 September 2014,
Edinburgh:
I have to write a review of the new film *Pride*, the tale of the
unlikely alliance between the London Lesbians and Gays
Support the Miners group and the communities of the Dulais
valley in south Wales during the 1984–5 miners' strike. It's
showing at a multiplex near our hotel, so we go to the first
showing at noon.

I've been nervous of seeing this film, fearing it might leave
me feeling doubly patronised. The worry wasn't assuaged
when I kept hearing it compared with *The Full Monty*, a
film that left me as cold as a January picket line. Thankfully,
my doubts are blown away in seconds. It is big-hearted and
politically unabashed, and the closest I've ever seen to my
own life reflected up there on the big screen. By the time the
credits roll to the Communards' elegiac 'For a Friend', I am a
blubbering mess.

We are spat back out onto the bustling streets by two. There
had been talk of going shopping or sightseeing, but my sludgy
old blood has been given a rocket boost by *Pride*, and I march
us to the nearest Yes office to volunteer our services. Preds
stays there to help with admin – mainly the blowing up of
hundreds of balloons – while I am shoved into a packed car
and sent to knock up voters on a huge social housing estate
on the city's western edge. It's just three miles from the dark
magnificence of Edinburgh city centre, but it is another world.

On the estate, the hope and excitement for a Yes vote are
palpable. People wave and toot their horns at us; they talk
excitedly of their dreams of a more equal country, and of
Scotland becoming a beacon of progressive possibility in a
difficult world. Most amazing are the children, who follow us
around on bikes and scooters, cadging balloons and stickers,
and firing questions about what an independent Scotland
might look like. They are so bright and engaged; Scotland's
future is surely safe in these hands, I think. Kids from estates
like this rarely end up in positions of power, and for a few

sweet minutes, I forget the polls and begin to believe that their day is coming.

Back in town, Preds and I wander, and bump into numerous comrades from Wales. This morning, almost every Yes street stall seemed to be staffed by Plaid and Cymdeithas yr Iaith activists. As the close of poll nears, we break for a pint in a pub on the Royal Mile, where we get into conversation with a lovely retired couple from Dundee at the next table. They have voted No, as have a large proportion of their generation. The raw emotions dredged up by the campaign have genuinely unnerved them, though they accept that Scotland's independence is probably inevitable, if not tonight, then within a decade or so. At one point, a journalist from Finland walks by and asks us which side we're on. "It's all square here," laughs the Dundonian man, "We're No, and they're Yes." "True," I say, "but you've voted, and we can't, so it's 2–0 to you."

The Royal Mile is heaving, and as the polls close, the rush is on to find a good pub in which to watch the results. To my amazement, very few seem to be staying open late, so we stalk the city, our phones chirruping with messages from friends also on the prowl for the same thing. I hook up with Parthian publisher Richard Lewis Davies and Jasmine Donahaye, author, academic and Ceredigion friend, whose daughter lives here. Richard, a renowned expert in great pubs, says he knows one somewhere off Leith Walk, but by the time we have walked the couple of miles there, it is closing.

On the strength of the first few results, it is clear that the No campaign is well ahead. The night is unravelling, and I am suddenly exhausted and grouchy. I've left Preds somewhere in town, so walk back to find him. He and some mates have discovered a club showing the results on a big screen, but by the time I get there, he's been refused re-entry after coming out for a cigarette. The bouncers insist that he's drunk, and will not hear otherwise. We head off into the night, Preds muttering furiously that they took against him because he is wearing Yes stickers. It's well past 3am by now.

We wander down the Royal Mile in the direction of Holyrood, to see if there's any action there. Towards the bottom, there's a sign pointing down an alleyway to a café promising an all-night results party. It's a social centre for people in recovery from addiction; the atmosphere is tired and overwrought. A few people are in tears as the results roll in, their hopes dashed further with every announcement. We sip hot chocolate and watch the gloom unfurl. On the stroke of four, there's a half-hearted cheer as Dundee votes Yes, but it's the first such victory after hours of No votes from all over the country, and it's not enough. We leave the café, briefly join the truculent crowds outside the parliament building, and then shuffle off under a brightening sky back to the hotel.

We doze off with the TV blaring, and wake to find it all over. At 6.11am, Fife had declared its result, a 55–45 for No, a figure that put their victory beyond doubt. At 7.06am, David Cameron bounced out of Number Ten, looking much relieved, and gave a particularly graceless speech, talking not of the democratic deficit for Scotland, and certainly not for Wales, but for England. This was to be he said his priority, his mission. Project Fear had prevailed.

Saturday 20 September 2014,
Aberystwyth University:

After a subdued journey back from Edinburgh, it's back into the fray with a gathering in central Aberystwyth, and then a march up to the university for a rally in support of the strike there. It's in response to a sudden change in pension contributions by the university's management; some have been cut by fifty per cent.

Elin and I walk together up Penglais Hill and get some great responses. Many of the people here are by inclination Labour or Green voters, though I know a lot of them voted LibDem last time. They are horrified that they helped bring in this Tory-led government. It's safe to say that Mark Williams is going to struggle to get their vote again. After my speech at the rally, I get a few people telling me that they are seriously considering voting Plaid for the first time.

In today's *Western Mail*, former First Minister Rhodri Morgan writes that Wales now deserves some treats from Westminster, because we "didn't put the whole of the UK through the mincer of a referendum". It's an echo of comments made by his successor, Carwyn Jones, the other day, that the referendum had been a "serious injury" to the country. This was the greatest political engagement in British history. Every night, there were thousands packed into public meetings from Stranraer to Stornoway. People read up, educated themselves, and discussed the kind of country they wanted. And then last Thursday, 84.6 per cent of the electorate voted, the highest figure since universal franchise almost a century ago. To Welsh Labour, that's a serious injury. They are such anti-democratic bawbags.

Thursday 25 September 2014,
Village hall, Llannon, Ceredigion:
The official launch event of my campaign, and I'm terrified. Normally, I get a bit nervous before speaking, but I am an absolute bag of panic tonight, and a little tearful, for some reason. I'm scared that if anyone says anything nice to me, I'll dissolve on the spot.

When planning the event, we were hoping of course that it would happen in the slipstream of a Yes vote in Scotland, and that that would have a hugely galvanising effect on our troops back in the west. As it transpires, a No vote has been equally electrifying. Well over a hundred people show up, and the atmosphere crackles with political fervour.

It's a wonderful evening, full of passion and comradeship, music, poetry, speeches and laughter. I'm especially glad that it is one of those all-too-rare occasions where the two languages slip and slide over each other with no friction at all, which is exactly what I am trying to represent and promote – and not just for political reasons, but because it's so much more *fun* that way. Dafydd Iwan introduces me for my speech, and talks of coming to see my recent stand-up show about the Welsh language in Caernarfon. "Mae Mike yn deall y Cymry'n well na'r Cymry eu hunain",[1] he says, which overwhelms me. With a build-up like that, I'm full of *hwyl* and deliver my speech, much of it about what has just happened in Scotland, to massive approval. All I can see are rapt, enthusiastic faces. It is a fantastic, intoxicating feeling.

Eurig Salisbury does a slick and heartfelt job as the evening's MC, there's poetry from the divine Samantha Wynne-Rhydderch, and I'm thrilled that my friend Elliw Iwan, Dafydd's daughter and a brilliant musician in her own right, does a duet with her dad for the first time in public. Elin Jones wraps things up with a lovely little spiel too, and reminds everyone that I've given up two years of my life to do this, and that therefore they could perhaps spare a little time too between now and May. I appreciate hearing that, because I really have given up my life for this right now. It's not the lack of time that prohibits anything else useful being done, but the absolute lack of spare headspace.

Saturday 27 September 2014,
Lampeter:
Everyone it seems is going through a weird rollercoaster of emotions in the wake of the Scottish referendum. When we left Edinburgh last Friday, I'd felt for a while a sense of relief that the vote, 55 per cent No to 45 per cent Yes, had been sufficiently decisive. A knife-edge result either way – the Welsh referendum of 1997 writ very much larger – would have been incendiary. Anger returned the following day; anger that those bullies who cloaked themselves in the shabby rags of the underdog and the oppressed but were nothing of the sort, had got away with it yet again.

The anger has subsided through a busy, full-on week. Now, I

---

1   "Mike understands the Welsh better than the Welsh themselves."

feel calm yet energised by the whole thing, and from the turnout at my adoption meeting, it seems that plenty feel the same. Today, canvassing in Lampeter, there are some fascinating discussions about the aftermath of the referendum, and what it means for the UK and Wales. Things are really shifting, though god only knows where they'll settle.

Tuesday 7 October 2014,
Waunfawr, Aberystwyth:
Owen and I are trying to sort out the copy for the next edition of our *Ceredigion Post* newspaper. Much against my better judgment, the front page story will be about health, despite the fact that it is a devolved matter and therefore not strictly on the table in this election. Elin is insistent on this, and although I disagree, I see why. Concern about Bronglais, especially, is the number one topic on the doorstep, and has been since I started canvassing sixteen months ago.

Really, though, this is playing the LibDems' game. They shove outrageously scaremongering health stuff on the front of all their leaflets, because it plays so effectively on people's worst fears. It also lets them muddy the waters as to which layer of government deals with what, while dodging any responsibility themselves. Keeping people scared and ignorant has long been their schtick, and the weight of government seems to have done nothing to change that.

They play it fast and loose on the doorstep too. When healthcare concerns are brought up, I always acknowledge that both Mark Williams and Elin Jones work tirelessly to protect what we have, and to say that I would too if elected. None of that from LibDem canvassers, who glibly tell people that somehow Elin and Plaid have made things worse. It's dirty, irresponsible stuff.

I rewrite some of the health copy to include mention of the Transatlantic Trade and Investment Partnership (TTIP), an EU-US deal that could allow much greater foreign private sector involvement in the NHS. The campaign against it is gathering pace, our MEP Jill Evans has been doing some sterling work on it, and I think we need to nail our colours to the mast. Elin disagrees. She says that "TTIP is an important issue, but one that very few people will engage with." I stand my ground. Plenty are already nervous about it, and they're exactly the sort of wavering Labour, LibDem or Green voters that we need to be attracting. More importantly, as a vital but bone-dry campaign, it needs as much publicity as possible – something delivered through every letterbox in Ceredigion, for instance. As my pompous *coup de grâce*, I write in an email: "As a principle, I'd always rather over-estimate people's understanding than under-estimate it." TTIP goes in, probably just to shut me up.

Great canvass this evening around Waunfawr, and great news too from a poll conducted by the NUS. At the 2010 election, student support for the Liberal Democrats was getting on for 50 per cent. It's down to 5 per cent now. Vroom vroom.

Thursday 9 October 2014,
Llanfarian school:
I'm chairing a public meeting that we've organised to discuss environmental issues, with an extremely impressive panel, all local. Organising it has reminded me once again what an incredible array of talent and skill there is lurking here on the west coast. There's Hywel Griffiths, the geographer-poet of Aberystwyth University, scientist Iolo ap Gwynn, Alun Williams, chair of the county council's environment committee, activist and film-maker Sara Penrhyn Jones, and Kelvin Mason, the stalwart of local green campaigns who also teaches in Liverpool.

Not quite so impressive is the venue, a last-minute switch. Panel and audience alike are squeezed onto tiny primary school chairs, which makes for an uncomfortable evening. One couple make a noisy exit halfway through. The debate is fascinating though, and covers much ground. I'm especially impressed with what Alun has to report about the pioneering work of

Ceredigion council, in transport, recycling, street lighting, carbon reduction and renewable energy. It is way ahead of any other authority in Wales. We have been on the receiving end, every year, of some of the worst cuts of all Welsh councils, and services are stretched to breaking point. The LibDems are going to bash the Plaid-led council all they can in the coming campaign; we need to be celebrating its many achievements, against considerable odds. As well as pointing out that most of the council's problems come from massive cuts, and who's responsible for those?

Saturday 11 October 2014,
Pontrhydfendigaid:
A chaotic day's canvassing in and around Swyddffynnon and Bont. We keep losing people and being late for arranged rendezvous, and you can't afford that in a part of the county where the phone signal is as occasional and unexpected as old Hamlet's ghost. Reactions are reasonable, if cautious. I have a long chat with a woman in Swyddffynnon who thinks I'm a real breath of fresh air as a candidate, who worries about the erosion of Welshness in the area, who is with us totally on our anti-austerity message, but who cannot get past the fact that she works with some Plaid members "and they are complete bastards". She may be right, but we don't have the monopoly on that.

UKIP have finally gained their first elected MP this week, after winning the Clacton by-election. It feels like a turning point, and a grim one at that.

Wednesday 15 October 2014,
Hafod, near Pontrhydygroes:
An enjoyable two days of filming some video shorts about places in Ceredigion. We're going to put them out in the new year under the title *Mike Parker's Rough-ish Guide to Ceredigion*. Director Emyr Jenkins, originally from Penrhyn-coch but now in Cardiff, has volunteered to help. We had a great time making

TV programmes together ten years ago or so. Working with him again is like slipping on a comfortable old coat.

Unfortunately, coats are the theme of both days, as regular downpours sweep in from the west and send us scuttling into the nearest doorway. Yesterday, we filmed two videos, one in each language, in Aberystwyth, before I headed off for a few hours canvassing with a team in Llanbadarn. This morning, we do two in Cardigan, and then finish off trying to film at possibly my favourite place in the county, Thomas Johnes' ghostly Picturesque estate at Hafod. By then, it is pouring with rain, and after an age sheltering in the church porch, we have to give up.

Saturday 18 October 2014,
Cardigan:
In the last few weeks there's been a noticeable increase in the size of our canvassing teams, particularly in and around Aberystwyth and Aberaeron. A decent turnout today in Cardigan too, and some excellent responses. Owen was with us, and as he much prefers being the man in charge of the canvass sheets rather than doing the doorstep stuff, I get a running commentary on how much the vote seems to be slowly but steadily moving in our direction. As we finish, he tweets, entirely truthfully, that we had been canvassing solidly since 10.30 this morning, and that it had taken until our very last door at 2.45 to find someone saying that they were going to stick with the LibDems. And him only because his father used to be big buddies with Geraint Howells.[2]

Thursday 23 October 2014,
Home:
Put the finishing touches to my speech for the Plaid conference this weekend in Llangollen, and it makes me realise something. My writing has definitely changed in the last year and a half.

---

2   Liberal/LibDem MP for Ceredigion 1974–92.

I seem to have lost the ability, and indeed the urge, to hold an idea up to the light, to turn it around and look at it from every side to test its robustness. Truths are usually found tucked away in nuance, and nuance has vanished from my words. Politics is inevitably far more black-and-white, right-and-wrong, and I seem to have absorbed that way of writing almost by osmosis. Will the opposite happen if I lose the election? Or have I dulled a sense that I will never again recover? The thought terrifies me.

Friday 24 October 2014,
Llangollen:
Six o'clock start for the drive to Llangollen. In the car, Radio 4 kicks into life and I hear Jim Naughtie introduce Leanne on the *Today* programme. He's in a haughtily aggressive mood, ridiculing Plaid for our lack of traction compared with the SNP. Much is made of a recent rogue poll, taken immediately after the Scottish vote, that had only 3 per cent of the Welsh population wanting outright independence; the figure has usually been around 10 per cent. It's amazing how far and wide the 3 per cent statistic has gone, and how it's being used by journalists and our opponents alike as the first stick with which to hit us. Leanne does OK, but transparently ducks a few questions, instead trotting out lines that we've heard a thousand times before.

I arrive at the International Pavilion in time for the first rendezvous, a photocall of all Plaid's 2015 candidates in front of a shabby advan emblazoned with the slogan *Gweithio Dros Gymru / Working For Wales*. I end up next to Leanne at the front. Later, she says to me that when she looked round at that point, she was so excited by our variety and talent as a group. It's true. We are a formidable cross-section of Welsh life, and for all my grumpiness, I'm very proud to be part of it.

I spend the morning in a candidates' training session run by Claire Howell, the guru loved by Tŷ Gwynfor. It's largely the same as the session I attended in Machynlleth two years ago, but it's good to hear some of the core messages restated, though one relatively trivial observation makes me snap in disagreement. It comes when Claire says that all male candidates should wear collar and tie at all times. I've not worn a tie once yet, and have no intention of starting. Surely, I say, so much of the disaffection in the political status quo means that if we are serious about being different, it is no bad thing if we look a little different too. Tielessness seems to be working well enough for Alexis Tsipras and Syriza in Greece. Cerith Griffiths, the genial firefighter who's the candidate in Cynon Valley, is the only one to agree with me. Dafydd Wigley, in attendance as the co-ordinator of the party's general election campaign, is foursquare with Claire. He says that in his long experience, he reckons that eighty percent of people don't care about ties, but for the twenty percent who do, politicians looking the part is important. I take his point, but think it's an observation from thirty years ago.

Leanne's speech this afternoon is good. She starts off hesitantly, but warms up nicely and really gets into her stride laying into the austerity agenda of all three main parties. "Austerity has failed," she says a couple of times, the venom dripping from her voice, before going on to list some of the catastrophic consequences it is having in our communities. It is passionate and moving stuff, and I know that it comes straight from the heart. Unfortunately, about twenty minutes in, a fire alarm goes off, stopping her dead in her tracks, and she never quite recovers.

Owen and I head out for an evening curry. Afterwards, I go back to my hotel, and am woken a little later with guts that have turned to fiery liquid. I'm sweaty and sick for hours, and just when I finally manage to get back to bed at about half past five, the hotel's fire alarm goes off and I have to make my way down to the car park. There, in various states of dishevelment, are Rhuanedd and Sioned from Tŷ Gwynfor, and Adrian Masters from ITV Wales. We manage a few weak jokes about how Plaid have really set Llangollen ablaze, before being allowed back to bed, or in my case, back to hugging the toilet bowl.

Saturday 25 October 2014,
Llangollen:

I'm still feeling dreadful, and have to pull it together to get back to the conference hall and deliver my speech. In it, I try and answer that regular doorstep question which comes even from people happy to vote for us at local or Assembly level, namely what's the point of voting Plaid for Westminster? My answer is to look at the towering record of the ten Plaid MPs since Gwynfor's first victory in 1966. From his lonely crusades against American imperialism in Vietnam and British brutality in Biafra, through the two Dafydds' ahead-of-its-time work in the Seventies on issues such as disability rights, domestic violence, homelessness and mental health, through the pioneering environmental work of Cynog Dafis and Simon Thomas, to the uncompromising stance by Elfyn Llwyd and Adam Price against Tony Blair's rush to war in Iraq, Plaid MPs, I argue, have always punched far above their weight. They never took the easy option, but as the benefit of hindsight shows us, they almost always took the right one.

It goes down well, and my stomach troubles subside just long enough to follow it up with a live BBC interview, a two-hander with the hugely impressive Carrie Harper, the candidate in Wrexham. As soon as that is over, and the adrenaline subsides, my guts begin to grumble again, and I have to take a few hours out to doze and sip Coke in my room.

My last appointment is to address a Plaid Youth meeting at the end of the afternoon. It takes place in St Collen's church hall, so we all walk down into town from the Pavilion. With us is Luke James, journalist on the *Morning Star*, who is very exercised by the idea that we might once again try and forge an electoral alliance in Ceredigion with the Greens. I'd mentioned the original pact that got Cynog elected in 1992 in my speech, but it's very unlikely to happen again in the same formal way, however much anyone hopes that it might. My point really is that the work we, the SNP and the Greens are already doing together, both in the European Parliament and at Westminster, is what we need to build on; that even with only ten MPs between us, the group has been a far more effective opposition than the tongue-tied Labour party.

Monday 27 October 2014,
Home:
Luke James has taken considerable poetic licence with our converstion on Saturday. His article is headed *Plaid Cymru Conference 2014: Plaid and Green Party Discuss Electoral Pact*. Fortunately, it's the *Morning Star*, so unlikely to be making many headlines elsewhere.

Thursday 30 October 2014,
Bow Street:
Owen gave me grief about the stuff in the *Morning Star*, which has been picked over on social media and in a few blogs – all part of a pretty tough week since getting back from Llangollen, with little time to rest. It's plunged me into quite a downer, which isn't alleviated by tonight's public meeting in Bow Street to discuss what next for Wales in the light of the Scottish referendum. I say "public meeting", and that was how it was advertised, but yet again, it's just a small gathering of the old faithful. We are not bringing in new blood, even on an issue as meaty as this. The only newcomer is my American neighbour Alma, who thought that it sounded interesting and opted to cadge a lift with me.

I'm chairing, with a panel of Cynog Dafis, Elin Jones, Leanne's adviser Steffan Lewis and Dr Elin Royles of Aberystwyth University's International Politics Department. It's an interesting discussion, though I'm semi-detached. The acoustics in the hall are appalling, and I can barely hear anything being said by anyone in the audience. Add that to the fact that it is nearly all in Welsh, and I really struggle to keep up. There is translation – Alma is the only one using it – but I'm too ashamed to admit that I need proceedings delivered through headphones, and in a language I can fully understand. Cynog, the stern voice of my conscience in all matters Cymraeg, is sat right by my side, and is already huffing and puffing at some of the things I've come out with. It is not a fun evening, and it should have been. On the drive home, Alma assures me that I looked in control, but I'm sure she's just being kind.

Friday 31 October 2014,
Aberporth:
It's an eerily warm Hallowe'en, and I'm in no mood for a day's canvassing. Driving down to pick Elin up in Aberaeron, I feel stressed and begin to see how easily I could give myself a stroke – everything just swirls around my brain, getting hotter and hotter, and I can picture it just fusing one day.

A day in Aberporth doesn't help. From the moment we arrive, I feel a strange tension in the place. There are dogs barking everywhere, hollering in windows, snapping behind letterboxes. People refuse to answer the door, or scream at us through net curtains to go away. Those who will talk tell us they'd never vote Plaid because they don't like the Assembly; no amount of explanation that we're not actually running it will dissuade them. And there are so many angry older men, hurtling towards UKIP as they shout into our faces word-perfect *Daily Mail* editorials about immigrants, Muslims and benefits.

This is how it happens. In the latest Welsh opinion poll, all four main parties slipped back, while UKIP doubled their score to 14 per cent. We've been too smug in the past in thinking that Wales was somehow immune to this poison. In fact, with its Labour wastelands and embittered retirees, it is ripe for it.

Monday 3 November 2014,
Cardiff:

Although I'm nervous about doing *Sharp End* on ITV Wales
this evening, it's a glorious drive down to Cardiff, punctuated
by rainbows, sudden shafts of sunlight and billowing showers
sweeping across the landscape, all to the tune of Radio 3.
On arrival, I head to the Assembly for a briefing from Plaid
researchers on tonight's topics: the living wage, the Barnett
formula (Lord Barnett's death was announced yesterday),
housing and the devolution package just announced by George
Osborne for Greater Manchester.

I'm a big fan of Adrian Masters, the ITV Wales political
editor and presenter of *Sharp End*. From my years of making
travelogues for them, I know how thin a shoestring the whole
operation is, especially compared with the BBC. Adrian is a
fine example of how to turn that to your advantage, for he can
be and invariably is far more fleet of foot in his coverage than
his opponents. I saw it myself when I was doing *Coast to Coast*
and *Great Welsh Roads*. They'd just tell us to go away and come
back with a complete series. You feel trusted, and therefore
do a better job. Had it been the Beeb, we'd have been micro-
managed to death.

Adrian settles me, Mick Antoniw of Labour and William
Powell of the LibDems into the studio, and we're off. It goes
in a blur, but fairly well, I think. I manage to get a couple of
decent lines out, and a few good digs. The only sticky point
comes when the questions on housing go in an unexpected
direction, and I flounder through, my cheeks burning.

I drive home just in time to catch it going out at 11.20pm,
and fire up Twitter to accompany it. As ever, Plaid people
are tweeting and retweeting far more than anyone else, so
I get a pleasantly distorted sense of how well I've done. The
only negative voice is Gethin James, the UKIP councillor in
Aberporth, who tweets a couple of times that I obviously don't
know my way around Ceredigion council's housing policy.
He's quite right, in truth, and I feel a prickle of shame to have

been found out, and by him of all people. But he is shouting into the void, for no-one retweets him or picks up the point. Meanwhile, Plaid supporters continue their perfect circle of mutual backslapping.

Friday 7 November 2014,
Llety Parc Hotel, Aberystwyth:
To the National Library this afternoon to speak at the launch of Cynefin, their project to digitise the old tithe maps of Wales. I've visited before to look at how they're doing it and was predictably blown away. It's such a pleasure to be thinking and talking about maps, art and history for a couple of hours.

A swift return to my new normality straight afterwards, as I have to rush to Glynpadarn, a sheltered accommodation complex in Llanbadarn for a meeting with the residents there, organised by their local councillor, Paul James. Paul is a force of nature, a former legionnaire who battles on behalf of his constituents with the tenacity of a terrier. Residents at Glynpadarn have been hit by new individual bills from Welsh Water; many have seen their charges rocket. Elin is there too, and we vow to take on their case. We finish off having tea and biscuits with some of the residents. They adore Paul.

An email from Alun Williams: "I've been in a meeting in Cardiff this morning and just been speaking to Pippa Bartolotti. Unfortunately she says (in the nicest possible way) that the Greens will be standing in Ceredigion in both the Westminster and Assembly elections." This is no surprise. And, in my opinion, no bad thing either. We can't recreate the early 1990s, and there's no point trying. A Green candidate is just as likely to take votes from the LibDems as from us. More so actually, as things stand at the moment.

Off to Llety Parc for a fundraising auction for the campaign. Mererid and the finance committee have done a superb job of collecting some real treats for sale, from original artwork and bespoke poetry, to whisky, wine, food and holidays. People have been very generous, and by the end of an enjoyable evening, we've raised six grand.

Saturday 8 November 2014,
Aberystwyth Arts Centre:
The second Aberration LGBT night, organised by a gang that includes Helen Sandler, a mate since our time together at London University in the late 1980s. At our tiny college (Westfield, long gone), Helen and I were pretty much the sum total of both the Labour Club and the Lesbian and Gay Society.

They've managed to turn the great hall of the Arts Centre into a dark, glittering cabaret cave, and it's packed. The bill is wonderfully varied, including music, poetry and prose reading, comedy, burlesque and magic. Helen has slyly given me a slot to run a limerick competition, and makes sure as she introduces me that everyone knows I'm the local Plaid Cymru candidate. It gets quickly – and predictably – smutty.

There's a big group in from Tregaron, and although the little voice in my head is telling me to shut up, I hear myself recounting to hundreds of people the story of my first time there, twenty years ago, for the initial *Rough Guide to Wales*. Drinking in Y Llew Coch, I got chatting to some locals and told them what I was doing. One bloke looked at me, sucked on his rollie and said slowly "well, the only fact you need to know about Tregaron is that *everyone* fucks everyone else."

On getting home, I anxiously check Twitter to see if anyone has mentioned it. It's been a real uphill struggle to get me in the *Cambrian News*, but this would be on their front page in seconds. Luckily, there seems to be no mention, though I'm chuffed to see that someone from the gig has tweeted what a funky Plaid Cymru candidate Ceredigion has.

Tuesday 11 November 2014,
Aberystwyth:
Been an up-and-down few weeks, generally positive but with some bleak moments. One threatens to surface this afternoon,

when I am cosily ensconced at home just as the light is starting to fade and *Pointless* about to begin, but have to get my candidate drag on instead and head out into the rain for an evening's canvassing. As often happens when expectations are rock bottom, it proves to be much better than I feared. It's a good crew, we have a laugh, and the reaction is excellent – from the people who open their doors, that is. So many don't on these dark evenings, and I can't say I blame them.

Wednesday 19 November 2014,
Plas Penglais, Aberystwyth:
An invitation from the Vice-Chancellor of Aberystwyth University to a dinner in honour of artist Mary Lloyd Jones. It's in the VC's private house, a fine Georgian plas, and driving there, I'm apprehensive. It is, after all, only a few weeks since I was hollering through a loudhailer at a rally for striking university staff. I'd prevaricated about accepting, but I'm so fond of Mary. If she wants me there, I wouldn't dream of spurning it.

On arrival, I get a sneaking suspicion that my attendance is not at Mary's request, but the VC herself. We've only met once, when she gave Leanne and a crew of us a tour of IBERS. Most of the people I know who work at the university, or who I've met while canvassing, have very little that's positive to say about her tumultuous three years in Aber. My resolve is to listen a lot, and say very little. There's plenty to listen to, for she goes out of her way to tell me how much she loves it here, how settled her son is at school and how passionate she is about Aberystwyth, Wales and Welsh. She is very convincing, but it's hard to escape the feeling that I am being slathered in the softest of soaps, whilst also being very carefully scrutinised.

Thursday 20 November 2014,
Belle Vue Royal Hotel, Aberystwyth:
A public meeting with the Plaid Shadow Cabinet, and it's pretty much a capacity crowd. The idea of promoting the five

of them as a talented team-in-waiting is potentially high risk, but they've done a few of these meetings together, and they do it very well. Everyone is on good form. Leanne is relaxed and sparky, Elin and Simon play well to a home crowd, Llŷr and Rhun are in command of their portfolios. There is a real buzz to the night, and we are all thrilled.

Saturday 22 November 2014,
Lampeter:
Another day of canvassing, and another day talking about bloody UKIP. They won their second by-election this week, in Rochester. As had happened six weeks earlier in Clacton, the incumbent Conservative MP had switched sides, forced a by-election, and then won it for the purple-and-yellows – the colour of spreading bruises, as Manon Steffan Ros pointedly wrote in one of her recent stories in *Golwg*.

In Lampeter, there is real hatred towards the eastern Europeans in the town, most of whom work at the Dunbia plant in Llanybydder. One man tells me about "a friend" who is "very considerate, not an extremist at all, who's going to vote UKIP". This isn't happening in a vacuum. The media really do have to take some responsibility here, for their bulletins and their front pages scream about little else but MIGRANTS and MUSLIMS. Day in, day out, constant drip drip drip, like a water torture. And like a water torture, it is sending people quite mad.

Monday 24 November 2014,
Home:
In Scotland, *The National*, a newspaper supporting independence, makes its debut this morning. It's very exciting, not least the idea of launching a newspaper – any newspaper – in the current climate. Instead of allowing it to turn inwards and fester, the profound disappointment of the Yes campaign is being channelled outwards in so many ways, this new paper included. From a Welsh perspective though, it's hard not to

feel raging jealousy. The last attempt to establish a newspaper here, *Y Byd* in 2008, collapsed in an all-too-familiar cloud of betrayal and recrimination. It's a sobering contrast.

Tuesday 25 November 2014,
Polly's Wine Bar, Cardigan:
One of the things that I'd wanted to do differently as a candidate was to try and have a few cultural evenings, mixing musicians and poets, writers and film-makers, mixing the languages and audiences too. It would, I felt, represent the unique selling point of me as a candidate, and perhaps help break down some of the barriers in our communities, and towards Plaid too. Owen humoured me, but was never keen on, as he put it, "wasting hours trying to organise these things, and maybe picking up one or two extra votes as a result." Tonight is what has been billed as my launch night for the south of the county, and I see that he has a point. It's a decent turnout, but there are hardly any curious newcomers, and more to the point, organising it has been like herding cats. Organising anything in Cardigan tends that way.

On the plus side, it's a brilliant evening. Dewi Pws is the MC, cheerfully sailing close to the wind every time he opens his mouth. Ceri Wyn Jones performs some of the Cardigan-themed *awdl* that won him the chair at this year's National Eisteddfod. He is superb, introducing it with bilingual dexterity and hilarious, deadpan humour. There's more of that from brothers Richard and Wyn "Fflach" Jones, whose band, Ail Symudiad, has been a staple of the Aberteifi scene for decades. Richard is one of the most naturally funny people I have ever seen on stage; he has us all in stitches with his surreal stream-of-consciousness monologues, and his constant reference to me as "Trevor", i.e. Trevor Fishlock, my erstwhile elder on ITV Wales travelogues. Carwyn Tywyn, a lovely man and an old friend of Owen's, glues the evening together with some fine harp action.

Owen and I are both demob happy on the late drive home, so relieved are we to have got this evening out of the way. He is even happier when I tell him that yes, it was more trouble than it was worth and that he was absolutely right. He loves hearing that.

Wednesday 26 November 2014,
Capel Tŷ'n-y-Gwndwn, Felinfach, Ceredigion:
Guest speaker at a Merched y Wawr[3] branch meeting in Dyffryn Aeron. No direct politicking, of course; I give a talk about my travel writing. Lovely reception by all, and some terrific conversations, plus a few furtive nods that votes are coming my way. Great cakes too, and as the guest speaker, it is my solemn duty to sample them all. The ensuing sugar rush gets me home in what feels like no time. I seem to be doing fine with the women of Ceredigion, but I'm not so sure about the blokes.

Saturday 29 November 2014,
Home:
This week I've been like a yo-yo up and down that coast road. Tuesday in Cardigan, Wednesday Felinfach, Thursday night an excellent Traws Link Cymru rail campaign meeting in Llanybydder, last night a trip to Pembrokeshire for John Osmond's[4] launch evening, and today back to Cardigan for a typically chaotic, but pretty encouraging, canvassing session. That's nearly six hundred miles in five days. Most years, I drive eight or nine thousand miles, but at the car's MOT the other week they told me I'd done over 22,000 in the last year. This is costing me a small fortune.

Owen emails me to say that, as of today, Gethin James is officially our UKIP candidate, and that the Greens have also

---

3   Literally "Women of the Dawn", the Welsh-speaking version of the WI.
4   John Osmond, former boss of the Institute of Welsh Affairs, now Plaid candidate in Stephen Crabb's seat of Preseli Pembrokeshire.

chosen theirs, a guy called Daniel Thompson who lives in Ffos-y-ffin.

Friday 5 December 2014,
Home:

Leanne is in town. It's Small Business Saturday tomorrow, so she and I do a whistlestop photo-op tour of some of the shops and cafés in Aberystwyth, before we head off to a Plaid Cymru Youth meeting upstairs at the Cŵps.

As it's a last-minute pub session, there's no translation equipment, so Leanne starts by saying that she's going to speak in English, but that she's sure I'll do mine in Welsh. She flashes me a grateful-but-stern smile. I start in Welsh, but after a couple of minutes, notice that there is someone who evidently doesn't speak it, as their neighbour is having to translate me in a loud whisper. "Oh sorry," I say, "I hadn't realised there was someone here without Welsh. I'll carry on in English." That makes someone else get up and walk out. Oh god.

Much of Leanne's address is about Scotland. She's been there countless times over the last year, even more so since the referendum and Nicola Sturgeon's ascent to the top job. She is far closer, politically and personally, to Sturgeon than she was to Salmond. They have become firm friends, and Leanne's regular trips north have made her extremely wistful about the contrasting positions of their two parties. Since losing the referendum, the SNP have seen their membership more than treble to eighty thousand. Opinion polls are putting them on unprecedented, insanely high figures. There is talk of them wiping the board come the election in May. Sturgeon is walking on water, while Leanne has to wade through it in leaking wellies.

While I'm as excited as anyone about the revolution that's rumbling on in Scotland, I'm fed up with hearing that it's the only show in town. It reminds me too much of when I first got to know Plaid Cymru, when Ireland was always held up as our blueprint. Way before their economy collapsed under the weight of its own avarice, there were plenty of warning signs that things were far from rosy for the vast majority of people, and that some terrible social and cultural problems were being rapidly exacerbated by the Celtic Tiger. I wrote about it a few times, but it was a subject few wanted to acknowledge, let alone discuss.

It's no different with Scotland. Plenty to be inspired by, for sure, but plenty to be quizzical about too – the readiness of supposedly green politicians to stake their all on fossil fuels, for starters; or the pungent stench of the SNP cosying up to Donald Trump and Rupert Murdoch. And one for us here, so I share it with the meeting, "You know that Salmond and Sturgeon made the calculated decision not to have the referendum ballot paper bilingual? Numerous Gaelic organisations pressured them to, but they decided to keep it in English only, out of a fear that the presence of Gaelic would subliminally frighten people wavering over voting Yes." A couple of people in the audience nod. Leanne looks cross. "Well, I'd never heard that," she says, and changes the subject.

She's staying over at ours, and as we're both back in Aberystwyth in the morning, we leave her car in town and I drive us home. I'm not sure if I've annoyed her with my comments in the meeting. There's definitely a bit of an atmosphere, and although we have a lovely evening at home with Preds, there's none of our usual high-jinks. I feel sad that the closer we become as colleagues, the further away we seem to be as mates. It's an irony I never saw coming.

Saturday 6 December 2014,
Richmond Hotel, Aberystwyth:
The Plaid Ceredigion Christmas dinner, and flashbacks to being the guest speaker at the same event, in the same room, eight or so years earlier. If someone had told me then that I would be here as the constituency's candidate for Westminster, I would have thought that they'd lost the plot.

Tonight it's Dafydd Wigley doing the honours. He gives a

typically rumbustious speech, in which he roars with approval about me as candidate and the campaign we're running. This provokes a huge, boozy cheer and round of applause.

Giving the vote of thanks, I tell the story of a recent canvass in Lampeter, where I met a very well-spoken, very English lady who'd always voted Liberal. "But," she told me, "one must punish them for their actions, in giving us this horrible, philistine government. The Liberals really have proved themselves to be the most terrible tarts." I laughed, thanked her and started to head back down the path. She called me back. "And, my dear, I'm afraid to say not just any old tarts, but the very cheapest tarts of all. They've sold themselves for nothing."

I'm sat next to Wigley, who is keen to probe me on the finer details of how the campaign is going. I tell him of the apparent drift of some of our traditional Welsh-speaking vote, and our ongoing difficulty in appealing to non-Welsh-speaking voters, even with me as the candidate. Both illuminate our central problem in Ceredigion, that we are perceived by some traditional Plaid voters as too soft on the language, while many others think we're obsessed by it.

With his decades of experience in public life, Wigley has a dexterous and pragmatic attitude to the Cymraeg faultline. Certainly, whenever I've met him over the years, he has been brilliant at smoothing the way in conversations, whatever the company. Sometimes, we converse in Welsh, sometimes English, and unlike some people, he never makes me feel the slightest bit guilty about needing to use English to get through more complicated or technical stuff. He evidently loves good conversation, and that is his priority, whatever the route taken to get there.

He does manage to give me a guilty twinge about something else though. "At some stage in the campaign, you're going to be asked whether you'll move to Ceredigion if you win," he says as we eat. "And the answer to that must be a resounding yes!" He stabs his fork in the air for emphasis.

Monday 15 December 2014,
Morlan Centre, Aberystwyth:
A public meeting called by Hywel Dda Health Board for local residents to air their concerns. It is the same stalemate as always: on the one side, Health Board smoothies agreeing with everyone, but promising nothing, and on the other, an audience of furious sceptics. Some see the bigger picture, but many of the most vocal and habitual contributors at these meetings seem unable ever to go beyond the specifics of their own individual experience.

After the meeting, I go to say goodbye to Elin, as we're off to India on Wednesday for Preds' fortieth and the festive season. She is being harangued by a constituent, a well-spoken, grey grump who seeps dissatisfaction like an open wound. She introduces us, and we discuss the meeting. As I leave, she tells me to have a good holiday, and to make the most of it, as the campaign will be relentless from the minute I get back.

"You going away then?" says the grump. "Yes, to India for three weeks. First time, I can't wait." He is unimpressed, and snorts his derision. "I suppose it's all on expenses," he sneers, his runaway eyebrows locked in a furious frown.

My fantasy self head-butts him and tells him to piss off, that you don't get a penny for being a candidate, that it's costing me a fortune in petrol, food and accommodation, that as a self-employed writer it was also costing me thousands in lost earnings, that I've made my own way for over two decades, sometimes earning only seven or eight grand a year.

My real self shrugs his shoulders, mumbles a vague goodbye, slides out of the room, and curses him all the way home.

TARGET PRACTICE
January – March 2015

Thursday 15 January 2015,
Morlan Centre, Aberystwyth:
Back in political drag for the first time after India. A relatively
gentle return, an upbeat campaign committee, followed by a
public meeting of Traws Link Cymru, the campaign to rebuild
a railway between Aberystwyth and Carmarthen. I've been
involved from the start, and have spoken at all of the public
meetings to date, in Lampeter, Tregaron and Llanybydder, but
sensibilities dictate that there's no official place for me tonight,
so that if I want to speak, I'll have to do so from the floor. The
election campaign has gone up a few gears now that we are
in 2015; what might or might not happen in May is already
dominating the news media.

As ever with these railway meetings, it's a great turnout.
There is such massive public goodwill behind this campaign;
small wonder that it is catnip to politicians. Around a hundred
people turn up, and although I've got a question primed in my
head, I just cannot go for it, and look like yet another carpet-
bagger. This is ridiculous, I realise. It's a subject I know very
well and care passionately about; if there is one single thing
that I would like to help achieve as Ceredigion's MP, it would
be this railway line, and I would work tirelessly to help make it
happen. Yet I say nothing.

It is Huw Thomas, the Labour candidate, who puts me off.
He is seated just behind me, and leaps in so shamelessly that
it makes me squirm. He kicks off with a faux humble "Well, I
suppose I'd better – ha! – introduce myself to those who don't
know me, and say that I'm Huw Thomas, the Labour candidate
for Ceredigion", and then proceeds to tick every box: that he
had grown up in Aber and as a youngster desperately wanted
to visit his own capital city; that it was the lack of transport
that made him have to pack his spotted hanky and trek to the
bright lights (of Oxford University, he forgets to say); that his
first language is Welsh and his many relatives locally would
weep at the chance for a day return to Llanilar; that he now
works for a sustainable transport charity, so that on every

possible level, he passionately supports the campaign. At this point, he remembers that his contribution is supposed to be a question rather than a commercial, so he swiftly bolts on something straight out of his last Cardiff council meeting, and asks have we thought about guided bus lanes as a good option? The suggestion is tactfully ignored by everyone.

I've just re-read my diary entry of a year ago, from a public meeting about Bronglais. It was the same thing there – I couldn't and didn't speak, and was overcome with hot embarrassment at the bandwagon-jumping of the many politicians there. I concluded my entry with the words that I "probably needed to become more shameless". It seems I haven't. Seems I must.

Wednesday 21 January 2015,
Aberystwyth prom:
Filming Plaid Cymru's five-minute *Political Slot* for Channel 4, on an icy but sunny Aberystwyth prom. The cameraman is thrilled by the quality of light and photogenic possibilities of the town, even more so because they've just hotfooted it from filming the UKIP slot in a rainswept Clacton-on-Sea. The only way is up on all counts.

It's an honour to do this, and I've worked hard on a script. I want to do something in praise of well resourced, well run local government, and how it is increasingly under threat from savage cuts and their background ideology. The perfect idea came to me on a very different beach in Kerala over Christmas: to look at the massive storm damage suffered by Aberystwyth a year ago, when it was all over the news, and how it was the public sector that so swiftly sorted it out. In the film, I'm interviewing the novelist Niall Griffiths and Sue Jones-Davies, star of Monty Python's *Life of Brian*, now a Plaid town councillor and Aberystwyth's funkiest yoga teacher.

Had dinner last night with Linda McDougall, the director. She tells me that she loves doing Plaid films, though she's a Labour member and married to the veteran MP for Grimsby, Austin Mitchell. He's standing down this time, and she cannot wait, for lots of reasons. "As soon as the election is called, the minute they break up in March," she tells me, "I'm leaving the Labour party, and joining the SNP. They're the ones getting it right at the moment. And you lot too, if you can only get your act together." She is certain that I am going to win, and says that she will put a hundred quid on me at the bookies.

Tuesday 27 January 2015,
Tŷ'n-y-Rhyd Farm, near Devil's Bridge:
An early start for a breakfast organised by the Farmers Union of Wales. I get there for 9.00, and it's already humming. Dozens of people, an S4C film crew included, and a great atmosphere. Farmers spend so much time on their own, so when they get together it's always voluble and laced with laughter. A brilliant full cooked breakfast too, which sets me up nicely for a day's canvassing around Lledrod with a very spirited crew.

Friday 30 January 2015,
Llandyfrïog:
Enjoyable day canvassing in the villages on the Ceredigion side of the river around Newcastle Emlyn. Met some real characters, and there seems to be a decent sense of community cohesion so sorely lacking in some places. I'm especially inspired by a local bloke with whom I have a long and fascinating conversation, *yn Gymraeg*, in Llandyfrïog. He organises all kinds of community events, from Welsh classes to music nights, and goes out of his way to invite newcomers. It's all kept pretty informal, and has a very high success rate.

Monday 2 February 2015,
Home:
Oh god, I've managed to annoy Cornwall now. I posted a blog last week about the anti-austerity alliance between Plaid, the SNP and the Greens, and how for us as a party, in Ceredigion especially, this was something of a leap of faith, as the Greens have refused to countenance any deals between us in Wales. It

received a fair few comments, positive and sceptical, but the thing that gained the most attention was the illustration I used for the piece:

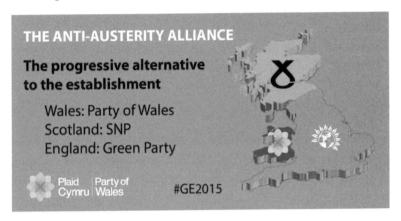

THE ANTI-AUSTERITY ALLIANCE

The progressive alternative
to the establishment

Wales: Party of Wales
Scotland: SNP
England: Green Party

Plaid | Party of
Cymru | Wales   #GE2015

I'm not even sure where it came from. Tŷ Gwynfor I think, as it was posted from an official Plaid account and it certainly looks like one of theirs. It's vanished now, inevitably. But of course there's no distinction on the map for Cornwall, and that has enraged Mebyon Kernow[1], who are supposed to be our sister party.

There's a blog doing the rounds headed "It's official! Plaid Cymru consider Cornwall to be a county of England", and my Facebook page is full of apoplectic Cornishmen demanding that I amend the map. I can't believe that I've tumbled not only into the trap of enraging supposed comrades, but enraging them by means of a map. I've written and talked so much over the years about how easily maps cause offence, deliberate or inadvertent, for they burrow straight into a very deep sense of identity. I somehow forgot my own lesson.

It only confirms that politics now is almost exclusively fuelled by what I describe in the latest *Planet* as "the adrenaline of umbrage". We are hooked on it. Find something to get upset about, foghorn it across social media, watch it grow and

1   The Cornish nationalist party.

mutate into all sorts of horrors, while the real culprits escape unscathed as we punch six bells out of each other.

Wednesday 4 February 2015,
Llandre:
Kicked off the afternoon by giving a presentation in Welsh to Cymdeithas y Chwiorydd[2] at Capel y Garn in Bow Street. Llinos Dafis had kindly organised it, but told me to keep it free of party politics, so I do a map talk, which people seem to enjoy.

Cynog and a few others meet me afterwards for a canvass in Bow Street and Llandre. Under Owen's strict orders, now that we are in the official campaign, we are canvassing only targeted electors. He gave the last campaign committee meeting a presentation about this apparently infallible system, one that calibrates people's propensity to vote at all with their level of fondness for Plaid. An A1 is someone who always votes, and always votes for us; an E5 someone who hates us, but never votes anyway. It is the fifteen thousand or so people in the middling categories that we must concentrate on. This targeted system is held responsible for the thumping win in the Ynys Môn by-election the summer before last, and now it has been rolled out for us all.

As ever though, any statistical data is only as good as the human input that created it. In Ynys Môn, there had been council elections just a few months earlier, so data was plentiful and recent. In Ceredigion, much of our data is quite old but, even more unreliably, is filtered through the wildly erratic levels of canvassers' optimism. There are parts of the county notorious for their mismatch between startlingly good canvass data and the actual reaction on the doorstep. Some seem to have marked down every "Pob lwc i chi!"[3] as a

---

2   The Society of Sisters, a regular weekday group meeting of the chapel's women.
3   "Good luck to you!"

cast-iron Plaid vote. In this generally polite part of the world, it is not an assumption you can make.

Llandre seems to be a case in point, but the other way round. Cynog will not be told to knock only on targeted doors ("bloody nonsense!"), and as there are not many people in at all, I give in and do the same. That way, we find a few voters not on our list, who are firmly in the bag or seriously considering us.

Thursday 5 February 2015,
Plaid office, Aberystwyth:
Owen and I have a pre-meeting before the campaign committee. I report back yesterday's slightly chaotic canvass, and the positive reactions we got from some people who weren't on the targeted canvass sheets. Having checked his master list, he shrugs it off as a blip, but I'm not so sure. People's political habits seem more fluid now than ever, and I'm worried that we are missing potential supporters by sticking so religiously to the script. He points out that we would reach more people if I wasn't quite so verbose on the doorstep. Touché.

There's better news from the online videos about Ceredigion places that I've been making with Emyr. The Aberystwyth one in English has reached over twenty-two thousand people so far, which is just amazing. They look good, and people like them. We decide to finish the Hafod one, and do two more, Tregaron and Borth.

Matthew has been getting me to make little videos for Facebook, too, a "Minute with Mike" on some issue or other. These are nothing like Emyr's televisual treats; we film them on a phone. I'm very careful about how home-made they look though. I remember the last election campaign when a Plaid candidate did regular videos in her living room, which made her look like a junior jihadi.

The campaign committee meeting is buoyant: canvass returns are steady in our direction and people seem less fazed by a knock on the door now than they did before Christmas.

Afterwards, we pile over the road for an excellent curry at the Light of Asia. It is a great laugh, and a real morale boost. We haven't done enough socialising outside the grind of the campaign. It was something I'd wanted to encourage, but, as with so many other ideas and ideals I came into this with, it hasn't turned out that way.

Friday 6 February 2015,
New Quay:
Elin, Mary, Owen and I sweep through a chilly New Quay, but there's almost no-one in. I remember staying here midweek in October a few years ago, and being thunderstruck by the lack of lights in any house on the main street at nine in the evening. The few people I do meet today say that the proportion of holiday homes in the town is now around seventy per cent, and that community life is dying. Not helped, it has to be said, by the county council, who decided to close New Quay library the year before last, one of its last civic amenities. It has been saved for now by volunteers, but that cannot be guaranteed forever.

New Quay has always been my favourite seaside town. Walking the great stone claw of the harbour wall never fails to thrill, nor does a night in any of its famously boisterous pubs. One of my happiest memories is of sleeping two nights anchored in the harbour aboard the *Keewaydin*, a gorgeous wooden Edwardian sailing ketch that was taking us down the Ceredigion coast for one of my TV programmes. On the first night, we all took a dinghy into town and the pub, but on the second, I stayed alone on the boat and had a blissful couple of hours bobbing gently on deck, watching the town come and go; my own bespoke mime of *Under Milk Wood*. For all Laugharne's protestations, New Quay is the real Llareggub. Even in its reduced circumstances, there remains that irresistible tang of prudery and priapism.

Saturday 7 February 2015,
Aberarth:
I've never felt quite so instinctively enthusiastic about Aberaeron, New Quay's posher twin just up the coast. It's hard to explain why; something about the way it turns its back on the sea, or its enforced colourfulness masking a vibe that sometimes seemed slightly prissy. Maybe it's an age thing, because I'm liking Aberaeron more and more as the years roll by, and it is very good to me this morning. There's an enthusiastic crowd of volunteers, and the response is excellent.

Again though, and mainly because the canvass lists are so difficult to decipher in places, we end up calling on many people not on the targeted list, and getting a very encouraging response. While this is of course brilliant, it is worrying that we would have missed them had we stuck to our instructions.

The positive mood evaporates a couple of miles up the coast in Aberarth. A dozen-strong gang of Aberystwyth students has been door-knocking while I've been in Aberaeron, and I join them for the last haul. It has not gone well. Like many coastal villages, it appeals mainly to incomers and has never been good territory for Plaid. Our canvassers have been told to get lost by the majority of people they've encountered, sometimes in considerably more graphic terms. Many of the students, more used to life in a warm Welsh cocoon, are visibly downhearted, even disturbed, by the experience. I wish we'd sent them somewhere more promising, as I don't want to be losing our scant supply of youthful energy this early.

After dropping in to a gathering in Talybont, I head home for a couple of hours, coming back into Aberystwyth for a fundraising get-together at some members' house. The food is good, the wine flows readily and there are many keen to hear how it is going. Very well, I tell them, but we really do need the numbers out there now. I hope they hear that bit. There are very few faces here that I've seen out on the stump.

There are some people I know from the arts and media world, including Meic Birtwhistle, television producer and stalwart of the Ceredigion Labour Party. He's here, he tells me, because for the first time in his life he is going to support a candidate other than the Labour one. It's partly personal, in that he knows me well enough to think I'd be an interesting MP, but mainly political, because Plaid is offering a solid left choice against a highly conservative local Liberal party. I know that he will have thought about this very deeply, and I'm honoured.

Tuesday 10 February 2015,
12 noon, Y Tabernacl, Machynlleth:
A coffee with Duncan Kerridge, a long-time acquaintance and parent of kids at Ysgol Llangynfelyn in Taliesin, one of the Ceredigion primary schools facing the axe. I've read the report that recommends its closure, and like many of the parents, was troubled by its apparent bias towards the council's desired conclusion.

This is such a thorny topic, and there is no single answer that works everywhere. Sometimes the option of closing small village schools and opening a new combined facility works well; it was what the parents themselves wanted in the Synod Inn area a few years back, which resulted in the hugely impressive Ysgol Bro Siôn Cwilt. The same thing happened in the 1970s where I live near Machynlleth, and no-one would want to reverse that decision. Glantwymyn school is the keystone that keeps our scattered community together.

In Llangynfelyn, there is no option for a new, combined school. It is only a mile and a half to Talybont, and that is where the kids will be encouraged to go. I've asked some councillors about this, particularly the point that the main A487 between the villages is a terrible stretch of road, with no pavement or cycle path, so the effect will be to enslave yet more children into dependence on their parents and the car. I've floated the idea that if the council does close the school, they must have a safe walking/cycling route to Talybont in place by the time it happens, but no-one takes it up. That would be too much trouble, I'm told, as it would require the participation of the Highways Agency and, at a time of shrinking budgets, the compulsory purchase of land. I can fully understand why the parents feel so aggrieved.

It's difficult enough to work through the obvious practicalities in a discussion like this, but that's nothing compared with the implications that it has for the faultlines in people's sense of identity and belonging. As Duncan puts it, Llangynfelyn is seen as the school for hippy-ish English parents who want their kids educated in Welsh, while English parents who want an English-medium school send their kids to Comins Coch and Welsh-Welsh parents to Talybont. This is prickly turf indeed, and although those making the decision say that such matters have no bearing on the outcome, I don't think anyone really believes it.

6.00pm, Maes Deri, Talybont:
A small crew of us out to canvass in Talybont, although getting people to open their doors on these dark evenings is still difficult. There are plenty of snowdrops out, but any sense of spring is as faint as a lamb's bleat.

There's some enthusiastic support, but a fair bit of implacable opposition too. I've been told off again for spending too long talking to people, especially those who are almost certainly not going to vote for me, but once again, I commit the cardinal sin. Those conversations are often so much more interesting. Tonight, I spend far too long arguing with a man about economics. He is quite inclined towards Plaid and has voted for us in the past, but will not be doing so this time. He thinks that we are fiscally illiterate, and is especially venomous about our demand for an extra £1.2 billion to the National Assembly, the figure that has been cooked up as our shortfall because of the iniquitous Barnett Formula.

That Wales receives less than it needs and deserves is accepted by almost everyone across the political spectrum, and I wish that we'd concentrated on that rather than nail a precise figure on it. It sounds so plucked from thin air; worse, it sustains the hoary image of us crouching behind a begging bowl. In this part of Wales, people find that really offensive to their sense of self-esteem, and I can see why. I've always said it's a strategic mistake to bang on about £1.2 billion, and it's a figure we've quietly decided to ignore in Ceredigion. It will not be appearing in our literature.

The real trouble with it is that it gives voters like this man, someone who would quite like to be persuaded to vote Plaid, an insurmountable reason why he can't. As he says, "If I can't believe this figure that you're making so much of, then why should I believe any of your other statements about the economy? 'We don't want austerity,' you say. Well, who the hell does? But the country's knackered, spent out, and there isn't any choice. And why? Because your lot, well Gordon Brown anyway, broke it. But it is your lot too. That Leanne Wood, it's all spend, spend, spend. She doesn't have the first idea about the economy – you can see it on her, every time she's on the telly."

It provokes a heated discussion about the national debt. I point out that the debt-to-GDP ratio has been higher than it currently stands for over half of the past century, the very times when we planned and rebuilt for the future. In 1945, it was three or four times higher than it is now. "Oh, 1945!" he snarls, "You can't compare now with then. Different times, different answers."

I know that I have failed to persuade him, and that I am not going to get his vote. There are many like him, though, people intellectually or emotionally attracted to Plaid, but put off by thinking that we sound like a toddler when it comes to how we intend to pay for our extensive wish list. In Ceredigion, this really matters. Not for nothing are Cardis the butt of so many jokes regarding their caution with money. The prevailing narrative – that the left broke the economy, and the right have fixed it – is utter horseshit on several levels, but it has been repeated so often that most people take it as read. We should be challenging that, not getting stuck in the cul-de-sac of having to justify a specific figure.

Another bloke is delighted to meet me, but only so that he can say something he's been saving up for ages. "I shall not be voting for you," he declares, "I am not interested at all. All you believe in is Wales for the Welsh." With that, he slams the door, thrilled to have got it off his chest. I try to put a leaflet through his letterbox. "No THANK YOU!" he roars from the other side.

Once again, there is much debate amongst the canvassers about our targeted lists. No-one likes them, and again we find supporters we didn't know about by knocking on doors we shouldn't.

Thursday 12 February 2015,
Aberystwyth University:
There are ten of us out this afternoon for a canvass in Llanilar, including the party's Chief Executive Rhuanedd Richards. If we do get into the TV debates, she's nervous about how Leanne will manage, for it is going to be such a big deal. Like me, she wants to see more of Leanne's passion, even anger. There has been much in the news this week about tax avoidance, implicating both Tories and Labour; there's no shortage of things to be angry about. Rhuanedd's a whizz at canvassing too, even though Llanilar is, by some distance, the most loyally Liberal Democrat village I've yet encountered. It has always been that way apparently.

Even though the election is yet to be called, it's the first hustings tonight, and all six candidates are here. I am terrified. The audience consists mainly of bussed-in cheerleaders; by far the most obedient are the Labour lot. Every time Huw Thomas coughs, they break into applause. There are not many Pleidwyr here, but a fair few Tories, LibDems and even Kippers. They don't look like they get out very often.

Mark Williams spends most of the evening attempting

to put as much distance as possible between himself and the government. He speaks well, but seems a little weary. I'm sure he must be thinking, "Here we go again", for this is his fifth Ceredigion campaign. It's the first time I've met my Conservative opponent, Henrietta Hensher, and the Green, Daniel Thompson. Henrietta is polished but slightly patronising, and ends almost every answer with the buzz phrase "going forward", using it as a kind of verbal full stop whether it fits or not. Labour candidate Huw Thomas is fond of it too. I smell candidate training. Daniel seems likable, but very earnest and terribly nervous. Gethin James for UKIP is sat next to me, and I'm startled to see that he reads every answer, word for word, from notes. When a question is asked for which we're not prepared, he's all over the shop. I'm amazed; he's been a county councillor for ten years, and I expected him to be better than that.

Huw makes a telling slip, which I pounce on. At one point, he is cranking up the rhetoric against the coalition government's cuts and privatisation. When it's my turn to answer, I say that I'll take no lessons from Labour on this, the party of dubious PFI schemes and, via their Assembly government, flagrantly biased financial settlements for Welsh councils. The pattern of non-Labour areas having to take a far greater hit has been unchanged for the last three years, whereupon Huw shouts "Well, that just shows that if you don't want bigger cuts, you should vote for a Labour council!" I call that out as the authentic voice of Labour cronyism.

None of us shine especially, but I'm happy to get it out of the way without any damage being done.

Friday 13 February 2015,
Home:
Pippa Bartolotti, the leader of the Welsh Greens, tweets a link to a Left Unity essay about how the only chance of success for the anti-austerity left is if we all attempt to compromise and forge new alliances. It's an excellent piece, which stirs me

greatly. In a fug of optimistic bonhomie, assisted by a glass of wine, it inspires me to tweet Bartolotti. It soon gets bizarre:

@pippabartolotti: "It takes big hearts to put aside little differences. Thanks to LU for this pledge which we all see as progressive... [link to article]"

@mikeparkerwales: "So agree. Would love to see some of that same reciprocity with my campaign in Ceredigion. Any chance of that?"

@pippabartolotti: "Have you approached the local party bearing organic and fair trade gifts with floral tributes from the hedgerows?"

@mikeparkerwales: "They can gladly have a pot of my home made marmalade if they want! Seriously though, we need to talk. Too much at stake."

@pippabartolotti: "I am being serious. You have to approach the local party with something more appealing than Plaid have delivered before."

@mikeparkerwales: "Could we talk please? Can't squeeze it all into tweets. My email is parkerplaid@gmail.com. Hope to hear from you."

Sunday 15 February 2015,
Manchester:

Preds and I have come to Manchester for the stadium show of *Phoenix Nights*, starring my old stand-up partner Janice Connolly. Any hopes that I might get twenty-four hours free of politics are soon dashed, as my phone goes into meltdown all morning. Pippa Bartolotti has turned our little Twitter exchange on Friday night into an extraordinary public statement, complaining of "harassment" and "threats", particularly from Plaid supporters.

She's written it very carefully, not to state directly that I harassed her, but to imply that our six tweets were part of a bigger, more orchestrated campaign of abuse. It's very cheeky. So much for "it takes big hearts to put aside little differences." It has of course alerted journalists, and Owen too. He's furious, and in a terse phone call as we sit in a Manchester café, orders me to keep quiet. I'm on holiday, mate, even if only for one sweet day, so no danger on that score.

Monday 16 February 2015,
Home:
On the run back from Manchester, we pick up a *Western Mail*. They have run the story, which includes this priceless paragraph:

> The comments came after Plaid's Ceredigion candidate Mike Parker appealed for help from the Greens with his campaign, only to find the Welsh Green Party leader Pippa Bartolotti asking him on Twitter if he had approached the local Greens "bearing organic and fair trade gifts".
> After a jokey response from Mr Parker, the Wales Green Party leader said she was serious.

The BBC have run it too, under the headline "Greens accuse Plaid Cymru of 'harassment' over election". I get some indignant Green Party members shouting at me on Twitter and Facebook, though there's a fair few supporting me too. Bartolotti is not universally popular in her own ranks. The words "drama queen" are used by a few.

Brilliant. I've not yet so much as grazed the skin of the Tories or Labour, or even – more pertinently – the LibDems. But in the space of a couple of weeks, I have managed to infuriate Mebyon Kernow and the Green Party, our supposed allies.

Tuesday 17 February 2015,
ITV studios, Cardiff:
A drive down to Cardiff for an interview with BBC Wales about public disenchantment with political parties, and to attend an ITV Wales reception for election candidates. There are only

eight of us there: five Labour women from the south, and one each from the other three main parties. I'm very glad I bothered, otherwise Plaid would have been unrepresented.

On top of that, it's good to catch up with old colleagues from ITV Wales, and to pick up some gossip. I particularly like the nugget from Owain Phillips, the genial political reporter. He tells me that a few weeks ago an ITN political correspondent was dispatched from London to do a piece about the election in Wales. He swept in, refused to talk to any of the local journalists, and, despite people pleading with him not to, went to record his piece at Blaenafon, with the wheel of Big Pit as his backdrop.

Friday 20 February 2015,
Y Buarth, Aberystwyth:
Lively, excitable afternoon with Leanne, Elin and a big crowd of supporters, plus a TV crew and a couple of journalists in hot pursuit. It looks increasingly likely that Leanne will be part of the TV election debates, although Cameron is still trying to duck his way out of them. Press interest in Plaid is increasing as a result.

After a visit to the Aberystwyth food bank, we all squeeze into the office of the Penparcau Forum, before heading out to canvass the Edwardian villas of the Buarth, on the north side of the town centre. Canvassing while being trailed by a TV crew is excruciating. The sight completely freaks out most people, while others ham it up terribly. All the same, the response is excellent, especially from otherwise Labour and Green voters who are lending us their support this time. Leanne is so good on the doorstep. Her warmth is entirely natural and her command of the issues far stronger than comes across sometimes in her media appearances. I wish more people could see the real her.

There's a journalist, Jamie Merrill, from the *Independent on Sunday* trailing us too. He wants to write a piece about the election in Ceredigion, and is intrigued by what he has seen so far. What most struck him as he travelled here from

London was how different things are here, politically as much as anything else. "Once I'd passed into Wales," he says, "I was travelling through lovely countryside and tiny little market towns – in England, that would be rock solid Tory territory. But here, it's a scrap between two centre-left options. It's very strange, very unexpected."

At the beginning of the day, he tells me we are deluding ourselves if we think we can overturn a LibDem majority of over eight thousand. By the time we have pounded our way up and down the hilly streets of the Buarth, and he has listened in on the conversations, he is a lot less sure. "I think the real vote here is where it was in 2005, rather than 2010," he says as he comes to leave. "I wouldn't want to bet on who'll win it."

First use today of the new campaign posters with my name on them. It is so strange to see them. I had noticed from photos on Twitter that most other Plaid candidates seem to have had their personalised posters for months now, and had quietly wondered where mine were. I suspect that no-one had wanted to commit the money until the very last minute, just in case I didn't last the course.

Tuesday 24 February 2015,
Village hall, Taliesin:
In the office, Owen and I have yet another difficult discussion about the targeted canvassing, and how, every time we go off-piste from the lists, we find new potential supporters that we know nothing about. Whenever this has happened, I report it back to him, whereupon he scampers off to his database to see why they were missing. His relief at finding a reason – that they don't often vote or aren't on the register, mainly – far outweighs any concern he should have that perhaps we are missing people. And we are, unquestionably. I'm the one out on the cold pavements four days a week, hearing it time and again. Meanwhile Owen, in the office with his spreadsheets, will not accept that there is any ambiguity in the system, much less a margin for error.

Neither can I believe that he is leaning so hard on the gaps in the electoral register as a reason. When the draft new one was published last month, Ceredigion had lost seven thousand voters in a year, well over ten per cent of the total. It is one of the largest falls of any constituency in the UK, and there is a huge effort being made to get people back on.

I'm meeting the missing voters all the time, and can see the patterns. They are frequently people who care about the issues and follow events, but who have lost faith in party politics, so haven't bothered voting lately. Many of them are also incomers, and have felt even more semi-detached from the system since moving to rural Wales, and finding it even less familiar than they expected. More than most wannabe MPs, I know that I can reach them, and have been. Trying to entice them back into participating and breaking down the barriers to Plaid Cymru – and to Cymru itself – were significant reasons for me being chosen as candidate. It's only going to work as a strategy, however, if we find and talk to the people likely to be receptive to it.

To Taliesin, where I'm giving a map talk to the Llangynfelyn Heritage Group. It's a great mix of locals, incomers and everything in between, amongst whom are a few old neighbours. Everyone seems pleased to have me, and to enjoy the talk.

As I near the end, I suddenly feel ill. My innards dissolve, my head starts to thump and sweat begins to bead across my forehead. The minute it is over, I have to make my excuses and scarper, feeling steadily worse by the minute. By the time I get home, I am shivering and properly sick.

Saturday 28 February 2015,
Cardigan:
Back in the Wild West for a lively street stall outside the Guildhall in Cardigan. We are asking people what proportion of the price of milk they think goes to dairy farmers (it is about 25p per litre). Almost everyone over-estimates it, some substantially. There is real trouble brewing in the dairy sector,

exacerbated by the strong-arm tactics of the supermarkets who often use milk as a loss leader to bring in the shoppers, and screw their suppliers as a result. Richard and I spend a long, cold two hours in a farmyard this afternoon hearing more about the problem. It is fast reaching crisis point.

Wednesday 4 March 2015,
Plaid office, Aberystwyth:
Weeks after the event, the *Cambrian News* has run a spiteful piece about us – me in particular – "bullying" Pippa Bartolotti and the Greens. They never warned us it was coming, nor contacted us for a comment. Owen is furious: "Six months of acceptable impartiality by the CN's standards, but today is horrid" he writes in a round robin email. Elin's main concern is that I'll open my big gob again on social media and make things worse. Richard, love him, manages to find the positive, writing "O leiaf mae enw a llun Mike yn y CN!"[4]

We have a good number of former and otherwise Greens promising to support me; a few are even taking an active part in the campaign. Encouraging them to speak up is the best retort.

Saturday 7 March 2015,
Galeri, Caernarfon:
The party spring conference, and there are more journalists here than I've ever seen at a Plaid event. I do a number of media interviews, including one with someone from the new Welsh edition of *The Sunday Times*. I ask him why the big interest in us all of a sudden, and he says that it is because a hung parliament looks inevitable, in which case they – and their readers – need to know more about the smaller parties, who may well end up as kingmakers. On top of that, it looks almost certain that Leanne will be in the UK-wide television debates. It is quite bizarre being treated as if we are some new

---

4   "At least Mike's name and picture are in the *Cambrian News*!"

kids on the block: a party that's ninety years old this year and has been in the Commons for all but four of the last fifty years. I do a live interview too with BBC TV, who are broadcasting throughout today, to an audience that probably consists of Preds' mum and a dozen others. The interviewer keeps pushing me about how popular Mark is in Ceredigion, which eventually elicits a tetchy response from me that "so are certain brands of washing powder and trips to Borth beach". I surprise myself sometimes.

Owen is not pleased that I've written a piece for the *Morning Star* about working with the Greens. It is entitled "A Leap of Faith", and that is exactly what we need right now, even when we have Green candidates standing against us in most Welsh seats. He is worried that it might provoke another haughty backlash from Pippa Bartolotti, but so far, she's kept uncharacteristically quiet. I don't think it will, and I don't care. The most important thing is to raise the profile of the anti-austerity alliance in Westminster, and Bartolotti is of no relevance to that.

A difficult moment too with a Ceredigion councillor. I ask about some of the school closures being proposed, and how loaded the consultation processes seem to be. The conversation confirms some of my worst fears, and together with a few sharp comments about "pushy incomers", infuriates me.

Now though, we're notching up a gear. The election is two months today; Owen tells me that from here on in we will be campaigning pretty much all day, every day.

Sunday 8 March 2015,
Gwesty'r Celt, Caernarfon:
I pick up the *Independent on Sunday*, which contains Jamie Merrill's take on his day trip to Aberystwyth the other week. "Plaid Cymru scent Lib Dem blood in Wales" is the headline, even if – to be pedantic – we're hardly likely to be scenting their blood anywhere but Wales. The piece is favourable, too, and thankfully digs no deeper into the recent spat with the

Greens, something he'd been quizzing both Leanne and me about when he was with us.

Owen sends a text, saying how chuffed he is with it, but that he hasn't yet managed to see *The Sunday Times*, which also carries an interview with me. He won't be quite as pleased when he finds a copy, as they have focused entirely on my thoughts about breaking up the UK. "English hopeful in call for split" is the headline, and although there's not a word in it that I regret, it is doubtless well off-message. The larger story above it is headlined "Labour alliance with SNP would break up Britain, says Cameron". That is obviously the context into which they have slotted me.

I'm staying on in Caernarfon for an all-day session of candidates' media training, led by Ashok Ahir, someone I've long wanted to meet. He's another West Midlander turned *Cymro manqué*, and was a finalist in the 2012 Welsh Learner of the Year award. His Welsh, and the session as a whole, are excellent, though I fall spectacularly flat on my face at one point.

There are a dozen or so candidates, with widely varying amounts of media experience between us. Because I've been on TV many times, everyone expects me to be a whizz at the whole thing, and it's a belief I'm happy to stoke. On camera, so that we can all watch our efforts, they get us to give a thirty-second introduction to ourselves; most are forcibly stopped mid sentence as they massively underestimate what thirty seconds feels like. By sheer fluke, I finish bang on the mark, and am backslapped as an evident professional.

It doesn't last. They line us up in groups of three and four to fire questions at us as if it were a live news programme. When Ashok, as the questioner, turns my way, he throws me a challenge about Plaid's anti-austerity stance, and was it realistic with the country in such deep debt? This is a question I've answered scores of times, but my mind goes blank and I stare at him like a sullen teenager. All I manage to get out, after a long and awkward silence, is a nervous giggle and a request to start again.

People are genuinely shocked that I lost it so easily. So am I. No-one else fluffed so badly. Tŷ Gwynfor had said a month or so ago that they wanted to use me as one of the frontline media spokespeople in this election campaign. I wonder if they will after they've seen this.

Monday 9 March 2015,
Plaid office, Aberystwyth:
It's been agreed that Richard and I will attend the office staff meetings with Elin every Monday morning, so that we can deal quickly with any stuff coming in. I'm beginning to be inundated with emails about particular policy issues; most are cut and paste templates from supporters of 38 Degrees[5] and the like. As I'm out now every day, it's getting impossible for me to deal with them all, so it is agreed that Jordan, an American volunteer coming to work with us up to the election, will help me out.

We've commissioned a phone poll in the county amongst voters we believe to be fairly fluid in their loyalties, and the results are fascinating. Of the people who voted LibDem in 2010, about a third are sticking with them, a third don't know, and the final third is divided between us, the Greens, UKIP and not voting at all. Astonishingly, none of it seems to be going to Labour.

Tuesday 10 March 2015,
Penparcau, Aberystwyth:
Canvassing all day, in and around Tanygroes and Sarnau and then back up for the late afternoon and evening in Aberystwyth. It's the first properly warm day of spring, and what a difference it makes. People are so much more cheerful and willing to have a chat.

A couple of notable responses this evening. In Penparcau,

---

5   A UK-wide non-party political campaigning and lobbying organisation, with around two million members.

we whistle round a courtyard of houses knocking only on the targeted doors. As we finish, I notice a man in the central yard unpacking his car after a supermarket shopping trip, so go and have a quick word. He has voted Plaid before, and is considering doing so this time, but "You weren't going to knock on my door, were you? I've just seen you walk straight past it. Are we not worth it or something?" He's not pleased. Not only does sticking to the targeted list mean that we might miss potential support, it seems like it could even lose us votes.

Mererid Jones is in charge of this evening's canvass, and she marshals us all with military efficiency, hustling people to the right doors and chasing us up if we linger too long. It makes all the difference. I wish we had a Mererid on every canvass. At one point, I see her talking to an older man, and go to join them, just in time to hear the old chestnut that "Nigel Farage is the only one saying it like it is". I'm not in the mood to waste time, so just hold my hand up in resignation and say, "I'm sorry, Farage is not the answer. He's playing on people's fears, picking off the most vulnerable in our society and stirring up some extremely nasty forces. If that's how you're going to vote, that's your business, but let's agree to disagree", before stomping off and leaving Mererid to pick up the pieces. Afterwards, she tells me that he then said, "Blimey, your man speaks his mind, doesn't he? I like that. You might have my vote."

Wednesday 11 March 2015,
Plaid office, Aberystwyth:
A campaign committee at the end of a long, wet day out canvassing around Ystrad Meurig and Tynygraig. It was OK, though there were a lot of long drives and tracks to walk down only to find no-one in.

Had to write a five-hundred-word piece this morning for *Pink News*, the online LGBT news site. Plaid put out a party political broadcast last week, featuring a young man "coming out" to his parents as a Plaid voter. Our opponents have been making as much mischief as they can over it, accusing us of crass insensitivity, disrespect, opportunism and so on. Chris Bryant[6] has been the chief stirrer.

I've tried to dampen down the excitement with my response, though since when did that work online? Comments are coming in thick and fast, mostly favourable, but a few implacably angry. Broadly speaking, aside from political opponents trying to score points, those who hate it seem to be people who were, or still are, highly traumatised by coming out, or who had especially difficult times doing so. It is an intensely personal response.

"The personal is political" used to be the rallying cry of feminists, and then the wider liberation movements. It has been staggering to see how swiftly it has moved from the radical fringes of debate to become perhaps the defining philosophy of Western liberal democracies. Our politics are increasingly forged from our personal experience and sense of identity. I worry, though, that something intended to liberate is beginning to have the opposite effect, polarising and killing debate before it's even started. Now, it is not just that the personal is political, but that the political is in danger of becoming almost entirely personal.

Friday 13 March 2015,
Llanwnnen:
Unlucky Friday 13th, and so it transpires. A fairly pointless street stall in Lampeter which fails to engage with many people, and then a bollocking from Elin. During one conversation *yn Gymraeg* with a local couple, we were talking about the desirability of learning Welsh, and I mentioned that for all his promises, Mark Williams still hadn't done so. Elin was cross, and told me afterwards that I'd made them very uncomfortable. It didn't seem that way to me, but perhaps she's right. Or was the discomfort hers?

It gets worse. From there, we canvass Elin's home village

---

6   Labour MP for Rhondda (2001–).

of Llanwnnen, just down the road. As we're finishing, my phone goes. It is one of our more challenging activists, a gifted academic who is always phoning to berate me about something, or complain that he and his ideas are not getting enough kudos or attention. It's more, much more, of the same today, in a ceaseless monologue of woe. Fed up, I snap and end up shouting at him, while standing on the main street of the village, right by the church. By the time I've wrapped up the call, Elin has disappeared. I feel like I've really let her down today, and I'm furious with myself.

On getting home, I pour it all out to Preds. He is in no doubt: I owe the man I shouted at an unqualified apology. He's right, and I shuffle off to my office to try and make amends.

Tuesday 17 March 2015,
Beulah:
A slow drive south with Richard for a full day's door knocking in Beulah, Bryngwyn and Brynhoffnant. I am so glad of Richard's company; he is an absolute gentleman and was an inspired choice as agent. We share many enthusiasms and political perspectives; most importantly on these long, long days, punctuated only by the odd sandwich, we can really make each other laugh. And boy, do I need that right now.

Wednesday 18 March 2015,
Pentre Bach (Pentre Sali Mali), Blaenpennal:
Frantic day, kicking off with a drive to Tregaron for a Q&A session with final-year students at Ysgol Henry Richard. En route, I pick up Jordan, the American volunteer at the office; she's barely been out of Aber, so it's good to show off the Ceredigion countryside, bathed in watery spring sunshine. We arrive at the school, fail hopelessly to negotiate their labyrinthine security system and have to call for help.

It improves from there though; the session is great fun, the students are well clued up on the issues and bilingually eloquent in expressing them. Not surprisingly, patchy broadband and mobile signals are a massive concern. We always think about this in terms of its negative impact on business, but it is a huge matter for young people and, as it stands, threatens to be a significant factor in a new population exodus from the countryside. We are repeatedly assured by the Welsh government and BT that better communications are just around the corner, but the reality continues to defy the promises.

Tregaron looks glorious this morning, as if it is waking up from hibernation, and after giving Jordan a whistlestop tour of the town, we head back north to Bontgoch, on the other side of Aberystwyth, for a few hours' canvassing. There are the usual odd moments: one old farmer in a woolly cap declares that all our woes stem from there being too many "pobl liwgar"[7] in the country. Support though is solid, including from some who have never previously voted Plaid. Yesterday, pundit and publisher Iain Dale changed his prediction for Ceredigion, saying that he now thought we'd take it. Momentum is building.

Back to the Plaid office for a meeting with Cynog about how to do hustings meetings. His main message is to be accurate and positive, and that any demolition of the LibDems should be done precisely and politically, not personally. He says that our strategy should be clearer in this election than any other Westminster poll in living memory: the choice is more of the miserable same or something radical and different. To that end, we should be unashamed to promote the idea that this is the time for the state to invest, not cut, and that we absolutely uphold the ethos of public service and the public sector.

It is extremely useful, and as Jordan is with us, is conducted in English, for which I'm grateful. As soon as she leaves the room though, Cynog reverts to Welsh and proceeds to tear Owen and me off a strip about the recent edition of our newspaper, the *Ceredigion Post*. The front page headline – *Poll Boost for Mike* – is larger and more prominent than its equivalent in Welsh

---

7   "Colourful people", by which he presumably meant black and brown.

(*Hwb i Ymgyrch Mike*). This is, I know, a treasonable offence for many, especially those who fought for legal parity for Welsh through long and difficult years. "Mae pobl wedi eu carcharu am hyn,"[8] Cynog lectures us, his eyes blazing. He used to be a teacher of course, and we sit there like naughty fourteen-year-olds taking our punishment.

Final gig of the day is an informal public meeting in Pentre Sali Mali, home of the hit S4C kids' programme, and something of a village hall to the widely scattered community of Blaenpennal. I've never met the owners before, although we have friends in common, and it is a pleasure to do so at last. They obviously work so hard to knit the community together and it shows, for the evening is the perfect antidote to the scratchy language politics of earlier. It is a well-mixed crowd, locals and incomers all getting on pretty well, and in both languages, just as it was this morning in the school.

Thursday 19 March 2015,
Aberystwyth University:
Good day out and about doing more photographs with Marian Delyth. Then back to Aberystwyth for the second hustings organised by the university students' union, this time focusing on international students, immigration and associated issues. There's no Henrietta the Tory this time, so it's an all-male panel.

Once again, Mark Williams is happy to stick the boot in to the government of which he has been part for the last five years. He denounces the new visa regulations that have been imposed on visiting students as a "narrow and inflexible system". They have already succeeded in making the UK far less attractive to international students, to pander to the xenophobic media chorus of late.

There are marker pens and little whiteboards in front of each of us, and at various points we are asked questions

---

8   "People have been imprisoned for this."

and told to write the answers down and show them to the audience. One asks us how many international students we think there are in Aberystwyth. I put 2,500, and the right figure is just under two thousand. We're all fairly near that, except for Gethin, who guesses 20,000. In a town whose total population, student and resident alike, is less than that. Could there be a more perfect illustration of how the world looks through UKIP goggles?

Saturday 21 March 2015,
Neuadd Goffa, Talybont:
An interesting canvass this morning in Llannon. One conversation in particular has stayed with me, with a woman originally from Sardinia. She's a dispensing chemist and had recently moved jobs, from Aberystwyth to Llandysul, and has been truly shocked by the poverty that she's found in her new position. "Although there's quite a lot of deprivation in Aberystwyth," she tells me, "it's nothing to what I've found in Llandysul. It's rural poverty on a scale I haven't seen since I was growing up in a really poor part of Sardinia. It is getting worse, and quite quickly." This is alarming to hear, but no surprise either.

As we leave Llannon, we pass Mark Williams, Elizabeth Evans and a small gang of LibDems starting their rounds through the village. I'm very glad we got in first. With the Sardinian woman's words in my mind, seeing the opposition sharpens my resolve, for this is a fundamental battle of ideas. I cannot forgive the Liberal Democrats for bequeathing us this government. They didn't have to go into formal coalition with the Conservatives. Between them, they have wreaked irreversible havoc on society in just five years; dismantling the fabric of the country with indecent haste, and picking on the least deserving victims.

It's a race to get to a Plaid fundraising lunch in Talybont. The curries are excellent, and there's a good crowd of familiar faces, though most are grouped around a TV to watch the final

Wales match of the Six Nations, playing away to Italy. It's quite a relief not to be the main focus, especially when I realise how unhappy some people are about two of our recent leaflets. One was a questionnaire that had the English text above the Welsh, the other the newspaper that Cynog had already complained about, with its more prominent English headline. They were passed for publication by everyone, but it's my face on them, so it's up to me to take the rap.

And there is plenty of rap to be had in Talybont. Telling me off for this slur on Welsh is the very first thing some people want to say to me, even as I'm trying to eat my lunch. A wave of tired exasperation passes through me that yet again we are stalling at the first fence, the indignation of the comfortable middle-classes as they rock up atop their favourite hobbyhorse. Sod the poverty, forget the food banks, let's just make sure that the ears of a few librarians and lecturers are kept safe from the beastly *iaith fain*.[9] I nearly crack when one person says to me, "Well, you can see why people are thinking of voting for Huw Thomas".

In the pursuit of something gentler, I go and talk with a small group of elderly women sat at the back of the hall. It is no respite. One of them, a spry 95-year-old with piercing eyes, reaches down into her handbag and pulls out our questionnaire, together with a copy of Huw's latest Labour leaflet, in which the Welsh is first throughout. She waves our effort at me in clenched fists, and is inconsolably furious. It is a real shock to witness such passion in someone at her stage of life, and makes me re-assess my soreness. She has been witness to the language's every struggle for decades, a fighter all her life for the tortuous, inch-by-inch progress of Cymraeg into some kind of official recognition. With that as your life's backdrop, you could only see the leaflets as a step in the wrong direction.

---

9   "The thin language", i.e. English.

Sunday 22 March 2015,
Borth:
Sunday canvassing has never happened before. To many, it is heresy even to contemplate it, but the Plaid Cymru Youth conference is on in Aberystwyth this weekend (I went to speak to them yesterday), and they'd volunteered their services for today, so I insisted on it. In the last campaign committee, we'd pondered where would be the most suitably godless place in the county to try out a Sunday morning canvass. The answer was obvious: Borth.

It's a hoot. There are nearly twenty of us, and we sweep through the sun-dazzled village like a small hurricane. Unsurprisingly, Borth has never been especially strong for Plaid, all the more so since Mark Williams moved here after winning the seat in 2005. But the response today is terrific, and not a single person mentions Mark.

Matthew and I will be back here tomorrow to film another one of my Rough-ish Guide videos. I filmed here before with Emyr, for *Coast to Coast*, and I know that he loves it as much as I do. He will capture its beautiful bleakness and big skies, its perilous fragility and downright oddness. We're also filming in Tregaron tomorrow, so it will be a day of Ceredigion at its eccentric finest.

Tuesday 24 March 2015,
Ffosygrafel Uchaf Farm, near Clarach:
The National Farmers' Union (NFU) hustings in an ice-cold cow shed. One of the traditions of rural Welsh politics is that candidates have to do separate hustings for the NFU and the Farmers' Union of Wales (FUW), so this is just the first such outing.

I have been dreading this one, for despite the fact that Preds is from a local farming family and that nearly all of our neighbours are farmers, I feel more of a political fraud in this environment than in almost any other. From the candidates' opening speeches, it would seem that I'm not alone. Each of us rather pitifully tries to establish our agricultural credentials, turfing up old grannies, uncles, friends and neighbours in a bid to convince them that we too are of the soil. One look at us though is enough to tell anyone that we're not.

Thursday 26 March 2015,
Llandysul:
It is always a pleasure to come to Llandysul, and getting to know this area better has been one of the highlights of the last couple of years. The landscape is one that reveals its joys quite slowly, slyly even. It is not the stuff of stirring postcard views; rather a soft green sea dotted with hard nuggets of an old way of life. Discussions on doorsteps here are always fascinating, and often challenging.

I cannot shake off the conversation that I had last weekend with the pharmacist in Llannon, who had recently moved jobs from Aberystwyth to Llandysul and was horrified by its worsening poverty. Today, I am primed to spot any signs, and there are plenty, both in the town and surrounding villages. While it is inevitable on a daytime canvass that you will meet more people who are elderly, ill or unemployed, I suddenly notice the worn-out carpet slippers, the wafts of damp and decay, the cracked, dirty windows and sagging roofs. More than anything, I notice the haunted looks on so many grey faces, and it is heartbreaking.

Infuriating too. One of my terrors is that rural, Welsh-speaking Wales is sliding into the kind of social, economic, and cultural cul-de-sac that you can see, far farther down the line, in some of the Native American communities of the US, or amongst the Aborigines in Australia. Today, that seems as close as I've ever felt it.

Saturday 28 March 2015,
Aberystwyth:
A Morrisons' shop is not the best way to wrap up a long day's canvassing, and when I finally leave the store, my mind has

crumbled to dust. Heading past Llety Parc into Llanbadarn I suddenly see a series of Vote Mike Parker Plaid Cymru placards strung along the perimeter fence. I had completely forgotten that the first crews were going out to put them up today, and a hot flush of shock, horror, excitement and pride engulfs me. "Co ni off!"[10] as they say round here.

Sunday 29 March 2015,
Home:
An apologetic email from a friend who promised to help with the campaign, but who has never done so and is now crying off altogether. He's very sorry, but he has way too much to do, he's sure I'm going to win anyway and he's sure too that I'll understand. I do, for he's not been the only one. When I was first selected, I was inundated with promises of help by a staggering range of people. Few of those have come to much. I don't really mind, because I know that I've done the same, and that's life. We all intend to do more than we actually can.

There is, however, a curious pattern here. Most of the people who were so excited by my candidature, and who made extravagant promises to help that they couldn't keep, were fellow English incomers. Very noticeably, there was a great deal less promised initially by my Welsh mates, but it is they who have put the hours in, hugely in many cases, while making the minimum of noise about it. *Vive la différence.*

Monday 30 March 2015,
Home:
Radio 5 Live want to talk to representatives of each party about the experience of being a candidate, rather than any specific policies. I've been put forward for Plaid. As we are now in the period of electoral purdah, I can't mention the name of the constituency in which I'm standing – if I did, they'd have to invite all the other candidates on as well.

---

10 "And we're off!"

Interviewing me is Adrian Chiles, an old acquaintance from university days in London. We grew up just a few miles apart and he succeeded me as sabbatical President of the students' union. We haven't talked in over twenty years, and it is great to hear him again. He says in the interview that he's not surprised to find me standing for parliament as "You were the first properly political person I ever met". He is slightly more fazed though that I am standing for Plaid Cymru: "Last time I looked on the map Mike, Kidderminster was definitely still in England."

The election campaign officially began today. David Cameron went to Buckingham Palace to see the Queen and get parliament dissolved. Nick "me too" Clegg went separately to do the same an hour later. It's not often that I feel sorry for the Queen.

PLAID AND PREJUDICE
April 2015

Wednesday 1 April 2015,

12.40pm, Y Ferwig, near Cardigan:

Daytime canvassing in the villages north of Cardigan proves fairly fruitless; lots of "I don't know if I'll even bother to vote", "I can't decide" and even "I'll make my mind up when I get to the polling station". That is a terrifying response. Is it like closing your eyes and jabbing the newspaper to pick a horse for the Grand National?

It's April Fool's Day, but jokes are thin on the ground. It soon gets even less fun. I receive a Twitter message from Chris Betteley, a journalist at the *Cambrian News*, asking me to call him. On the journey back to Aberystwyth, I do so.

He tells me that he is investigating a piece I wrote in 2001 for "*The Planet* magazine", as he keeps calling it. It concerned the "white flight" phenomenon of incomers into rural Wales, focusing especially on the high command of the neo-fascist British National Party (BNP), many of whom had decamped to Montgomeryshire. Although they have now imploded, the BNP were on the march at the time; they were shortly to get councillors elected, and then a couple of MEPs. In Dyffryn Banwy that summer, they organised a festival whose guest of honour was veteran French fascist Jean-Marie Le Pen.

"White flight" was not just the preserve of paid-up BNP members. I was a new arrival in Wales myself at the time, and had been startled by how many fellow incomers told me that they had moved here principally to get away from multicultural English cities. That they were now the incomers into a different culture was an irony that didn't trouble them. It was a phenomenon that bewildered me, and I had wanted to write about it.

Betteley reads out the most florid sentences of my two-thousand-word article. "It's very extreme, don't you think?" he repeatedly goads me. I refuse to accept that it is. I ask him how he found it; he says it was "given" to him, but will not tell me by whom. I say that I need to re-read the article, and will call him later.

In the car as we rattle through Llannon and Llanrhystud, we discuss it. Hedydd, who works in Jill Evans's office in Brussels, sees the political implications immediately, and is thinking out loud a comprehensive plan of action to counter it. I nod along, but secretly think she's being a little over-dramatic.

2.00pm, Plaid office, Aberystwyth:
She's not the only one. Owen hears the news and goes very pale. "They'll have a bloody field day with this," he mutters, and starts to draft lines of response – that mine was a fierce piece attacking racism, and that we should always challenge such attitudes wherever they appear. I'd told him that the article, and the press reactions to it at the time, were out there on the internet, but it hadn't been followed up, and stupidly, I was quietly relieved that no-one seemed that bothered. We agree the line, and I say that I'll ring Betteley later.

4.40pm, BBC studios, Aberystwyth:
Radio 4's *The Media Show* is interviewing all of the parties, one by one, in the run-up to the election. On the strength of my TV and radio work over the years, Tŷ Gwynfor have put me forward as the Plaid spokesman.

It goes really badly. The presenter is clearly none too excited to be talking to Plaid Cymru, and focuses on the budget of S4C, over which we do not agree. It ends sourly, and leaves me shaken.

Back in the car, I decide to get the *Cambrian News* out of the way, so ring Betteley back. He is now fixating on one particular section towards the end of my 2001 article. After sifting through the chilling record of BNP leader Nick Griffin, who had moved to Dyffryn Banwy in order, in his words, "to escape multicultural Britain", I wrote: "Nick Griffin's politics are a warning to us all in Wales. He might be the most obvious race-obsessed import in the hills, but he is not, by a long way, the only one. To some extent, rural Wales has become the British equivalent of the American mountains inhabited by a sprinkling of paranoid conspiracy theorists, gun-toting Final Solution crackpots and anti-government obsessives."

Betteley insists that I am calling incomers "Nazis". I'm not; I never use the word, not even against Nick Griffin. "But what else can you possibly mean by the phrase 'Final Solution crackpots' then?" he demands.

I clearly remember the thought process that led me, all those years ago, to that choice of words. The sentence describes those American cults, usually far up in the mountains of Montana or Colorado, who had collectively lost the plot, and especially those, such as Waco, Heaven's Gate and the Mansons, where it all ended in the grimly final solution of mass murder or suicide. With the arrival of the BNP's leadership in mid Wales (Griffin was far from the only one), my new patch was becoming the bolthole of choice for all sorts of violent extremists. While house-hunting out in the boondocks of Ceredigion and Montgomeryshire, I'd met a few myself and heard some terrifying, sinister stuff. Writing that "to some extent, rural Wales has become the British equivalent" of such places in the States was hyperbolic, for sure, but not unwarranted.

Betteley will not accept that this is what I meant, and insists that "Final Solution crackpots" can only mean the Nazis. I'm too naïve to see where this is going: it is the word "Nazi" to which he is wedded, and it sounds as if this is a decision that has been taken at the top. Neither do I spot that he is nailing these words to Wales, rather than America, as written.

"Were you vetted as a candidate?" he asks. I tell him of the process by which you join the Plaid Cymru register of candidates: a formal application and a grueling interview. As I know he's seen the *Telegraph* and *Guardian* pieces from 2001 about it, I tell him too how badly it was misconstrued at the time. I quickly realise that saying that was probably a mistake.

4.55pm, Plaid office, Aberystwyth:
It turns out that saying anything at all was the mistake. So keen was I to get it out of the way after my doleful interview

on Radio 4 that I didn't check my emails before calling him back from the BBC car park. I still hadn't when I get back to the office. "I called Betteley," I tell Owen. "You did *what?!*" he shouts. "Didn't you get the message saying to email him, not phone?" I open my emails. "Ah yes," I say, "there it is."

This is, I'm told in no uncertain terms, a potential disaster in the making. It had been mentioned before that, in particular with the *Cambrian News*, it was better to communicate with them by email, for that way no words could be misattributed. That felt overly paranoid to me, so I'd developed the policy of speaking to their journalists, hoping that the human touch might play in my favour. I see now that that was a very forlorn hope.

10.30pm, home:
Email from Elin:

"I understand from Owen that you rang the *Cambrian News* journalist to discuss the *Guardian* article. I had been discussing the lines to take with Owen and was waiting for your return from the studio.

I very strongly advise you NEVER to ring a journalist with a response to a request – always put it in a considered email. Especially from the *CN*. It allows a third party – such as Owen and me – to know what you have said, and more importantly allows you to be far more in control.

We will live by our nerves now until next week's *Cambrian News*."

This is going to run and run. Preds thinks I should face it full on, publish my 2001 article online, and write an update on the issues it raises. After all, those kind of bigots have hardly vanished. Quite the opposite, and now they've got their very own political party to play with, a party that unlike the BNP in 2001, is actually winning seats. He's right, I should do that, but I know that is going to be a tough sell to Plaid, in Ceredigion or Cardiff. They want this buried stone dead.

Thursday 2 April 2015,
Home:

First day canvassing with the election battle bus, an aged black Range Rover that has been customized with a loudspeaker system and my name all over it. It's been christened the Mikemobile, and will be driven most days by Brython, a delightful man from Devil's Bridge. Sitting in it made me feel painfully self-conscious, but it's very comfortable, and it will be a joy not to have to drive everywhere myself.

I get home just in time for the first UK-wide leaders' debate on ITV. There is a gathering in the Cŵps pub in Aberystwyth for those who want to watch it with other members of #TeamLeanne, as we're being encouraged to call ourselves. I bottle out, though, and scuttle home, where I can at least watch the two-hour marathon through my fingers or the bottom of a glass.

Leanne starts quite nervously, but soon gets into her stride. Her crowning moment comes almost an hour in, when Nigel Farage makes a flagrant pitch to shore up his bigots' vote by rattling chains about health tourism, and picking on the loaded target of HIV sufferers.

Leanne ploughs straight in and tells him that he is scaremongering and should be ashamed of himself. It gets her the first applause of the evening, and makes her performance one of the main headlines of the night. That it should be for this thrills me especially, for it chimes in perfectly with the fact that Plaid are consistently the only party prepared to call UKIP out for who they really are, and what they really represent.

It has been a shock to me how nervously the other parties tiptoe around UKIP. You can see them agonising over how to tackle them, terrified how it will play out in focus groups or on Facebook. I saw it the other week at the Aberystwyth University hustings on the issues of immigration and international students. Only when I went for the UKIP candidate, who was coming out with some utter bilge, did they weigh in too – and only once they'd seen that it went down well with the audience.

The same pattern kicks in tonight. It is Leanne's intervention that they all try to emulate. Two hours after the debate has ended, Ed Miliband tweets "I want to say, Nigel Farage's comment about the NHS and HIV was disgusting." *The Sun*'s political editor fires back "If only Ed had been standing five feet away with a microphone, eh?"

Saturday 4 April 2015,
Aberystwyth:
A street stall and some canvassing in Aberystwyth, before I have to shoot off to a party in Birmingham to remember my friend Ulrike, who would have been fifty today.

Yesterday's *Daily Telegraph* led with a story headlined "Sturgeon's secret backing for Cameron", and it has blown everything else off the agenda. It concerns a leaked civil servant's memo about a conversation that supposedly happened between Nicola Sturgeon and the French consul general in Edinburgh. She has denied it, and today, so has the French consul general. There's something very fishy about it, from every angle.

[After the election, we learned that the leak had been authorised by Alastair Carmichael, then LibDem Secretary of State for Scotland. To cover his tracks, he lied in TV and press interviews about his knowledge of the memo, and instigated at public expense a Cabinet Office inquiry into the source of the leak, knowing all along that it was him. In December 2015, he survived on a technicality a rare election court, convened to investigate the case, and remains the LibDems' only MP in Scotland.]

Tuesday 7 April 2015,
7.30pm, Neuadd Goffa car park, Penparcau, Aberystwyth:
I return from a day's canvassing in Llandysul and Lampeter to meet Richard, who has a copy of the brand-new Aberystwyth edition of the *Cambrian News*. Just from the look on his face, I know that it is not good. The story is on the front page, though down at the bottom and thankfully not the main item. The

headline though is hideous: "Plaid election hopeful defends 'Nazi' slur".

Half an hour before arriving back in Aberystwyth, the first comments on Twitter started to trickle in. First up was something supportive from a member who works in a newsagent's, and who had presumably seen it as the paper arrived. That quickly elicited a response – "Not something I would be proud of comparing people to Nazi!" – from "Joe", an anonymous Twitter account that was set up a few weeks ago, and which has been bombarding me with complaints ever since. It's as if he knew this was coming and was eagerly waiting for it.

8.50pm, home:
As I walk though the front door, the landline phone is ringing. It's Leanne, who gives me a rousing keep-calm-and-carry-on talk, tells me how proud she is of me, but warns me not to do or say anything without checking it with Owen and Elin. "Don't get down though," she assures me, "it's only tomorrow's chip paper". "Tomorrow's toilet paper, I'm hoping," I reply. The call is much appreciated, though, and it helps to know they're not about to drop me from a great height.

9.15pm:
Oh shit. The other Ceredigion editions of the paper have led with the story. The headlines are a disgrace.

Just to grind my face in it with my neighbours too, they've even made it the main story in the Machynlleth and Llanidloes edition, despite the fact that it has barely any cross-over into Ceredigion. I notice that in all the versions, they have quoted the most colourful line of my original article, but have changed its punctuation. This has the effect of changing the subject of the all-important "Final Solution crackpots" line from America to rural Wales. Whether this was done by accident or design, it's a very poor advert for their journalism.

Four different pictures, four different headlines, all of them

CARDIGAN & NEWCASTLE EMLYN

Cambrian News

Established 1860 WELSH WEEKLY NEWSPAPER OF THE YEAR 2015 Thursday 9 April 2015 80p

Staff at Cardigan store in anxious wait to see if jobs are safe
page 13

Grand National runners and riders

Don't miss our sweepstake kit, pages 16 & 17

Plaid Cymru candidate Mike Parker pictured on the campaign trail in Cardigan

Incomers are 'Nazis', says would-be MP

Plaid candidate defends criticism of English

A CEREDIGION Westminster candidate has defended comments he made comparing the county's English immigrants to Nazis and labelling the area a racist "safe haven" for "gun-toting Final Solution analogous".

Plaid Cymru candidate Mike Parker said in a magazine article in 2001 that the level of racism he encountered from people who had moved to the area from across the border had "taken him by surprise".

He wrote: "It is a sad truth that many English migrants into rural Wales are out-and-out racists.

"Their principal reason for leaving English cities was to get away from the multicultural society, from black and Asian people in particular, and they are rural Wales, with its largely white population as a safe haven."

Mr Parker, who came from near Machynlleth, added in the article: "To some extent, rural Wales has become the British equivalent of the American mountains, inhabited by a sprinkling of paranoid conspiracy theorists, gun-toting Final Solution crackpots and anti-government obsessives."

The Final Solution was a Nazi Germany plan to eradicate the Jewish population in Europe.

EXCLUSIVE by Chris Betteley

This week, while admitting that he would not use the type of language today he used "as a younger man", he was bit at the time of writing the piece – Mr Parker defended his comments as "valid".

"Never in a million years did I think I would be doing something like this [standing for MP] when I wrote that," Mr Parker told the Cambrian News.

"I was younger and angrier when it was written and would never apologise itself like that time. However, the point I was making is definitely still valid."

The 47-year-old – an English travel writer, television presenter and stand-up comic – moved to Llangwyrfon near Aberystwyth from Kidderminster in 2000 and, after joining Plaid, was named the party's 2015 General Election hope to regain the Ceredigion seat it lost a decade ago.

Mr Parker is expected to be the main challenger to incumbent Liberal Democrat Mark Williams at the election when Ceredigion goes to the polls on Thursday, 7 May.

→ Story continues on page 3

9 new jobs announced for Emlyn cheese factory
page 4

ISSN 2058-1795

SOUTH

Cambrian News

Established 1860 WELSH WEEKLY NEWSPAPER OF THE YEAR 2015 Thursday 9 April 2015 80p

Angry protests as leisure centre hours slashed

Grand National runners and riders

Plaid candidate says incomers are 'Nazis'

Racism accusations defended by would-be MP

Lifeline thrown to Aberaeron swimming pool

FREE MOT FOR LIFE

Cawdor Aberystwyth
Tel. 01970 577562

www.cawdorcars.co.uk

Come Dine Caribbean Style
Now 7 Days!

Irie

10% off

MACHYNLLETH & LLANIDLOES

Cambrian News

Established 1860 WELSH WEEKLY NEWSPAPER OF THE YEAR 2015 Thursday 9 April 2015 80p

Groups in spat over future of Llanidloes woodland

Double award for inspiring volunteer

Candidate compares incomers to Nazis

Would-be MP from Mach claims area is 'haven for racists'

Piece of rock history for project

FREE MOT FOR LIFE

Cawdor Aberystwyth
Tel. 01970 577562

www.cawdorcars.co.uk

Come Dine Caribbean Style
Now 7 Days!

Irie

10% off

dropping the N-bomb. That, of course, is the word now hurtling around the internet. The BBC, Sky and most of the UK papers have taken it up, Nazi this and Nazi that; the further it goes from the source, the more it is reduced to a bald core, namely "Plaid Cymru candidate says the English are Nazis". Round and round it spins.

My Twitter feed is in meltdown. My sacking is being demanded by numerous Tories, UKIPpers, LibDems and – most of all – Labour people. Peter Hain is one of the first off the mark, tweeting an image of the worst of the *Cambrian News* front pages with the message "Plaid Cymru must sack Candidate after this 'Nazi' attack on English constituents". Alastair Campbell, who knows a thing or two about spin, tweets the same image and "What will nice TV debate Leanne say about Plaid candidate saying English people in Wales are Nazis? Nats ain't nice." They are both retweeted hundreds of times.

Preds and I sit in the kitchen, glued to our phones, which are buzzing and bleeping like anxious robots. Messages are pouring in from all corners, even abroad. Most are positive, though there are some horrors.

9.38pm:
Chris Betteley of the *Cambrian News* is loving himself on Twitter. As a finale to various arguments he has been having about the paper's coverage, he pugnaciously tweets an image of all four front pages that attack me. His accompanying message is equally defiant: "If you write something it stays written: Plaid candidate: English migrants are 'gun-toting Final Solution crackpots'."

This is retweeted dozens of times, by LibDem, Tory and Labour candidates and officials, now joined in unholy alliance with various Kippers, EDL supporters and other actual fascists.

Betteley gets a little carried away though when challenged by some Plaid supporters. In answer to the question "Which part of a quote from 2001 is 'news'?" he replies: "It became news when a writer who labelled a 3rd of the county racist stood for MP to represent them."

The biggest irony is that tomorrow, I will be meeting the charming Mr Betteley for the very first time, as it's my long-standing candidate's interview with the *Cambrian News* – and it's him doing it.

10.25pm:
Difficult phone conversation with Owen, who is panicking. Earlier today in the office, I asked if someone could accompany me tomorrow to the *Cambrian News*, as I didn't think then – and I certainly don't now – that I could cope alone. He took that entirely the wrong way and shouted that if I didn't believe he trusted me, what was the fucking point of me being the candidate? I just didn't understand what he was ranting about at first, because that was nowhere in my thinking.

Minutes later, the BBC call, wanting me to go on *Good Morning Wales*. As instructed, I say no.

11.45pm:
It's a late night for Plaid Cymru. The midnight oil is being burned up and down Wales as responses are drawn up. Helen Bradley, the chief media officer, has sent out the line to all party officers and candidates, and now we are shuttling between us, and Owen and Elin, my statement that is to go up in the morning.

Her first effort makes me wince. It is desperately hand-wringing, and doesn't sound like anything I'd write myself. I respond by saying thanks, and that I'll write something, incorporating the spirit of what she is saying, and have it ready for the morning. Just as I send that, an email pings in from Elin Jones, who has been uncontactable all evening, in response to Helen's piece: "I think that's excellent. And I would go with it first thing 8am tomorrow morning. On Mike's Twitter and Facebook and then to be shared. No prevarication on this please."

Within a minute, an email lands from Owen in response, saying simply: "Spot on".

Wednesday 8 April 2015,
03.07am, home:
A couple of hours skittish doze before waking up, my heart and head racing immediately. I make a pot of tea and return to my study to work on the statement that must be out there by 8am. The night is so still, but alone at my desk, I feel suddenly terrified by this. It's not even really begun yet. Most people will be picking up their copy of the paper in the morning, and at ten o'clock I'll be out there again knocking on doors. What sort of response am I going to get?

07.05am:
A much-needed dog walk over the hills as the sun rises; I return to find Preds up and poring over Twitter. The messages, mostly positive, keep flooding in, and in the small hours I was apparently trending. I've finished my piece, and it's been agreed, so it'll go online by eight o'clock. Preds wants me to eat, but I feel so sick that the thought of food repulses me. As a compromise, I have a banana and nearly gag.

07.50am:
Nick Servini[1] delivers a piece about me on *Good Morning Wales*. He manages to get the word Nazi in by reading out the *Cambrian News* headlines. The BBC website has headlined it "Plaid Cymru candidate in Nazi slur row". Nowhere is it mentioned that I never actually used the word.

In the online piece, Huw Thomas, my Labour opponent, calls for me to be sacked and says "There should be no place in our politics or our society for such divisive and hateful language." His party says I am "not fit" to represent Ceredigion. My Conservative opponent Henrietta Hensher says that I

---

1   Political Editor at BBC Cymru Wales.

have tarnished "a section of the population within Wales as a whole", while Liberal Democrat AM Peter Black demands a "full public apology" as my "offensive views shouldn't just be swept under the carpet."

Mark Williams is keeping out of it. His sidekick Elizabeth Evans was merrily re-tweeting calls for my sacking last night, but he will leave the dirty work to others, as he always does.

Tŷ Gwynfor's daily candidates' briefing lands in my email inbox. Today's topics, in order: Mike Parker, Non Doms, Energy, Rural Fuel Debate and Bedroom Tax. On me, the line is clear: "Mike Parker used language that he now recognises as inappropriate". I have never said that, and neither would I. This is the sound of the party galloping in the opposite direction. My party.

9.30am:

Time to leave home, and get back out there. Part of me is eager to do just that, though it is scrapping hard with the other part of me that wants to hide under the duvet or, better still, head off for a day's walking and wallowing in a lovely pub somewhere, anywhere but Ceredigion. Preds waves me off, as he does every morning, and I feel overwhelmed by his love and strength. No way could I cope with this alone.

I've put my phone on silent, as I cannot bear its incessant chirruping. Instead, I tune into Radio 3 and let the morning concert drift me on my way.

10.55am, Eglwys Fach, Ceredigion:

A small gang meet to canvass the northernmost villages in the county. My mouth is dry as I knock the first door, but no-one mentions anything and the response is pretty good. On my fourth door, the subject finally comes up, courtesy of a widowed lady in her sixties. "So you're in the headlines this morning, I see," she says. "Yes," I reply, nervously. She pulls a face. "It's just tittle-tattle, dear. Don't worry."

12.10pm, *Cambrian News* offices, Aberystwyth:
Quick stop to pick up Hedydd, my chaperone for the *Cambrian News* interview. As I walk in to the Plaid office, everyone starts applauding, and it nearly makes me cry. Messages are pouring in, and the overwhelming majority are wholly supportive. People know a stitch-up when they see it.

Hedydd and I arrive at the paper's offices, and are bundled into a stale meeting room where Chris Betteley awaits us. He gets up, and shakes our hands. I had expected to feel like punching him, but instead, I'm overtaken by a contemptuous calm. "First things first, I guess," says Betteley. "Are there any issues about this week's coverage that you'd like to discuss?" I reply that I have plenty of issues about it, but that I'm not going to discuss them now.

We get on with the interview, about Plaid's manifesto for the election and what I am bringing to the campaign locally. Betteley has at least skimmed the manifesto, and asks some decent questions. Perhaps they'll feel obliged to give me a slightly fairer ride in the next few weeks.

3.30pm, Aberystwyth prom:
TV interviews with the BBC, in English and Welsh, and ITV. Rhuanedd has come up from Tŷ Gwynfor to marshal the troops, and me in particular. She does it brilliantly, with a sweet calmness that is just what I need right now. In preparing me for the interviews, her advice is to keep repeating the central message, that racism is a scourge, must always be challenged, and would people rather sweep it under the carpet?

The interviews are tough, as I will not apologise for what I wrote, and that is all they want. We go back to the office, to find it humming with excitement. There are people everywhere, the phones are ringing constantly and everyone is jabbing at their screens and reading out the latest comments. There has been a steady stream of people coming in since first thing wanting election posters, so many in fact that we have just had to order an unexpected reprint. Two *Cambrian News* employees came in during the lunch hour to get posters and express their horror and embarrassment.

There is a huge backlash roaring towards the paper. Their Twitter account is being inundated by complaints. On Facebook, some advertisers are discussing boycotting them. The basic story, with the all-important N-word, has made it into many of the UK papers unsifted, but every single piece of analysis, on numerous blogs and forums, is disgusted by what they've done, and calling it for what it is, a crass attempt to throw the election. The hundreds of messages I'm getting, and that are flooding into the office, are almost universally supportive, many from political opponents.

Having started the day feeling so scared, this turnaround is intoxicating. Even Elin, normally so steady-as-she-goes, is lit up by it. "We've beaten them!" she beams. "We've taken them on and we've beaten them! I can't believe it!" I think back to all the Ceredigion Plaid meetings I've attended, and how terror of the *Cambrian News* has overshadowed every one. Elin has had to suffer their passive-aggressive ways for years; no wonder she is so thrilled at the prospect of the tables turning.

6.30pm, BBC1 Wales:

I am the top item on *Wales Today*. From the interview I filmed this afternoon, they have of course selected the bit where I am most stubbornly refusing to apologise. It is not good to watch; I appear not to give a shit if I've offended anyone. Everyone said that I should keep re-stating the same rebuttal whatever the question, but I was conceited enough to think that I could do something better than that. I was wrong.

This being election TV, everyone has to have a look in. Huw is oily, Henrietta haughty, Gethin bemused and Daniel absent (thank you, Dan, for not hurling yourself aboard the bandwagon). Mark is at his twinkling best, huffing and puffing incredulity that any such thing could happen in his manor. "These comments don't relate to anything I've ever observed in my time living here," he assures us. Really Mark?

7.15pm, Community Hall, Borth:
Off to a hustings meeting at Borth's community hall. I opt for the back road via Clarach, as I want the ever-reliable thrill of the view over sea, bog, estuary and mountain from the top of the hill before the final descent into town. The sun is going down in a pink blaze, and the scene calms me down profoundly. None of this nonsense matters.

Preds and his mum are also soaking up the sunset, having driven down and parked on the front. We chat, and they are relieved to find that I'm in genuinely good spirits, fired up even. Adrenaline is coursing through me, blanking out the exhaustion and a nagging headache I cannot shift.

As I arrive at the community hall, there is a woman waiting for me outside. She is a local resident, a fellow Midlander, and warns me not to come too close as she is laid low with a contagious virus. Despite that, she says, she had to come and tell me of her experiences as a nurse locally. In her work, she hears incomers every day telling her how much they love living here because there are so few black or brown people, although this is usually couched in far more revolting ways. "You're absolutely right to challenge this," she tells me. "It's everywhere. I'm fed up of hearing it. Don't resign, don't give up. Fight on." I shall, I assure her, before she heads off back to her sick bed.

This diversion means that I am the last candidate to arrive in the hall. As I climb up on to the stage, Huw, who has been doing such sterling work in calling for my sacking, turns to me with a sickly grin. "Well, we didn't expect to see you here tonight!" he says. I grunt in reply. Yet again, there is no Henrietta, and there has been no word from her either, so it is just the five men. The only seat left is next to Mark. For the first time at these events, we do not shake hands. He glances at me, doesn't quite catch my eye and mumbles a greeting. I nod one back. This is going to be fiery.

The meeting is brilliant: an old-school community meeting with around a hundred in attendance. Nice one, dear Borth.

For the first time in any hustings, it is not dominated by clap-happy party tribalists. There are actual undecided voters, dozens of them, keen to hear what we have to say and to offer their perspective.

Some, I'm sure, have come in the hope of a dust-up over the *Cambrian News* and its rapidly ballooning repercussions ("Come on love, it'll be even better than *Corrie*"). A BBC film crew has shown up too for the same reason, but they are firmly told by the organisers that this is a community event, and they are not allowed to film. It is a guilty pleasure to see their bubble of self-importance pricked so adroitly.

There's no elephant in Borth's bizarre Animalarium, but there is one in the room, and I know that I have to address it as quickly as possible. I finish my opening speech with a reminder that this proudly independent county deserves an MP unafraid to say what he sees. "If you're in any doubt as to whether I fit that bill, I can only refer you to today's *Cambrian News*," I say, to some laughter.

Questions are varied, from the hyper-local to the international. One about the UK's role in the world and our defence strategy produces a strange moment: Plaid, the LibDems, the Greens and UKIP all condemning the replacement of Trident, while the Labour candidate is a lone voice in its favour.

A Plaid member is called to ask a question, and he does so splendidly. He voted LibDem in 2010, he tells us (it's true, he did, and we never let him forget it), before reeling off a list of Mark Williams's worst votes in the Commons over the last five years, and finishing with "I'm ashamed of my voting record, Mr Williams – are you?" He's built me a wide open goal, handed me the ball and I'm determined not to miss.

Mark gets to answer before me; his defence consists mainly of talking about his staunch opposition to the bedroom tax, one of the issues mentioned in the question. I have the vote-by-vote statistics on the bedroom tax in front of me, and point out that at different times he has managed to vote for it, against it and abstain on it. This gets the audience quite excited and Mark very flustered.

There are lots of thumbs-up and smiles from people as the meeting comes to an end. A few come to tell me that what I've said tonight has made them decide to vote for me. As I'm talking to some of them, I'm aware that there is a man who has placed himself in my line of sight and is trying to get my attention. He is hopping from foot to foot and looks seriously agitated. The second he knows that I have spotted him, he barges over and elbows the person I was talking to out of the way.

He is an army veteran, and wants to talk at me about Plaid and the military. He is especially furious about a group of Aberystwyth Plaid town councillors who, last year, organised a white poppy ceremony on Remembrance Sunday. A recollection tinkles in the back of my mind, of a few furious tweets lately about Plaid and the white poppies from "Joe", my anonymous online bugbear. His Twitter avatar is an armed forces veterans' badge. So this is him.

11.20pm, home:
The relief to be home is indescribable. I plough through hundreds more messages on Twitter and answer as many as I can. I haven't yet managed to look at those stacking up on Facebook. Our broadband is atrocious at the moment.

I was a topic on this evening's *Sharp End* on ITV Wales. Tory AM Byron Rogers says that he wants to "see this man disappear off the face of politics", for "a racist leopard never changes its spots". The UKIP rep, Blair Smillie, retorts that "he should stand down, no question about it. There is no place for racism. You can't just go around and call people Nazis."

Adrian Masters, the presenter, says calmly, "But he didn't call them Nazis."

Smillie: "But comparing people to Nazis…"

Masters: "But he didn't. He never used that word."

Smillie: "Oh… er… right."

Would that one single BBC reporter had bothered to mention it.

Thursday 9 April 2015,
7.05am, home:
Alastair Campbell has retracted his tweet of Tuesday evening, after various people pointed him towards some facts about the case. He tweets "Fair enough" and that he was "misled by paper and Twitter reaction", which is as near to an apology from him as I suspect anyone's ever got. Hundreds of other tweets that condemned me without hesitation have also vanished.

11.10am, Cilcennin:
The police have been trying to get hold of me, and at last we manage to speak. Someone has put in a complaint of incitement to racial hatred against me, though the sergeant I speak to tells me that she doesn't think it has much chance of success. Generally though, she wants to warn me about my security, and, having seen some of the social media hatred towards me, fears that I might be vulnerable to some idiot's attack. She asks for our home and car details, my movements in the coming days, and gives me a number to contact in case of emergency.

I call Preds immediately afterwards. This is not something he signed up for. He is even more of a home bird than me, and I cannot bear the idea that I am making him feel in any way exposed or vulnerable. He is typically emollient, but I know damn well that he is scared. So am I.

After all this, and calls back to the office to sort out my input to the letters that are now shuttling between Tŷ Gwynfor and the *Cambrian News*, I manage to knock a few doors. No-one is much interested.

4.20pm, Aberaeron:
A good lunch in Aberaeron's Castle Hotel, with everyone in slightly hysterical high spirits. A good response too when we canvass the town; Elin having moved here makes it a whole lot

easier. When I first canvassed Aberaeron, most people told me that they automatically voted for Elizabeth Evans, the LibDem councillor. That seems to be changing; we are definitely getting a better response here now.

I steel myself to go and buy a copy for my records of the Aeron valley edition of the *Cambrian News*. As I place it on the conveyor belt in Costcutter, I fold it to try and mask the picture of me that dominates the front page. Slightly desperately, I engage the woman on the till in bright chit-chat and piercing eye contact, so that she won't look down and make the connection. Too little, far too late.

10.10pm, Aberaeron Rugby Club:
As if these last couple of days haven't been mad enough, there's another hustings tonight. It is the one I was already dreading more than any other: organised jointly by the FUW[2] and CLA[3], and to be held, as far as possible, in Welsh. Unlike the Borth crowd last night, this is not my natural constituency.

As we arrive, my phone goes, and for the third time today, it is the police. The PC I speak to tells me that they have consulted lawyers over the incitement to racial hatred charge against me, and have decided not to prosecute. In telling me this, he lets slip, deliberately I'm sure, the name of the person that has attempted to lay the charge. All becomes clear: it is a notorious and fanatical anti-Plaid activist, a man of many aliases, a longtime scourge of anything too Welsh for his liking and, I would hazard a bet, an habitual time-waster of the police.

There is quite a crowd hanging outside the rugby club, soaking up the evening sunshine before we head inside. Mark Williams is there, and pretends not to notice me. I was determined to steer clear of Nazigate, and not say anything to my opponents, but when I see Huw Thomas's grinning face

---

2   Farmers Union of Wales.
3   Country Land and Business Association.

scan me for any visible signs of damage, something inside me quietly snaps.

"Evening Huw," I say, "have you noticed that Alastair Campbell has backed down on his comments? Are you going to do the same?"

"It wasn't us that leaked it, promise!" he squeals. I notice that Mark has edged closer and is earwigging our conversation, while skillfully carrying on one of his own. "Honestly, it wasn't us!" I believe him. Although the reaction from Labour has been by far the worst of any party, there's no gain for them spiking the contest in Ceredigion. As for his own comments about it, on social media and in news reports, he tells me proudly that he has no intention of retracting them. "I've read your original article you know, and I'm completely right to challenge it." With that, he sails into the hall.

The evening is horrible; the room packed and hot. Although it is conducted mainly in English, I know that I do quite badly, and really fluff a question on the badger cull. Mark, as ever, is in man-of-the-people mode. He employs his regular rhetorical knack of asking and answering his own questions ("Am I comfortable with all that the Coalition government has done? No, I am not."), while breaking free from behind the table to get amongst the audience. Henrietta the Conservative makes a rare appearance, and again sprinkles plenty of "going forwards" into her answers. By the end of it, my head is throbbing mercilessly, and although a few Plaid stalwarts reassure me that I did OK, they can't look me in the eye as they say so.

12.45pm, home:
Preds assures me that he is fine, but I know he's not. When I got home, I noticed that he'd removed the sign with our house name on it from the front. We make a bit of a joke of it, but both know that this is far from funny. We sit at the kitchen table once again, poring over our phones as the messages continue to roll ceaselessly in, like a raging sea of shite. I receive a message from Rhuanedd, linking to a blogpost. "You

need to see this – but not get involved", she writes. "It could turn interesting tomorrow."

Our broadband connection is about two candlepower at the moment, and the link from Rhuanedd will only half load. It's in Welsh, about someone apparently advocating chucking Tippex over cars displaying the England flag during football tournaments. I can't see who wrote it, or when. Presumably, it's some other Plaid candidate in this election, and this will be tomorrow's storm in a teacup. Though why it's anything to do with me, I'm not sure, and Rhuanedd's brief note doesn't much illuminate. Perhaps she's just reassuring me that it's someone else's turn in the village stocks.

Friday 10 April 2015,
7.50am, home:
Alles ist klar – and bloody hilarious. The remarks about vandalising cars with Tippex, and so very much more, were made in 2006, by the young man who is now my Labour opponent. Twitter has already gone ballistic over it, most pointing out Huw's spectacular level of hypocrisy after all that he hurled at me.

11.15am, Plaid office, Aberystwyth:
The *Cambrian News* has changed its headline online; I am now only getting at "racist" rather than "Nazi" incomers. While negotiations continue with them regarding a rebuttal or right of reply, as well as drawing up a case for the Independent Press Standards Organisation (IPSO), we need to get a leaflet together putting my case directly to the voters. Owen and I have formulated an agreed version. I've talked him out of using "The Truth" as a headline, for the simple reason that it sounds so comically pompous, the kind of thing used by people who finish their sentences with "FACT" or "End of".

The Huw Thomas story, Tippexgate as it is inevitably nicknamed, has been picked up by all the London tabloids. They are thrilled to have something that so readily tickles two of their itchiest g-spots in this election: stoking English resentment towards their neighbours, and bashing Ed Miliband. Looking at Twitter, it is horribly evident how successful it has been as a strategy. Huw's timeline is putrid, as are numerous message boards. Unsurprisingly, as it concerns both flags and football, the row has activated the real meatheads of the English Defence League and their ilk. There is not a word being said in Huw's defence. It is a massive contrast to the reaction I got, where about ninety-five per cent of messages were supportive.

It gains extra currency of course because of the proximity to my headlines over the last couple of days. What is it about Ceredigion, many punters ask. What is it, indeed? It also means that the TV crews are once again hotfooting it our way, and that I will have to give my response to them. At the moment, all I can think of to say is "what goes round, comes round, dear Huw", while wagging my finger at the camera. I'd better come up with something a little less Jeremy Kyle.

2.25pm, Waunfawr, Aberystwyth:
The controversy has certainly put fire in Plaid bellies; there is a massive crowd out for the afternoon canvass around Waunfawr. The BBC crew film us, and then conduct an interview with me about Huw's comments.

So far, I've resisted the advice to say the same thing again and again in TV interviews, the only way, I'm told, to ensure that what you want to say is what they will have to use. It seems so coldly cynical, but today, I get it, and trot out variations on the same theme – that I have no interest in combing through the back utterances of my fellow candidates, and wish only to take on the LibDems for their actions in government – to all of the journalist's four questions. It feels more like a GCSE Drama lesson than a real interview, but it'll have to do.

7.20pm, Tan y Cae, Aberystwyth:
The perfect end to this bloody week: a parking ticket.

9.40pm, home:

The *Cambrian News* has now pulled the story entirely from their website, though the damage continues to spread ever wider. I hear a podcast, one of a regular series by former BBC Wales journalist Phil Parry, who never misses a chance to kick Plaid. He reads out the worst of Wednesday's press coverage in a tone of sarcastic incredulity, before saying of me "How racist can you get?" One of his little helpers sings *Deutschland über Alles* in the background.

Much more entertaining is tonight's *Gogglebox* on Channel 4, featuring a recent Plaid party political broadcast. It is priceless watching the Goggleboxers make sense of it ("What's Played Simroo?"). The lovely lady vicar is much taken with us, as are the sweet old soaks Giles and Mary in their rambling West Country homestead. After watching it, Giles says "Well, I think I might vote for Plaid Cymru you know Mary". She looks at him scornfully and sighs, "But we live in *Wiltshire*."

Saturday 11 April 2015,

10.50am, street stall, Aberystwyth town centre:

Although the reaction to the *Cambrian News* has been mostly fine, I wake up feeling extremely nervous, as we're doing a street stall in the middle of Aberystwyth all morning. Anything might happen.

Leanne is coming to support me, and I really appreciate it. At last week's Saturday street stall in Aber, hot on the heels of the first TV debate, she was the talk of the town. It was Easter weekend, so there were tourists everywhere, and I lost count of the number of people who said in broad Black Country tones, "Sorry fella, can't vote for yow, but I wish I could. Yower girl did great on the telly the other noight." She has been so strong in her public support of me, including in TV interviews. It can't be easy, because I know that she'll be getting grief from some people in the party. There are a few who would love to have quietly dumped me this week.

As I walk down the main street, a LibDem councillor spots

me and comes bustling over the road. "You need to know, it wasn't us behind this," he says anxiously. "You've got to believe that. It wasn't us." I say as little as possible, and carry on to the stall.

We've got boxfuls of the rebuttal leaflets, but it's difficult to know how to play it. Do we go charging up to people offering to put the record straight, on something they perhaps hadn't even noticed? Within the first few minutes, though, it becomes evident that almost everyone has seen the *Cambrian News*. Of course they have. It's been sat on half the counters of the county for the past four days, shrieking into the face of anyone who pops in for a can of Coke or a chat. A couple of people refuse to shake my hand, a few even run away and one bloke screeches "Fucking Nazi!" at me as he thunders past.

None of this is as upsetting as my very first encounter on the stall. It's someone I know slightly from art and theatre nights; her face crumples when she sees me. I go to her, but she recoils as if I'd hit her. She tells me how disappointed she is in me, and how could I say such cruel things, before starting to cry. We have an anguished chat for quarter of an hour, and I hope that I'm able to put her mind at rest, to show her that I'm not the person they're trying to paint me as.

When Leanne arrives, everything goes up a notch. I am so pleased to see her. We hug, the deep bear hug of old friends meeting in the aftermath of a crisis. She is glowing with crisp-cut health and efficiency, streaked with a determination to lift our collective spirits. Elin is buoyed up too, and the three of us get into a great stride as we tour the pavements, shops and cafés. There is much laughter and encouragement, and it's all considerably livelier than the LibDem stall just down the street.

2.10pm, Lampeter:

After a lunch of toasted sandwiches and much tweeting, it's off to Lampeter for more of the same. It goes well, though none of us know whether to bring up Nazigate when talking with people, or to let them do so should they want to. I cannot work out how to play it, but we muddle through. It does come up a great deal though.

Elin steers us into a women's boutique opposite the university. Leanne tries on and buys some stuff, while I take photos of her, the shop manager and Elin posing with the merchandise. I post one on Twitter, with the message "Shopping with the girls in @lanlloft Lampeter. Not sure whether I'm playing Carrie or Samantha". I wanted to add the hashtag "#SexAndTheCountry" to underline the reference, but thought that would probably get me into trouble. As it's the irascible Republic of Twitter, I get into trouble anyway, with a few people shouting at me for being sexist.

5.40pm, St Michael's Church car park, Aberystwyth:
Returning to my car, there's something almost as unwelcome as yesterday's parking ticket under the wiper: a LibDem leaflet. "What has Mark Williams done for us?" it is headed, a question we've been trying to pose as well. Among the list of achievements, one leaps out, that he "opposed going to war in Syria". He abstained! Nine LibDems and thirty Tories did the right thing; he wasn't one of them. Utterly shameless, and quite literally on a matter of life and death.

11.10pm, home:
A meal out with friends, at a pub very deliberately not in Ceredigion. All the same, our entrance causes a bit of a stir, and during the evening a few people sidle over to ask me what the hell is going on. After a couple of pints and some food, I am suddenly completely spent. As we drive back through Machynlleth, Preds asks if I want him to stop at the Co-op and pick up a local edition of the *Cambrian News* for my records.

I don't look at it until we get home, and chuck it onto the kitchen table. It unfurls and the front page glares back. The picture, an arch promotional shot for a book I wrote a few years ago, is bad enough, but the banner headline – "Candidate compares incomers to Nazis", with no inverted commas around the N-word, unlike the others – drills into my pounding head. This is the edition sat like a steaming turd in the parlours and kitchens of my friends and neighbours, people who thought that they knew me, and thought that they liked me. The words start to blur, and I realise that I'm crying, and then sobbing. The week tumbles out of me in skeins of hot snot.

Sunday 12 April 2015,
11.30am, Plaid office, Aberystwyth:
There are more tears as I drive to Aber for a campaign committee meeting. Adrenaline (and paracetomol) have been keeping me going for days, but as that has faded, I feel utterly knackered, with a headache I cannot shift, and a sense of despair at how this whole thing has gone.

Everyone else is shell-shocked too, and it's a sombre meeting. The reaction on social media has been overwhelmingly positive, but social media is not the real world, something Plaid activists are prone to forget. No chance of that in this instance: people report numerous canvassers' tales of doors slammed in our faces and verbal abuse. To those who already hated Plaid, this has been a godsend, for it has given them carte blanche to vent their spleen. Aled Morgan Hughes tells us that on Wednesday, he tried to give one of our leaflets to a woman in Llandre. Seeing that it was bilingual, she put her hand up to refuse it, screeching "No! I won't have that language touching my skin!" We're in the realm of pathological phobias now.

The game-changing enormity of the paper's spite is beginning to hit home, and we know it is having all kinds of as yet unclear ramifications. We discuss the complaint that has been filed with IPSO, the possibility of a legal challenge under the Representation of the People's Act and the ongoing negotiations with the *Cambrian News* for some sort of response. They have offered to explain in next week's paper that I never used the word Nazi, but that is nowhere near enough. The IPSO and legal cases could go on for ages, and we just don't have time. Something has to go out there soon. The only way to guarantee that, I'm told, is for us to take out a half-page advert in the *Cambrian News*, in which we can say whatever we want.

Elin mentioned this idea to me on Friday, and I refused point-blank to countenance it. It's like being booted in the bollocks, I said, and then handing over fifty quid as a thank you to your assailant; I cannot stomach the idea. I'd rather lose with my head up than go crawling to them. And other people are withdrawing advertising from them out of solidarity with us; why in god's name would we give them more? Elin replied that I was too upset, and that we'd have to come back to the issue at a later date, i.e. this will happen and you'd better think yourself round to it.

Two days later, and I still can't accept the idea. I can see how much this annoys Elin and Owen, but surely, they can see my point of view? And for the thousands of people – and I think it is thousands – who have seen right through this for the charade that it is, won't it just annoy them intensely to see us handing over hard-won campaign money to the very source of the problem? Yes, it may win back a few wavering votes, but the grovelling hypocrisy of it could actually lose us more. I want to remind Elin of her glee on Wednesday evening, when her eyes shone with excitement that we had taken them on, and were winning. Her eyes today are dark and unfathomable.

8.40pm, home:
I check Huw Thomas's Twitter feed, and shudder at the horrors on it. Huw himself, normally a prolific tweeter, has been silent over the past three days. He's not been seen in public since Thursday night's hustings either. Despite their evident pall of shame, Labour have tried to spin the saga as a point in his favour, to demonstrate that his snivelling apologies showed that at least he was man enough to own up to his mistakes. As opposed to me, is the implication.

Although I've not received anything like the number of hateful messages that Huw has, there are nonetheless some real peaches. A few are brutally homophobic ("Fucking cocksucker" seems to be the insult *de jour*), others are just pathetic. One tonight comes from Lampeter:

"I sincerely hope you don't get a single vote and you are humiliated in the election.

I'm starting my own election campaign, going door to door to bring awareness of you sick, sick, sick anti English nazi comments!

I will, till may 7th bring awareness to the people of ceredigion of your poison and venom, how can you expect to represent us all if you see us as Nazis!?!?!?

You bring shame on Ceredigion!

SHAME ON YOU!!!!"

He sends this from a named email account, so a quick google and there's his LinkedIn profile. He is apparently "a dedicated and solution-oriented professional" who is "recognised for my positive attitude, high level of energy and excellent interpersonal and communication skills which I use to great effect to successfully build positive relationships." I'd never have guessed.

Monday 13 April 2015,
5.00pm, Plaid office, Aberystwyth:
The pressure continues for me to OK a half-page advert in the *Cambrian News*. I still can't abide the idea, but offer a compromise: if they go for it, then I don't want my name or picture anywhere on it. They can do it as a general advert for Plaid and our policies, with a photo of Leanne if anyone, and that is it.

Elin is not happy. "There's no point in taking out an advert unless it's got your name on it," she says. "You must see that, surely?" She shifts a gear when she sees that I'm not for turning, and goes straight for my ego. "Your good name, and your reputation as a writer, have taken a knocking, and this is our chance to put it right." Normally, such an exhortation might work, but not any more, and I continue to say no. Right now, my reputation feels far beyond both my control and my caring, but my integrity, though badly battered, is hanging on by a thread. Paying the *Cambrian News* a penny would destroy that. We leave it unresolved and hanging in the air as a scratchy stalemate.

My opinion doesn't seem to count for much though, and as I leave the office, I wonder if she and Owen might simply override me, and do it anyway. If they do, then the next time they see me will be at the count on election night.

9.45pm, Aberystwyth University students' union:
To the third and final student union hustings, this time a general Q&A. What a night. Huw Thomas shows up in public for the first time since Tippexgate, and handles it very well. I shake his hand at the beginning, and he says "I know what you went through now." "Not very nice, is it?" I reply. "No, it's not". And that was it.

I want a quiet word with Mark Williams too about recent events, particularly the nasty stuff that has been coming my way on Twitter from "Joe", my noisy troll. This included a response to some frothing right-winger who claimed to have spotted "that nasty racist #PlaidCymru prospective candidate #MikeParker" in a pub in Aberaeron last Wednesday evening. "Joe" – evidently monitoring Twitter for references to me – replied that it couldn't be as "he was defiantly in the hustings at Borth". "Balls. Twatted the wrong bloke" came the reply, to which "Joe" said a simple "lol".

This is someone who has been working on Mark's campaign, making films for him. He's forever tagging Mark and Elizabeth Evans into tweets and appending them with "#TeamWilliams". Mark is all wide-eyed innocence. He's never *heard* of this Twitter account, has no *idea* who's behind it, despite having followed it from day one of its existence three weeks ago and being copied in to scores of its messages. Never heard of it at all – what was it called again? And, no, wishing violence on me is not acceptable at all. He will, he promises, make inquiries and get back to me.

We file onto the stage, depleted in number. There's no Gethin of UKIP nor Henrietta the Tory, so the political see-saw is firmly weighted to the left, which is tedious as a participant and must be hellish dull for the audience. Not that they mind much; at the beginning, the chair asks for a show of hands from anyone undecided about how they're voting. There are two. The rest of the crowd divide evenly, the only difference to previous hustings being that Huw's cheerleaders are considerably more subdued than usual.

At the end, Mark says to me, "Would you come and tell Elizabeth what you told me before the meeting please?" It soon gets heated: she too claims never to have heard of the Twitter account, and to prove the point, theatrically tugs her iPad out of her bag and looks it up. "Gosh no, never seen *that.*" Preds, who has joined us, asks how can that be when they have both followed it from the beginning and are regularly copied in. "I followed it, because he followed me," says Elizabeth. "I follow lots of things back." Mark nods along.

I can see that Preds' blood is up, which makes me both proud and wary. He asks Elizabeth about her re-tweeting Peter Hain's call for my sacking for what he described as my "'Nazi' attack on English constituents". She deleted it once it became clear that the tide had turned. A LibDem helper with them suddenly explodes into life, squawking "A re-tweet is not an endorsement! A re-tweet is not an endorsement!" like a protocol parrot.

Voices are raised, fingers are jabbed, faces get flushed, and a small crowd gathers to watch. My agent Richard, and another Plaid member, Gwynfryn, get stuck in as the insinuations and accusations fly. The LibDems are very rattled, and try to buy us off with a wide-eyed assurance that no-one, not a single person, has mentioned Nazigate to them on the doorstep. I only wish I could say the same.

As our little gang leaves the building, our danders well and truly up, Gwynfryn turns to me with a rueful grin. He's an imposing man, and was on fire up against Mark and Elizabeth just now. "Do you know," he says, "the last thing my wife said to me before I came out this evening was, 'For God's sake, don't get into a fight tonight'. Oops."

Tuesday 14 April 2015,
Tregaron:
To Tregaron for the livestock mart and canvassing. We meet up with the first batch of helpers in the Talbot for morning coffee. The woman cleaning in the bar sees me, and drops her vacuum cleaner in shock. "Oh, it's you!" she exclaims. "We've been talking about you all weekend." My heart sinks. She too is English and has a lot of questions. I answer them as best I can, and we have a good talk. "Are you English?" she suddenly says. "You sound it." "Yes, I'm from Worcestershire," I reply. "Really? Gosh. I never realised that."

This sets alarm bells clanging. She and her friends had evidently been provoked by what they'd read in the paper, but not enough to have gone much beyond the headline. The article states quite clearly that I am English, where I come from and that I moved here in 2000, yet they'd not noticed any of that. They will not be the only ones.

To the mart, and just as I'm trying to record a video message for Facebook, I hear a lovely, familiar liquid chirrup above me: the swallows are back. On a wire sit two sleek little fellas, and I idly imagine that they are on the last leg of their journey from southern Africa to our barn. It's far more of a pleasure to see them than it is Mark and Elizabeth, who I soon spot arriving. After last night's scrap, we all studiously ignore each other.

There's a good reaction to us though – lots of handshakes, back pats and laughter, in a furry old fusion of English, Welsh and pure Cardi. When Mark stood in the 2001 election, he promised to learn Welsh, and did so again when he won the seat four years later. He still hasn't. It is a subject I am told never to mention, but today, chatting and chuckling with farmers, it boils up inside me: how the hell can you represent this place when you can't understand the mother tongue of half of its population? And even ignoring the political imperative to learn the language, he's been in Wales for thirty years. Where's his respect? Where's his *curiosity*?

Good reaction too on the sun-baked doorsteps. Nazigate comes up a few times, and one or two have a go at me, but that seems to have calmed down. I'm sure the good weather is helping. There is a small but steady drift in our direction from previous canvassing sessions, and the LibDem vote seems to have evaporated. Then to Llanilar for an evening canvass. It was very lukewarm last time I was here, two months ago, and I meet many people for the second time. They are noticeably more enthusiastic this time round. Owen, who is marking the canvass sheets, cannot quite believe how much people have shifted our way. I don't think I've ever seen him look so excited.

Wednesday 15 April 2015,
3.10pm, Rhydlewis:
Spring is at full-throttle, and nowhere more impressive than Rhydlewis, a village I've never visited before. It is a beautiful spot, bursting with new greenery, daffodils and birdsong, and it puts a decent-sized crew of us in a great mood as we sweep our way around the village. Support seems solid, and there are some converts too, even from a houseful of badger-loving hippies.

The news is dominated by the polls, which consistently point to a hung parliament. In Wales, Plaid's ratings are inching up, but little and slowly.

11.50pm, home:
People's postal votes have evidently arrived, as photos of the ballot paper start appearing in my Twitter feed. Although

they are proudly supporting me, and it's undeniably exciting to see an X next to my name, the photos also make me feel unexpectedly panicky. It's because they have my home address on them, and I don't want that flashed around Twitter and wherever else it might lead.

The realisation is so strong that it makes me gasp for breath, and my omnipresent headache takes a sharper turn. I know that it is an over-reaction fed by sleeplessness and stress, but I feel under siege, my home the only place I feel secure. I cannot bear the idea of that being broadcast to any idiots on my case.

Electoral law is as creaky as old floorboards, publishing the home addresses of candidates on ballot papers and posters one of its more dilapidated elements. We discussed this a while ago, for the options were either to have my home address on the ballot, or a bald statement that I live in the Montgomeryshire constituency. The latter option was felt to be worse, for it made more of an issue out of it. Northernmost villages of Ceredigion have Machynlleth as their postal address, the same as ours, and that was felt to be less specific. That I'd be divulging my home address to everyone hadn't seemed a problem a month ago. Now it feels awful.

This is how paranoia sets in, I know, but going to bed, I feel watched. It's a horrible feeling – the first time I have ever felt insecure in the house that has been such a haven for the last four years. I look out into the darkness and imagine unseen eyes keeping a vigil out there, biding their time, unsettling us further.

I cannot sleep, and return instead to my office to message those who have posted pictures online of the ballot paper, asking if they'd delete them. I'm pretty sure that posting such images contravenes electoral law, so at least I can use that as the excuse, and not the real reason, that it is making me terrified and paranoid for us both. What the hell have I put Preds through? Though as I return to bed, he is sleeping soundly, and that's some comfort. I draw the curtains (normally we don't bother), snuggle in with him, and soon fall into an erratic slumber.

Thursday 16 April 2015,
10.15am, Llwyncelyn village hall, near Aberaeron:
The swallows arrived at ours just before I left at eight. It's taken them two days to get from Tregaron. I know the feeling.

To Llwyncelyn and a hustings for Mencap, attended by a few dozen of their clients. No Henrietta once again, and the remaining five of us seem to be on auto-pilot. No-one says anything in the least bit memorable.

12.45pm, Plaid office, Aberystwyth:
Discussions about where next in the Nazigate saga. IPSO's response: "We have conducted an assessment of your complaint against the *Cambrian News* and have decided that this falls within our remit and discloses a possible breach of the Editors' Code of Practice." So we can go ahead with that, but there is no guarantee of a decision this side of the election. There have been some unofficial discussions with the police about a case under the Representation of the People's Act, but nothing firm as yet.

Any hopes that the *Cambrian News* would let up on us have been blown asunder by this week's edition. Despite receiving numerous messages and letters of outrage at last week's slur, they have published none. Worse, they have dumped the story about Huw Thomas's Tippexgate remarks on our doorstep too, stating baldly that "The comments were uncovered by a Plaid-supporting blog, BlogMenai [true] and shared on social media by Plaid Cymru supporters [twaddle]." It's the handiwork of Betteley once again.

So, we have to get my side of the story in next week's paper, especially as the deadline for postal votes – and that's about twenty per cent of the constituency – is shortly afterwards. Negotiations are going on, with barely any input from me, for a right of reply. At least if that happens, there will be no further pressure to take out an advert in the *Cambrian News*, which would be a huge relief all round. If it does happen, the editor is demanding that we drop any legal and IPSO action, and that has been accepted by Plaid.

8.00pm, International Politics (InterPol) Department, Aberystwyth University:

A hustings to start the day, and one to end it too. The difference couldn't be starker from the limp walk-through this morning. I get up to the university campus to find the car parks full and people milling all over the terrace and foyer of InterPol. As I walk into the building, it is already standing room only. There are hundreds here and the sense of excitement is palpable.

The candidates have photos taken with the chair, Sara Gibson of the BBC. Once again there is no Henrietta, so it's just the boys. Pleasantries are strained; we're all a bit wide-eyed at the huge crowd and charged atmosphere awaiting us. I'm the only one not wearing a tie. Daniel the Green has been getting smarter with every hustings, and now, in a dark suit and green tie, looks like a bank manager, which is ironic, as almost every answer he has given in these events has been to deconstruct the banking system and how a debt-based economy is imprisoning us, a topic he has studied in depth. He's absolutely right, but it's not always what someone wants to hear when their question was about the future of acute care in Bronglais.

The evening takes off like a rocket. Each of us gives an opening statement: Mark's denunciation of the Coalition government has been getting stronger over the weeks, and tonight he really goes for it, describing it as "doing a deal with the devil".

I decide to make my opening gambit about what we need in the character of an MP. It's a concept that remains cheerfully intact in Ceredigion. I have met many older voters, I say, who happily voted for Elystan Morgan (Labour) in the Sixties and Seventies, Geraint Howells (Liberal) in the Seventies and

Eighties and Cynog Dafis (Plaid) in the Nineties; liberal, radical Welsh all. They voted for the man, not the party.

Going further back, I quote one of Ceredigion's greatest political heroes, Henry Richard of Tregaron, the nineteenth-century peacemaker and internationalist. When right-wing Liberals sabotaged the 1866 Reform Bill and its plans to widen the franchise, Richard rounded on those in his own party who were prepared "to sacrifice their professed principles rather than see the representation of the kingdom slip from the grasp of their class." I repeat the phrase, and can feel it sinking in around the room. In 2015, I say, we in Ceredigion know all about Liberals sacrificing their professed principles to keep their hands on power.

I finish with a simple plea, for everyone in the hall to listen to each of us tonight, and decide for themselves who fits that radical, independent Ceredigion tradition, one that we need now more than ever. And who, perhaps more importantly, does *not* fit it. It gets a huge round of applause.

The crowd buoys us all along; everyone is on very good form. Mark comes out with his best one-liner yet on me, a witheringly deadpan "Mike used to be a comedian. I used to be a teacher." I taunt him for representing only the Mark Williams Party, as his literature makes almost no mention of the Liberal Democrats, and there's been no sign of Nick Clegg in Ceredigion. "Is he coming? It's almost as if you don't want him here," I say. Mark grins back.

My line of the night, the one fired instantly around Twitter, isn't one I'd cooked up beforehand. I challenge Mark's voting record, specifically his 3.1 per cent of votes against the government – less than his former leader Charles Kennedy and former party President [and soon to be leader] Tim Farron. I suddenly hear myself roar, "We haven't got the Conservative here tonight, but really we don't need her, because Mark – you're ninety-seven percent Tory!" He opens and shuts his mouth like a goldfish, and a massive roar goes up in the hall.

Huw Thomas gifts another open goal. Talking about the

Labour policy of a mansion tax, he says it is "a happy accident" that it will disproportionately wallop those in the south-east of England. That's no happy accident, I bellow, it's decades of rapidly growing inequality encouraged by Labour, Conservative and Coalition governments alike.

While canvassing earlier today, Cynog Dafis asked me if I minded him putting a question along the lines of "Do the candidates agree that Mike Parker was treated disgracefully by the *Cambrian News*?" I tell him to go for it. Although it has been the biggest talking point of the campaign, in hustings it has only ever been glancingly referred to. I'd be quite happy to see it brought into the light.

From the platform, every time we pause for the next question, I can see Cynog bouncing in his chair, his arm held rigid in the air, like a six-year-old with the answer. You'd think a question from our erstwhile MP would be of interest, but he is ignored throughout, while Lisa Francis, a former Conservative AM who now works in Mark Williams's office, is allowed two questions, both asked specifically to me.

After two hours, with the windows steamed up and sweat pouring off us, it comes to an end. I have enjoyed this one so much, the politics *and* the theatre of it. It is intoxicating and quite addictive. Plaid supporters are in top spirits, and I know that I did well. The buzz reminds me of a good stand-up gig, albeit without the subsequent drunken debauchery. I spurn various offers of a pint, because my energy has just evaporated; it's a cup of tea at home that calls the loudest.

10.45pm, home:
I catch up with tonight's BBC *Challengers' Debate*, the second UK-wide one to include Leanne. It's a very odd format: no Cameron or Clegg, so just Ed Miliband, Nicola Sturgeon, Leanne, Natalie Bennett and Nigel Farage. Inevitably, much of the focus is on Miliband as the only potential alternative PM in the line-up. All of the headlines come out of the scraps between Miliband and Sturgeon. The spin, and this is the story

topping the BBC news output, is that Sturgeon is offering to "help" Labour into government, and to make it more of the socialist party that it used to be. This will, for sure, be the Tory line to frighten the horses, and I fear it will be devastatingly effective.

Leanne is once again on good form, and particularly caustic towards Farage, or "my friend on the far right" as she calls him at one point, to considerable laughter (for viewers, he was on the furthest podium to the right of screen). But it is a single still image from the end of proceedings that makes my Twitter timeline melt into a puddle of goo, when Leanne, Natalie Bennett and Nicola Sturgeon cwtch up together, while Ed Miliband looks on awkwardly like a geeky big brother. The picture goes everywhere. To those sympathetic to the anti-austerity alliance of the Greens, the SNP and Plaid, it represents all our hopes for a new, softer, more human politics emerging from this election. To our enemies, it is doubtless a glimpse of harpy hell.

Friday 17 April 2015,
Home:
Sorting out emails before I head off to canvass, I pick through some of the responses to last night's hustings. A few write that they've decided to vote for me as a result, but a couple from Plaid supporters are less enthusiastic, and tell me in the nicest possible way that I was rather too forceful last night, and that's not really the way it's done in Ceredigion. I'm afraid it seems to be now.

Today's message from the LibDem attack dogs is to point out that I do not live in Ceredigion (they seem to be forgetting that when Mark was first elected, he was living sixty miles away in the Black Mountains of Breconshire). At 1.17, "Joe" tweets me a question as to whether I'll move if I win. Twelve minutes later, he follows it up with a complaint that I don't answer his questions. Which only makes me more determined to ignore him.

In the new edition of *Golwg*, columnist Dylan Iorwerth has written an interesting take on Nazigate. It is headed [my translation] "Dirty tricks and a new political order". He makes it quite plain from the start:

"In the old days, when I was living and working in the political world, there was no doubt whatsoever among other journalists who were the dirtiest fighters in electoral contests – the old Liberals.

With their beards and sandals (the stereotype of the day) they appeared harmless enough, but they had numerous officials who were legendary for fighting brutally as part of their box of tricks.

This is why it will be difficult to persuade many of us that it was not their successors, the Liberal Democrats, who were behind the dirtiest trick yet in this election – Ceredigion's Nazigate. I hope that this isn't true. It would be good to hear them condemn the story."

In truth, I don't think that it came from within the official LibDem campaign machine, but rather one of its rogue outriders, omnipresent "Joe". Over-enthusiastic supporters, well prepared to go far further than their parties would officially endorse, are a fact of every political organisation, especially in the furnace of election time and the age of social media.

It doesn't really matter who pointed the *Cambrian News* in the direction of the old newspaper articles about my 2001 piece. As "Joe" himself put it, when challenged about it on Twitter, "You really think its hard in the age of google to find something, please". What matters is how the paper chose to frame the story, and there, the buck stops with the newspaper's editor. Over the decade that she has been in the job, the paper's enthusiasm for Mark Williams has been noted by many, and not just in Plaid. Although this was the most extreme example, it is only the latest in a very long line.

[A month after the election, someone told me about a conversation they'd just had with the *Cambrian News* editor, in which she said that she regretted using the word 'Nazi' in the headlines. At best, this is disingenuous, for it was that word that went viral, just as she must have known it would. Once the N-word is out there, it takes on a life of its own. As was painfully obvious from the reactions I got for the remainder of the campaign, the subtleties of the story were lost. I'd called people Nazis, I was a Nazi, Plaid were Nazis – it all merged into one noxious cloud that hung over the campaign, and the damage was done.]

Saturday 18 April 2015,
10.05am, Aberystwyth town centre:

Another street stall this morning in Aberystwyth, and again some unpleasant reactions. It starts immediately. I see a man, about mid sixties, staring my way, so go up and say hello, putting my hand out. He shakes his head and says "No mate, I'm not shaking your hand. I'm disgusted by what you've said. You're a disgrace." I try to interject, but he is having none of it, and walks off up the street, turning to shout, "My dad fought the Nazis, you know, and your generation haven't got a clue what that means." I follow him, protesting that I was, however imperfectly, taking on fascism in my original *Planet* article, but he continues to walk away, shouting "No mate!" and "You're a disgrace!" as he recedes into the distance. He is shaking with fury. From his manner, I can tell that he's not one of life's inveterate complainers; it is clear that his outburst has taken him as much by surprise as it has me. It's a grim start to the day, and leaves me rattled. Someone goes and gets me a coffee.

Although there are some other nasty moments – a few choice names, and someone even spitting at me – the reaction is reasonable. No Leanne this week though, and it's all a little more subdued. Most people are heartily sick of the election, and are not pleased to have any reminder of it. I can't say that I disagree.

2.15pm, Talsarn, near Lampeter:

The day turns into a bright, brilliant spring day, as a crowd of us head to do a street stall in Aberaeron, and then to the annual Lampeter Stallion Show on a farm outside Talsarn. There's a healthy crowd there, and a cracking atmosphere. People have travelled from all over Wales and the border counties, so actual Ceredigion voters are fairly thin on the ground. Elin, though, can spot one a mile off, so there are plenty of introductions. More to the point, it's a cheerful and relaxing way to spend an hour or two, especially after the slightly tense street stalls this morning. My chips and curry sauce taste like nectar.

4.25pm, Goginan, near Aberystwyth:
The hedgerows are roaring back to life in the furzy lanes of Goginan. The reaction here has been great, and, as many of the properties here are old cottages, the kind that set the weekend property pages ablaze with desire, they're mainly filled with fellow incomers. I looked at a couple of places here when I was house-hunting in 2000 and 2001; it's a great spot that I've always loved.

I knock on the door of one cute place hunkered alone on a lane, and it is answered by a young man who stares at me with wide eyes. "God, that's amazing!" he starts, "I've just voted for you. Literally, about ten minutes ago." He and his partner have just done their postal votes, having discussed the matter for days. They'd moved from England a couple of years ago and never voted Plaid before. Nazigate had made them wobble, but they read up on it, and on me, realised that it was not as it seemed, and that my points were both valid and wilfully misconstrued.

There's also a bit of gay solidarity going on here, I'm certain, and I'm very happy to receive that. It makes a nice change. No-one has been overtly homophobic to my face, though it's made up a sizeable proportion of the online abuse I've received in recent weeks. I have heard, though, a few toe-curling things fed back from canvassers, of some people saying that they'd never vote for a bloody queer and so on.

6.50pm, Bow Street:
The end of a long, hot day, and there's a sizeable crew out for an early evening canvass in Bow Street. I approach one bloke pottering around his front garden. He sees my rosette and candidate's rictus smile, and calls in a Brummie twang "Don't waste your time, mate. It's Nigel Farage for me this time. He's the only one saying it like it is."

Normally when I meet a determined UKIP voter, I don't waste time engaging. It's like entering a very dark alley, hoping there's daylight at the end of it, but more often than not hitting a piss-soaked wall instead. On top of that, I get into enough trouble already for being too chatty on the doorstep. Sometimes though, the chance for a bit of sport proves irresistible, especially after an hour of stoic discussion about hospitals and speed limits. He tells me that he's lived here twenty-seven years, but that every time he goes into town (Aberystwyth), "I hear nothing but Romanian and bloody Polish being spoken". He says it three times. I can't say it's a common perception; perhaps it's that special UKIP hyper-sensitivity, like when Gethin guessed in a hustings that there were 20,000 overseas students in Aber. Never mind the facts though, all he hears is Romanian and bloody Polish, and it's finally made him see Nigel Farage's light.

"Oh, OK then," I reply, "so how's your Welsh?"

"You what?"

"Your Welsh. You've been here 27 years, you must be absolutely fluent by now."

"Eh, what are you talking about? I don't speak Welsh."

I leave him, and can hear the cogs slowly grinding. They're very rusted up though; they won't make a full turn.

The sun is dipping now, and it's almost time to call it a day. "Let's just do this last row of houses," I say to the crew. We do, and as I knock on the final door, I feel that the day has at least steadily improved from its shaky start.

The door opens and the occupant and I stare at each other in horrified disbelief. It is the man who got so upset with me this morning at the street stall. To paraphrase *Casablanca*, of all the doors in all the villages in Ceredigion, I had to go and knock on his.

I'm not sure who is the most embarrassed. As I guessed this morning, he is actually quite a polite chap, and he quickly stumbles over an apology for being "rather rude" by walking away from me earlier. "I was very upset," he says. We end up having a really interesting and honest conversation, which I appreciate enormously. As it winds up, he sticks his hand out and says, "I'm sorry I refused to shake your hand this morning. Will you accept it now?" "Of course," I say gratefully. The serendipity today has been wonderful.

"So, how's he going to vote then?" asks the person taking down the feedback, his biro poised hopefully over the canvass sheets. "I don't know," I say, "and to be honest, I don't really care."

Sunday 19 April 2015,
Home:
Author Patrick McGuinness emails me a piece he has been asked to write for the *Western Mail*[4]. In it, he calls Nazigate "a new low in Welsh politics", and ponders its larger lessons. He is not optimistic, and neither am I. He writes that I was "smeared and vilified by politicians who are prepared to misuse and to prostitute the language of race and racism for a quickly-scored point... This is a world Orwell foresaw: the shameless degradation of political language."

There has been so much said about it. Martin Shipton, the *Western Mail's* chief political reporter, wrote a very thoughtful piece, entitled "Incomers as Nazis? The Strange Case of Mike Parker and Huw Thomas" (it came out before Huw's own little problems). Chewing over Huw's strident calls for my sacking, Shipton writes that "there's a big leap of logic being undertaken here, both by the *Cambrian News* and by Mr Thomas" and that

4   They never print it.

"the condemnation of Mr Parker doesn't stack up". Examining the distortion that I called incomers Nazis, Shipton says "he wrote nothing of the sort" and that my 2001 *Planet* article was "carefully nuanced". Interestingly, he states too that the whole episode was "a Liberal Democrat bid to force the resignation of... Mike Parker", which no-one has contradicted.

Shipton concludes: "There are some sinister historical precedents for distorting the truth about one's opponents, as Mr Thomas, who holds a Master's degree in international relations from Aberystwyth University, will know very well. After this episode, we can say that writers who stand for election can expect not just their tweets and Facebook postings to be pored over by opponents, but their every published word that can be tracked down."

This concerns others too. BBC Political Editor Vaughan Roderick wrote in his blog that the calls of every party to bring in politicians from outside the bubble are all well and good, but that "people like that haven't been watching every word, while keeping an eye on the green benches, so that digging around is likely to produce a story that can be used against them" [my translation]. Author Jasmine Donahaye made a similar point in a piece on the IWA website, a defence so passionate it brought a tear to my eye.

There have been cautionary notes sounded too. While accepting I've been badly misrepresented, some criticise my choice of words in 2001. Some wonder why we haven't republished in full the original article, something I was keen to do but that was shot down by Plaid. A few have concentrated on something best expressed by *Golwg* journalist, Ifan Morgan Jones: "This was a glaring double failure of Plaid Cymru's PR operation" [my translation], in that they hadn't seen it coming, when it had been on the front page of some newspapers at the time, albeit in far less sensational ways, and that they hadn't prepared me, as a rookie candidate, sufficiently well.

Monday 20 April 2015,
5.47pm, Llanddewi Brefi:
Hellish day. Trying to canvass with Elin and others, while negotiations wing their way between Aberystwyth and Cardiff as to what I can and cannot say in my right of reply that's going in the *Cambrian News* this week. It all has to be agreed by four this afternoon.

I spent most of yesterday working on it. There are some bits that I only put in so that they can be taken out as bargaining chips, but they're all there for a reason. For instance, I quote Betteley's tweet from the night the paper came out, when he defended the story by saying that I was "calling a third of the county racist". There's no way they'll admit to that, but I want the editor to know what kind of careless bruiser she has on her team. Lo and behold, by the end of the day the tweet has vanished from his timeline. I hope he remembers his own sanctimonious homily to me from the same night: "If you write something, it stays written."

The documents, hurtling to and fro between Rhuanedd at Plaid and Beverly Thomas, editor of the *Cambrian News*, ping into our collective inboxes on a grimly frequent basis. At the beginning of the day, Ms Thomas claimed that she couldn't conduct any of the discussion by phone, as she had lost her voice. Shades of John Major's well-timed wisdom tooth, it would seem.

The misery is compounded by the fact that we are supposed to be canvassing around Talsarn and Cribyn, but have to repeatedly head for distant hilltops in order to find a phone signal for the next set of disputed documents to dribble in. Every phone call, and every email, gets unexpectedly truncated numerous times, sending everyone's stress levels sky-high.

After lunch in Lampeter, it's more of the same all afternoon: lots of frantic phone activity and breakneck driving around the lanes with handsets held aloft, interspersed with the occasional interruption in the form of some canvassing. In Llanddewi Brefi, Elin and I knock on a few doors. One is answered by a man who has been most engaged by Nazigate. He tells me that I have lost his vote, and that of many of his friends, though he at least asks "What's your side of it, then?"

The three of us debate it for fifteen minutes. I feel that we are winning him round. He can see that I was massively misquoted, and why, and is sympathetic to what I was saying fourteen years ago. He's under no illusions either about the press, local or national. "Something just doesn't smell right though," he says, and there is no shifting him. That's the territory we're in now: hunches, gut feelings, difficult reminders of a topic that everyone would rather pretend isn't really there.

That's the troupe of elephants in the room. If the controversy had been about transport or hospitals, it would all have been much clearer cut. As it is, I've been seen to throw a big rock into the dirtiest, darkest pool in these parts, the one that everyone peers nervously into and scuttles away from. Questions of identity and nationality lurk in every community. I've seen and heard it expressed from all angles, and in every tone from bemused incredulity to boiling fury. It is painful stuff, and I'm seen as the one prodding it.

While failing miserably to talk him round, a phone signal must have wafted briefly by as my pocket vibrates busily. Another urgent call from a despondent and furious Owen, another lot of obstreperous tactics from the *Cambrian News* as negotiations go down to the wire. They are refusing to let me use the words "right of reply", which we have caved in on, to my annoyance. They are also trying to excise all references to their deliberate distortion, but that at least is fought, and, to some extent, won. At 5.47pm, an uneasy truce is reached. We settle for less than I wanted, but it'll have to do.

9.20pm, Lampeter University:
Another hustings, another no-show from the Conservative candidate. Once again, there has been no contact from her to the organisers; she just doesn't show up. Even though the Tories last won Ceredigion in 1874, they are the senior partners

in the government upon whose record we are voting. It's plain rude for them not to face the electorate. Is her repeated absence deliberate? Has she been told to lay off, a tacit withdrawal to quietly bolster their coalition partners? They'd certainly rather have a LibDem MP return to the Commons than a Plaid one.

Shame she's not here really, as there are more blue rosettes and Tory badges in the audience than I've seen anywhere yet on the campaign trail, and they are in full, braying voice. Young Conservatives are such a curious combination of hubris and acne.

My headache throbs up a notch when I notice that "Joe", my Twitter bane, is in the crowd as well. He is a one-man Mark Williams clapping machine, and gets a question in too, on military veterans. As I begin my answer, saying that one of the most sobering statistics is that more Falklands veterans have died from suicide than were killed in the war itself, he starts shouting "That's not true! You can't say that! It's not true!" He may be right (later investigation is inconclusive), but he fully succeeds in derailing me.

At the end, there he is again, right in my face in agitated faux-chumminess, while haranguing me about the Falklands, and about the last-minute hustings meeting he has arranged for veterans. He emailed me about this a couple of days ago, and I replied that I couldn't do it, as I was going to be somewhere else that night. Anywhere else, in truth. It's exhausted paranoia, I know, but I just don't want any dealings with him.

He's not the only one who can google. On Twitter, "Joe" had already told me that he is gay, because he shouted at me about both the Plaid "coming out" party political broadcast, and my defence of it in *Pink News*. Now I find out from an article online that he only came out in his late thirties, and that it has been an almighty struggle. I don't doubt it. There are many ex-military men in the same, conflicted position, wrapped up, as in his case, with the unpredictable horrors of PTSD.

Since leaving the military, he's made attempts at writing and film-making careers, none of which have really taken off. On a personal level, I must push so many of his buttons, having come out as a teenager and never looked back, being happily settled with a boyfriend, and making a reasonable career out of my writing. And then I have the temerity to stand against the one politician, perhaps the one person, who has helped him out.

My heart should go out to him, and I wish I could say that it did, but I want to run. Foolishly, and because he has physically backed me into a corner, I tell him to cut out the matey stuff, because it hardly tallies with his Twitter taunts as "Joe". "Why do you say that's me?" he roars, "that's not me, you can't say that". He is livid. I'm just cold and snide: "So there's another veteran that's gay, has PTSD and an obsession with white poppies, living in Aberystwyth, making films and helping the LibDem campaign then, is there? What an amazing coincidence." I flounce off, and feel dreadful.

I'm really shaken up, and as I leave, I'm accosted by a strapping woman in a leather jacket festooned with badges. "If you get elected, will you support a bill to make ecocide illegal?" she barks. I must have looked confused, as she continues, "You know what ecocide is, don't you?" Yes, I sort of lie, and run through an exhausted checklist of Plaid's green credentials. She is semi-placated, and accompanies me out of the building, talking animatedly about climate change. We both stop dead in our tracks on the pavement. Iolo has kindly brought the Mikemobile round to the entrance, to get us all out of this horrible day as swiftly as possible. There it sits, four feet away from us, in all its black, gas-guzzling corpulence, covered in fluorescent posters with my name on them. "Hmm, yeah, ecocide eh?" says my Amazonian interlocutor. She punches me on the arm, vaguely affectionately I hope, and disappears into the night.

Tuesday 21 April 2015,
Abdul's Tandoori Spice, Cardigan:
An overnight stay in Cardigan. More than anywhere else in the constituency, the first question I'm often asked here is where I

live. I suspect that Machynlleth might as well be the moon to some this far down the map, but I often get the feeling that, for many, it's a better answer than Aberystwyth would be. They *really* hate Aberystwyth.

The *Cambrian News* is out this evening; reactions to my not-quite-a-right-of-reply have been very positive. We settled for too little though. Our conditions had been that it must be within the first seven pages, and with a flash on the top of the front page advertising it. They have put it on page 6, and made it as small as possible. It doesn't fill even half of the page. Directly beneath it is a much larger headline – "War of words erupts over 'gut instinct' politics" – giving a free run for Mark Williams to sound off against UKIP. It is obviously there to spike my piece, to flag up Mark's anti-racist credentials. His press officer has certainly swallowed the idea of banging home the message time and time again, even if it comes out as pure gibberish. In one quotation, he has Mark saying "For a right wing party to the right of the Conservatives – it will be the biggest right wing vote that any political force would have had in this country." Right.

One condition that had been agreed was that we should see the camera-ready piece before it went to press. Somehow in the frenzy of yesterday, it never happened. When earlier today Rhuanedd queried this, she was told that it had already gone to print. I can see now why they didn't want to show us. It is childishly pathetic, pushing the letter of our agreement to breaking point.

My piece, though, is fine. In all of the painstaking surgery applied to it yesterday, I'd lost sight of its strength. It does pack a punch, and numerous people tell me that it stands out a mile from the chuntering fare that usually fills the paper. And though I wish we'd fought for more, they have had to eat a fair slab of humble pie, printing a piece in their own pages stating quite unambiguously that the word "Nazi" was theirs not mine; that they changed the punctuation, and thus a crucial slant, of my original article; that I won an award for it in 2001; that their coverage had provoked threats of violence towards me, and police involvement; and that the whole episode had been one of "hysteria" and "sensationalism".

Thursday 23 April 2015,
11pm, home:
Leanne and Steffan Lewis[5] arrive late for a stopover at ours en route from the north. We drink and gossip into the night, despite everyone having a hideously early start tomorrow. Not that Leanne needs more than four or five hours sleep; she never has, as long as I've known her. On that score, if no other, she is very like Thatcher. It's not a comparison she likes me making.

Our leader is in her element, absolutely thriving on the buzz of the campaign; every phone-in, meeting and interview. On the ITV Wales leaders' debate the other night she was as sharp as a tack. She managed once again to slip out a headline-grabbing one-liner on UKIP, and totally outclassed her nearest rival, Kirsty Williams, who came across, even more than usual, as a holier-than-thou head girl – a real chip off the old Clegg. Green leader Pippa Bartolotti was straight out of Harry Potter; it was hard not to picture an owl on her shoulder.

Leanne tells us about the debate, and how Owen Smith dropped a clanger just before it started. Not realising that they were already being filmed, he replied to Leanne's polite chit-chat question as to whether he'd ever been on *Question Time* with a surly "no", before going on to credit her appearances not to the fact that she is the leader of a political party, but simply because she is a woman, and there to fill the quota. I do hope that footage emerges. You couldn't get a clearer example of the sour and reactionary worldview of Welsh Labour.

She has grown immeasurably throughout the last couple of

---

5   Leanne's chief of staff; since selected as the lead candidate for the regional list in south-east Wales for the 2016 Assembly elections.

months. Even the old guard of Plaid, initially *so* suspicious of her, have been warmed by her charm and telegenic steel, and one poll has named her the most popular party leader in the UK. Move over Cleggmania; now we are all getting Wood.

Friday 24 April 2015,
10.05am, Tregaron:
Strung out with coffee and adrenaline after a live hour-long hustings on Radio Wales from Tregaron, starting at nine. All six candidates and a stack of BBC people in puffa jackets are wedged into the Talbot's snug, in a sea of equipment and cabling (the BBC are here all day as part of their election roadshow). We all do pretty well in the circumstances, though no-one lands any killer blows.

Afterwards, Henrietta and I bond slightly over bacon sandwiches, though she starts with a thinly veiled warning about making "political capital" over her frequent no-shows at so many of the hustings, due, she says, to family illness. I point out that we've all had to miss one or two hustings, and managed to arrange stand-ins to cover us, and that failing that, it doesn't take much to let the organisers know that you won't be coming.

Now that we're in the final straits though, there is a strange warmth between us all. This is such an insane but unique experience, and only those also going through it really understand just how mad it is.

2.20pm:
There's another hour's live hustings on Radio Cymru's lunchtime *Taro Post*. I've been dreading it, but it goes well, and I even enjoy it. Garry Owen does a deft job of marshalling us and an audience of youngsters from Ysgol Henry Richard, many of whom I met when I went to speak there the other week. They are so impressive.

As it's in Welsh, Elizabeth Evans deputises for Mark Williams. There's no Green, so the only actual candidates are Huw Labour, Gethin UKIP and me. The Tories are represented by some grande dame on the line from Carmarthen, who gives me the best laugh of the hour. At the end, we are all fired one "light" question each. Hers is "Beth sy'n gwneud i chi chwerthin?" Without missing a beat, she harrumphs grandly "Coverage o'r etholiad gan y BBC".[6] Amen, sister.

The manufactured panic about the SNP is getting worse. Miliband has had to state repeatedly that there will be no deal of any kind with them, or us. Nick Clegg has followed suit today. On *Newsnight* the other evening, Charles Kennedy said that Tory, Labour and Liberal voters in Scotland should unite behind whichever non-SNP candidate has the best chance in every seat. It's infuriating. The SNP and Plaid have worked productively with both parties before, and have so much in common, especially against Cameron's Conservatives. The bigger picture is getting smaller by the minute.

Saturday 25 April 2015,
10.10am, Lampeter:
I meet Ellen and Iolo ap Gwynn, and we head south in the Mikemobile, which is starting to look very tatty by now. So are we all. I've used the old cliché of this being a marathon not a sprint a great deal lately, so we're coming into the final mile. I have hit the wall several times, and nothing feels quite real any more.

First stop is Lampeter, where we meet Elin and go to a Green Fair (or quite possibly "Fayre") at the Victoria Hall. It's a sweet event, and the response is polite, with a few people positively enthusiastic. One woman tells me with steely clarity that she won't be voting for me, because I'm not "suitable" for Ceredigion, though I'm still not much the wiser as to why. Nazigate, I suspect. Like most people, she never saw my reply to the story. We really did sell ourselves short on that one.

6   "What makes you laugh?" "The coverage of the election by the BBC."

12.40pm, Cardigan:

From there, it's a slow drive to Cardigan for Barley Saturday. It's all a little more edgy than last year, and no surprise to see most of my fellow candidates in town – everyone, in fact, except Henrietta. There's a slightly unseemly tussle between us and the LibDems for the optimum position on the raised pavement outside the Guildhall, which commands the best view up and down the long main street. Mark Williams and his crew don't even acknowledge our presence, and we end up yards apart, surveying the assembled populace like rival Popes scrapping it out on the same balcony.

Monday 27 April 2015,
8.15am, home:

I almost slice my face open shaving to the sound of the *Today* programme. The *Telegraph* has followed up on its "100 business chiefs support the Tories" front page of a few weeks ago with another one saying exactly the same, but this time with "5,000 small business owners". Radio 4 have decided that it is the headline of the morning.

So here is the BBC news: Tory donors, Tory members, Tory supporters and those who have been given honours by Tories are encouraging people to vote Tory. In other headlines, the Pope declares himself Catholic and a bear was seen scampering into the woods, clutching a roll of Andrex. The last *Telegraph* front page proved to be something cooked up in Conservative Central Office, and this is too. Fine if they want to make it into their story of the day, but much less fine that the BBC are so faithfully following suit.

11.15am, Cwrtnewydd:

A phone call from Owen with the first impression of the postal votes, which have been opened this morning for verification. It looks like we are neck and neck with the LibDems, and that Labour are a distant third. Plaid has never been as efficient as the LibDems in getting out the postal vote; usually the gap is massive, and considerably wider than the final result. Apparently, the LibDem representatives left the county council offices with faces like thunder. The news electrifies our happy band of canvassers, and we set off in great cheer. Even when we get hopelessly lost deep in the lanes, which would normally provoke much tutting and watch-checking, there is only laughter.

10pm, Llandysul:
A decent evening canvass in Llandysul, and then back to Siân and Guto ap Gwynfor's house for dinner, and a bed for the night. They look after me beautifully; I guess they know the election routine, and the needs of a candidate in the final few furlongs, better than most. Guto[7] will have seen it all his life. They're very optimistic, and say – as have many others – that there is a definite buzz out there around the campaign, one that reminds them of Cynog in 1992.

We watch the BBC news, which is still leading on the *Telegraph's* clarion call for the Tories, presented as straight fact. *The Guardian* and *Independent* have shown the letter to have come direct from Conservative headquarters, but that is not being discussed. It is very disheartening to see such shoddy journalism.

Even less appealing is the sight of David Cameron giving a speech today in the middle of a braying crowd. Smarting from criticism that the Tory campaign is lacklustre, the spin doctors have evidently told him to turn up the volume. "If I'm getting lively about it it's because I feel bloody lively about it!" he shouts, to raggedy cheers, having just hammered home that the fight "pumps me up!" Siân, Guto and I guffaw with laughter, and I distinctly hear the preacher's wife say a very rude word.

---

7   Guto, a chapel minister, is the son of Gwynfor Evans.

Tuesday 28 April 2015,
11.40am, Henllan:
Possibly the craziest canvassing session yet. A huge party of people turn out for the morning traipse around the village of Henllan, on the Carmarthenshire border. Most of the volunteers are lively ladies of a certain age, and I am passed around like a toy, and taken to meet all of their friends, family and neighbours. I'm not sure that I meet any actual undecided voters.

2.15pm, Daffodil Inn, Penrhiwllan:
Have to hide below the car park for a stealthy post-lunch fag. Possibly more than anything else in recent years, the smoking ban has been the most obvious cultural game-changer from a single law. Once the spell had been broken, and people had taken to the idea that their clothes didn't have to smell like they'd been used to wipe an ashtray, smoking shrivelled in acceptability far beyond the remit of the legislation. No-one forced people to hang outside the kitchen door in their own homes for a crafty smoke, but it soon became the norm. And now, having collapsed pathetically back into the arms of my old friend Nick O'Teen, I was having to meet him out of sight, out of mind and with a ready supply of mints. It's like being fifteen again.

9.45pm, home:
Considerably more productive canvassing this afternoon in Penrhiwllan, Croes-lan and Ffos-y-Ffin, before heading home. After a night away, it's even sweeter to be back. We've received the latest LibDem mock newspaper in the post, only the sorting by postcode has got a little confused around the county edges, as we've received both the Montgomeryshire paper ("JANE DODDS IS SET TO WIN!") and its Ceredigion stablemate ("MARK WILLIAMS IS SET TO WIN!").

Much of the content is identical throughout, with only the names changed. Breaking the Plaid rule of not tweeting after you've had a drink, I can't resist pointing this out. On both front pages are quotations from supposedly ordinary voters, who are both pictured: J— from Aberystwyth and F— from Welshpool [the leaflets use their names, but for obvious reasons, I shan't here]. J— says "The work that Mark Williams is doing for our area is really amazing and it's why I'm backing him on 7th May!" F— says "The work that Jane Dodds is doing for our area is really amazing and it's why I'm backing her on 7th May!"

My tweet includes a photo of the two front pages, alongside the message "J— from Aberystwyth meet F— from Welshpool. You have so much in common. Your exact words, for instance."

It quickly goes stratospheric, racking up over seven hundred retweets. There is much guffawing at the threadbare transparency of the LibDems' campaign machine. Someone from the Brecon and Radnor constituency posts an image of their newspaper ("ROGER WILLIAMS IS SET TO WIN!"); the three are then collected together and plastered everywhere.

Amid the general hilarity, I receive a furious message from the J— of Aberystwyth whose off-the-peg endorsement of Mark Williams provoked my tweet. I recognise his Twitter account immediately. He's been firing some strange messages at me lately, and the Plaid office too. He is another constituent with mental health issues whom Mark has helped, and who is repaying him by being an enthusiastic cheerleader for his re-election. Had I known it was him, I would not have tweeted anything that included his name, even though it's there on the front page of their paper, alongside his photo. Too late now; the retweets are pinging in every second or two, and the genie is well and truly out of the bottle.

J— contacts me on Facebook within the hour, demanding that I delete the tweet and apologise. I know from past experience that he will keep sending messages, on every available media, until he gets a response, so I compose what I hope is an even and emollient reply. Of course, that's not how he sees it, and as I go to bed, he is howling inconsolably into the night.

Wednesday 29 April 2015,
9.30am, Ysgol Penweddig, Aberystwyth:
In my old life, I'd often get to mid morning having barely uttered a word to anyone. Today, I am talking to three hundred teenagers at a school hustings just shy of nine o'clock. It's Aberystwyth's Welsh-medium secondary school, so *popeth yn Gymraeg*[8], except of course for the contributions by Mark Williams and Daniel Thompson. Once again, there's no Henrietta Hensher.

Someone asks a question about why we should believe any politician when they so regularly break their promises. I concentrate on the LibDems and tuition fees in my answer, though immediately afterwards I regret not making it slightly more barbed. If there was ever an audience and an occasion to mention Mark's broken promise to learn Welsh, this was it. Doing so would have sent Elin into orbit, but it would have been worth it to see his response.

8.45pm, St Anne's church, Penparcau, Aberystwyth:
The final hustings meeting. There have been around fifteen since the first tentative outing in February, well above average and a real testament to Ceredigion's hearty and human way of doing politics. Mainstream pundits, especially outside of Wales, tend to write Ceredigion off as an irrelevant electoral sideshow: a small party in a dust-up with an even smaller one, of no interest to those obsessing over the latest shifts in the Tory-Labour swingometer.

But therein lies its fascination, for it is an old-fashioned and uniquely calibrated contest, where the chief combatants are – whisper it if you dare – actually very close to each other.

---

8   "Everything in Welsh" – a famous poster slogan of the 1970s.

Were you to compare the Plaid and LibDem manifestoes over the past few decades, you'd find greater cross-over between them than probably any other two parties. One of the first things Mark Williams said to me was that he was sure we would find ideas and beliefs in common, and to some extent he was right. On the ground, however, there is a tribal divide that is deep, ancient and bilious, resulting in a campaign that is highly charged and personal. But never dull, and neither is it tonight.

It's a full house of candidates for our last outing together and there is a weary end-of-term feeling to proceedings. The meeting has been organised by the Ceredigion Association of Voluntary Organisations, so the subjects are mainly in the sphere of social policy. Someone asks: "Last year, the Conservative civil society Minister, Brooks Newmark, declared that charities should stick to knitting, and not get involved in politics. Do you agree?" which gives us all the chance to be withering about the Tories. Instead of being cowed by our scorn, Henrietta rounds on Huw and me in her answer by saying that we of all people should think twice before condemning people for remarks taken out of context. Though quite how you put "charities should stick to knitting" into a context that makes it palatable, she doesn't say.

Mark gets in a couple of sharp sideswipes at me. In his summing up speech, he says that we need an MP who "lives and works in the constituency", a reference I suspect few get, though more than another dig which is undoubtedly intended for my ears. It is about "J— of Aberystwyth", the man I managed to infuriate by tweeting about the homogenous rentaquote LibDem newspapers in which he had so prominently featured. Mark tells us a lachrymose version of his story: "J— is a real person," he says a couple of times, throwing a look my way as he does so. He's evidently quite angry about this episode, and wants me to know it. I growl quietly in my seat. If this lad is so vulnerable, why plaster him on the front of your leaflets with a generic quote that you knew would almost certainly be ridiculed? Who's the cynical operator here? They have used these fragile men as stooges, and Mark's cool self-righteousness raises something far more heated in me.

But it's handshakes all round when we finish; we even share a few good-natured recollections of the wildly varied hustings meetings in which we have sparred these last three months. The next time we all see each other will be a week tomorrow in the leisure centre at Aberaeron, at the count. Who will be on top? I have no idea.

Thursday 30 April 2015,
Lampeter:
Last day of April, one more week of *Groundhog Day* to go. We seem to be winning some and losing some. Yesterday in Pontrhydygroes, I saw a couple that I'd canvassed last summer, when we had an interesting discussion, albeit fruitless for me. They were lifelong Labour, with a visceral suspicion of Plaid. To my amazement, yesterday they told me they'd voted for me by post. There's still a great deal of apparent indecision out there, though. And if it's not indecision, it is people coming down against us, but being too polite to say so.

Question of the day from Cynog, asking about one of our liveliest volunteers in Lampeter, a young woman he'd met the previous day. "Ydy hi'n gweithio?" "Ydy, mae hi'n trefnu Ann Summers parties." "Beth yw Ann Summers party?"[9]

Another good one from Cynog, from when we were canvassing in Llangeitho earlier in the week. Some old boy had asked him about me. "Mae'n Sais, on'd yw e?" he'd said. "Ydy," replied Cynog. "Ydy e wedi dysgu Cymraeg?" "O, do". "Good, good, dyna'r main thing."[10]

---

9   "Does she work?" "Yes, she organises Ann Summers parties." "What's an Ann Summers party?"

10   "He's English, isn't he?" "Yes he is." "Has he learned Welsh?" "Oh, yes." "Good, good, that's the main thing."

WHISTLE: STOP

May 2015

Friday 1 May 2015,
8.05am, home:
On the leaders' interviews on TV last night, Ed Miliband
categorically ruled out working with the SNP and Plaid, even
in any post-election supply and command arrangement. What
a turnip that man is. Labour have pretty much abandoned
Scotland, so now it's Operation Cnut to shore up their support
in England. In Wales too – Scotland has become an increasingly
fraught topic of conversation on our doorsteps this last week,
and it is not playing well for us, or Labour. The Tory posters,
showing a tiny Ed Miliband in the pocket of a grinning Alex
Salmond, and one even portraying Salmond as a pickpocket of
"your cash", will be the defining ones of the campaign, I feel
sure.

The media are banging on about little else. Nicola
Sturgeon is on the front page of most of the papers every
day, and the language is brutal. In an echo of the referendum
campaign, the BBC have taken to showing any couple of
weegies hurling abuse at Jim Murphy as the main item on
the news, and the inference is clear: this is, all too literally,
that old cliché, the "ugly face of nationalism". It is working
a treat, as it always does, and it has boxed Labour and
the LibDems into a corner. They'd rather allow the Tories
back into power than try and champion a progressive and
collaborative alternative. It shows where the real battle lines
are drawn in this election, and indeed in the country: fifty
shades of unblinking austerity Unionism versus us, the SNP
and to some extent the Greens.

Some public support for me today from Andy Chyba, the
prominent Green, and Adam Ramsey on the Bright Green
website, who say that I am the only "other" candidate they
are endorsing. I've also been endorsed by campaign group
VoteSmart, who analyse each seat and throw their support
behind the progressive candidate most capable of winning
in each one. The Election Forecast website has changed its
prediction to me winning. It is looking close, but we have

momentum. At least we do according to the deskbound pundits; in the wild, I'm not so sure.

9.25am, Plaid office, Aberystwyth:
As people were wary of leaving the Mikemobile anywhere too prominent, Preds had to drive it back to ours last night, and it is up to me to get it back to the office this morning. I have never driven a Range Rover before, and this one is well over twenty years old.

It stalls fifty yards from our house on a steep slope. Efforts to re-start it come to nothing; all I manage is to roll it back and wedge it firmly into the hedgerow. I jump out and scream *"Preeeeedddds!"* at the top of my voice, like a small child on the cusp of a right paddy. He comes running, sorts me out, starts the car and even offers to drive it to Aberystwyth for me. I am sorely, sorely tempted, but I can't start the day being quite this pathetic, so reluctantly turn down the offer.

It is a horrible drive, and the traffic is awful. Worse, being on my own driving a clunky old jeep with my name emblazoned all over it, I feel hideously conspicuous. A few people give me a thumbs up as I bounce through Talybont and I wave back like the Queen.

As I climb the hill into Aberystwyth, my phone goes and sends my already jagged nerves into overdrive. It's Owen, checking up on me as I'm quarter of an hour late by now. "I'm on the way, I'm bloody driving!" I scream into the receiver, and kill it. By the time I arrive at the office, all of my frustration has coagulated into a cold fury with Owen, for not trusting me to come in, for phoning me when he knew I would be behind the wheel and – more to the point – behind the wheel of that old tank. I shriek at him never to do that again, that it was thoughtless and stupid. He looks at me, startled and equally angry. "Go, just go!" he shouts, and starts shooing me out of the room, his hands flapping me away, like I'm a puppy that has just shat on the hearth rug. Team morale is flaky this morning.

12.40pm, Lampeter:

It doesn't much improve on the doorstep; there are some very curious reactions now – a fair few new votes coming our way, and with real enthusiasm, but more drifting imperceptibly away. You can feel it, a sense of awkwardness, a reluctance to look me in the eye, a door closed just a little too hurriedly. Trepidation about Scotland is the main reason, and that even amongst *Cymry Cymraeg* supporters. And Nazigate still hasn't gone away. Those who saw my right of reply in the paper liked it very much, but most never noticed it at all, though they remember the initial headlines very well.

Worst reaction of the day, and the one that unsettles me profoundly and makes me think I'm really not cut out for this, comes as we arrive in Lampeter in the Mikemobile. As we head down one of the main streets, I see the bloke driving the car in front eyeing us in his rear view mirror. Suddenly, his brake lights snap on, and he leaps out of the car and runs around to my window. I wind it down to a torrent of abuse and anger, that I was full of shit, a bloody bullshitter, that he'd also moved here from Kidderminster and was fucking ashamed of what I said, for he had never – you hear that, *never* – encountered anyone with the kind of racist attitudes I described. I can't get a word in, and every attempt to do so only makes him shout even louder. It draws quite a crowd.

I cannot bear this. For starters, one of our volunteers is sat in the back of the car with her five-year-old daughter, and I feel awful that I have provoked this kind of scene in front of her. But I cannot bear it for me, and those supporting me, either. I'm so fed up with the tension, the lies, the anger, the feeling that I am being spotlit and carved open at every turn.

Mr Ranty, formerly of Kidderminster, finally dries up and runs back to his car, accelerating away as if on *Top Gear*. I catch a few people's faces on the pavement as we head quietly on. They are amused, perplexed and strangely blank. There is a shocked silence in the car. Even driver Brython, a man with the steadiest of nerves and the sunniest of demeanours, cannot quite find any words.

5.50pm, Plaid office, Aberystwyth:
I crawl back to the office with a mouthful of apologies to Owen for being such a prima donna this morning. He apologises too for shooing me away, though it was probably the only available response at the time. I tell him about our less-than-inspiring day, but he has a piece of crap news to trump that. Chris Betteley at the *Cambrian News* is poking around the "J— from Aberystwyth" outburst to see if he can make a nice eve-of-poll story out of it. I recall Mark Williams's pointed references ("J— is a real person") spat in my direction at the hustings the night before last, and I see all too clearly that I could well be strung up and kippered once again. I don't care now. Let them do their bloody worst, and let's get this thing over and done with.

9.30pm, home:
Email from Tŷ Gwynfor, which starts: "With less than a week to go it's important that we build towards a crescendo on social media." Can it get any louder? My social media feeds are already volcanic, and no-one needs any more "Great reaction on the doorstep!!" and pictures of squinting canvass teams. God knows what normal people must be making of it. Social media, Twitter especially, is the obsession of Plaid centrally. A few weeks ago, I was mildly admonished for not producing my requisite five tweets and two Facebook posts every day, which suggests they know neither the reality of canvassing nor the reality of Ceredigion telecommunications.

Saturday 2 May 2015,
11.15am, Aberystwyth town centre:
Last street stall of the campaign, and a bit of a hustle for the best spots. The LibDems are out too of course, but there are also stalls from Labour and the Greens. We're all a bit

over-excitable and demob happy. At one point, someone in the Labour gang is taking a group portrait around their stall, which I rush over to photo bomb. "It's never too late to rejoin Labour!" quips Huw Thomas to me as I skid to a halt in front of them. He's a sharp cookie, and although we've had our run-ins, I like him. Had it not been for Tippexgate, I'd say that he was guaranteed a glittering future in Welsh Labour. I wonder how that will play out for him.

Daniel Thompson of the Greens is on good form too. He has grown immeasurably in confidence throughout the campaign, and I think that he'll do quite well next week. I hope he does, though not at my expense of course. His take on our economic system is profoundly researched and urgently relevant; it's a far cry from the headline-grabbing histrionics of his Welsh party leader, Ms Bartolotti. I've tried to prod Daniel a few times to see what he makes of her, but he's always been scrupulously tactful, though tellingly non-committal. I can't imagine they'd have a lot in common.

Many people come up to shake my hand, slap me on the back and wish me well. I'm very touched by that, because it has been a filthy campaign, the worst Ceredigion has ever seen. I'm especially moved by the variety of people who tell me they are voting Plaid: from kids in hoodies to pensioners on sticks, dyed-in-the-wool Cardis to loquacious incomers. In these final few weeks, I've met many who tell me that they have registered to vote for the first time in their lives, so that they can vote for me. More often than not, they are the kind of people I partied with on the rave and road protest scenes of the 1990s, and are liberally covered with tattoos and piercings. I think of my banished ear-ring, sat in a drawer in the bathroom at home, and wonder if I'll be re-inserting it on Friday morning.

4.00pm, Waunfawr, Aberystwyth:
The complex doorstep discussions of a few months ago have long gone. Bit by bit, my spiel has been boiled down to the essential message, and I'm hammering it out repeatedly. As

every poll is showing, the only certainty in this election is a hung parliament. It's a stark choice between a return of the Tories, with the LibDems and possibly even the DUP and UKIP in tow, or a more progressive alliance of the centre-left. In Ceredigion, that means Mark Williams in the former camp, or me in the latter. Westminster only takes Wales seriously when Plaid does well.

I repeat this again and again on a last sweep around Waunfawr, though plenty don't even answer the door. I'm not surprised; we're trying to drum up a crowd for a last-minute rally with Leanne on Monday, the May Day bank holiday, so a message has been recorded to be played out of the speakers on top of the Mikemobile, which cruises the estate, hollering out its invitation. Whenever we've used the loudspeakers on arrival at a canvassing stop, the strike rate of doors even opening has plummeted. It has the exact opposite effect to an ice cream van.

Of the people I do meet, Scotland continues to exercise a lot of minds. Having hit so raw a nerve, the Tories cannot leave it alone. Boris Johnson has warned this weekend of an impending "Ajockalypse", while the press contrive to find new ways of demonising Nicola Sturgeon. From the *Mail*'s front page headline "The Most Dangerous Woman in Britain" to *The Sun* superimposing her face on Miley Cyrus astride her wrecking ball, nothing seems to be off limits. You cannot let this sort of racist genie out of the bottle, and then expect it to climb meekly back in this time next week. In a *Guardian* interview, the last Conservative Scottish Secretary, Michael Forsyth, warned that the anti-Scots rhetoric of their campaign is "short-term and dangerous" and "threatens the integrity of our country", but he is a whisper in the wilderness. Whatever happens, we are in for a rocky ride.

9.20pm, home:
Preds is out, so I have a few hours of luxurious solitude, and even manage a bit of the World Championship snooker

semi-final. I would have watched more, but inevitably, I fall asleep. The peace is overwhelming, and I can only sympathise with a woman in Waunfawr who sends me a furious email. She's got a migraine, and was just nodding off this afternoon when she was jolted awake by ten minutes of announcements inviting her to meet Leanne Wood on Monday. My precious peace is disturbed only by the soft clack of snooker balls, and I send her a heartfelt apology.

Roger Scully has crunched the numbers on the latest YouGov poll, and on two out of the three kinds of projection, he has us winning Ceredigion, and the LibDems being wiped off the map of Wales. Expectations are high.

Sunday 3 May 2015,
Home:
Labour's campaign staggers from hopeless to bonkers. Ed Miliband's last-minute secret weapon is a nine-foot, two-ton stone monolith, with their platitudinous pledges carved into it. Should they win, Miliband says, it will be positioned in the Downing Street garden as a daily reminder of his "contract with the British people". Twitter is gleefully taking the piss and has coined the name "Edstone" for this unfathomable folly. I know we're all tired, but even so. How many meetings must the idea have been floated past? Did no-one cough quietly and say, "Er, actually…"?

Stacks of messages wishing me well, from all over the world. Thanks partly to the scandals, but also to readers of my books, other writers and creative types, the Ceredigion election is being watched far beyond our borders. There's even an email from my all-time hero, Jan Morris: "Good luck dear Mike, for all our sakes!"

Monday 4 May 2015,
Aberystwyth University:
Bank Holiday Monday, and most normal people are having a day off. It's anything but for wannabe politicians. Farmers too.

Preds drives me down to Llanybydder, just over the border in Carmarthenshire, for the livestock mart and the chance for a joint sweep of the gathered tribes with Jonathan Edwards. I have to do two BBC interviews, in both languages, giving Plaid's official reaction to some gung-ho last-minute promises from Cameron. Because I'm just out of the constituency, they can interview me and not have to ask all the other Ceredigion candidates to offer their two penn'orth. Were I standing half a mile north, election rules would prevail. By the same token, Jonathan cannot do the interviews, as we are on his patch. The broadcasting rules are crazy.

After the two TV ones, I gallop around Llanybydder looking for a phone signal so that I can do a follow-up interview with Adrian Chiles on BBC Five Live. I find one in the nick of time, and am immediately on air, panting slightly from my run around the village. When I first spoke to Adrian a few weeks ago, it was all very light-hearted, particularly about our old college friendship. This time though, he quickly steers the conversation to Nazigate. He's very fair about it and says quite clearly that the headlines did not match the story, which is the first time anyone on the BBC has had the wit to say so. I say that yes, it has been difficult, but the support that has come my way because of it has been utterly overwhelming. And it truly has.

It becomes even more overwhelming within the hour. We drive back to Aberystwyth for the eve-of-poll rally with Leanne in a lecture theatre at the University. It's been organised and publicised quite late in the day, so I'm nervous that there might only be about twenty of our most hardcore members prepared to give up their bank holiday.

We arrive at the last minute, and there is a strange buzz around. As I walk into the lecture theatre, there is a murmur which swiftly explodes into applause, and then cheering, and then people stamping and standing up. I look behind to see if Matthew Rhys or Charlotte Church is following me in, and only then does it sink in that this wall of noise is mine.

It's all I can do not to burst into tears, but I can feel the passion and the affection flooding me, mainlining energy into my veins.

This is what I imagine some chapel meeting in the great revival of 1904–5 would have felt like. The *hwyl* is mighty, the atmosphere intense. There are hundreds here, faces – and phones – turned towards me, Elin and Leanne as we take the stage. Elin gives a tub-thumper of an introduction – even she, normally the most measured of politicians, is riffing wildly off the energy in the theatre. She gets hugely passionate that the slur thrown at me by the *Cambrian News* has been the lowpoint of modern Ceredigion politics, but that it cannot be allowed to prevail, a sentiment which, not surprisingly, receives tumultuous applause.

My speech is brief, its main purpose to rally the troops, get them out there over the next three days, and to introduce Leanne. She is on full beam today, and we are all putty in her hands. Afterwards, there are handshakes, hugs, selfies and jokes as we all spill outside for a photo-call.

The joyous mood is only slightly dented when a young man approaches me and asks if I'd answer something for him. Of course, I reply. "Is it true," he says, "that the reason you didn't go to the hustings meeting in St Michael's a fortnight ago[1] was because you refuse to set foot in any Christian church?" I'm taken aback, and have to ask him to repeat it. He does. It is really bothering him. I try and reassure him that it is nonsense, indeed that I spend a ridiculous amount of my time pootling around churches. I point out too that the very last hustings meeting was in St Anne's in Penparcau, and I managed that without being zapped into a pile of dust. Who told you this, I ask, already pretty sure of the answer. "A LibDem canvasser," he replies. He's a Christian, and says that other members of his congregation have been told the same too. I don't know

---

1   I had a pre-arranged meeting that evening in Llandysul, in the far south of the county.

whether to laugh or scream. Is there any barrel they won't scrape the bottom of?

Leanne, Elin and I bowl into town, where there is a street festival on to celebrate Aberystwyth winning the Urbanism Award for the best UK town last year. It's a lovely and lively event, and there is plenty of support, not least from the people working on the *Cambrian News* stall. They are giving away free bags for life with the paper's logo on them, but when they see me, they laugh and call, "I don't suppose you'll be wanting one of these, will you?" One of them takes a Plaid Cymru sticker and puts it next to the CN logo on her T-shirt.

Tuesday 4 May 2015,
Llandysul:
A wet whistlestop tour of the Teifi valley, calling at Penparc, Cardigan, Llechryd, Adpar and Llandysul. The Mikemobile is full of helpers, and the journey is spent, as it often is, conducting a running tally of our posters versus the opposition's. I cannot believe how much of an obsession this is for everyone. People even know on which properties there were LibDem posters last time, but not this, and announce it to a cheer. I've got strangely used to seeing my name on walls and gates, in windows and cars. It reminds me of my childhood, and seeing my dad's name poking out of hedges on For Sale boards. Estate agent and putative politician – we Parkers sure know how to court popularity.

The election really could not go on any longer. Everyone is on the brink of collapse. The office looks as if a bomb has been detonated there: mountains of boxes, leaflets, papers, placards, posters and canvass bags spilling all over the place, and a steady stream of volunteers pounding through. Somewhere in the middle of the maelstrom you can just about see an ashen-faced Owen and a grinning Gwen, holding it all together with punch-drunk good humour.

Upstairs, poor Jordan is having to spend most of every day now ploughing through emails that are pouring in and demanding answers. I've always been a little agnostic about online activism; ten seconds clicking on a petition isn't much of a commitment to the cause, and neither is bombarding people with generic emails. Much of it is just worthy spam, but it all has to be answered.

I nearly lost it completely in Penparc this morning. We were sent to knock on the doors of part of the village I canvassed only a few weeks ago, and a couple of months before that too. There are so many hamlets and villages in the county I have never canvassed at all, while some places are being done to death. It feels as if our organisation is on the brink of collapse too.

My hunch now, though, is that we are unlikely to win. There are some mysterious forces at work, many of which seem to contradict each other, but there's undoubtedly slippage among some traditional supporters, and I don't think we've done enough to convince others. Then there is the rapid demographic change in Ceredigion; there are whole villages and entire estates where you don't hear a single local accent.

Llechryd today was a case in point, although that did produce one of the more entertaining moments of the day. The door was opened by an Indian woman, who was charm and politeness itself, but told me, "I'm afraid I shan't be voting for you. I shall be voting UKIP." "Oh," I replied, a little nonplussed, "and is there any particular reason for that?" There was: "Well, Gethin James is my brother-in-law, so I suppose I have to vote for him." We laughed, and shook hands.

Will the shy LibDem vote, plus the anything-to-stop-Plaid brigade lending their votes to Mark, push us out once again? It feels that way, but who can honestly say? I'm knackered, but excited, nervous and a little scared too; proud of the integrity of our campaign, both locally and across Wales, and deeply grateful to the hundreds of volunteers. What an incredible experience this whole thing has been.

Wednesday 6 May 2015,
11.50pm, home:
So that's it. A dreary, wet day of last-minute canvassing in
Lampeter, Aberaeron and Aberystwyth. People are at snapping
point now; they have had enough. Many don't answer the door,
and they don't even bother pretending to be out either.
Cynog was with us once again canvassing. He'd intended to
sit this election out, but has found himself increasingly in the
thick of the action, and although he's hardly the most restful
of company, I am so glad to have him around. He is a force of
nature, well into his late seventies, but always at the head of
the pack, striding on purposefully.

More often than not, when I ask people if they have ever
supported Plaid in the past (it's a far easier question to ask
than "will you vote for me?"), the answer is yes, that they
used to vote for Cynog with great enthusiasm. He is hugely
respected. I'm not sure that I'm luring them sufficiently back
into the fold, but Cynog seems to think that it's going well, and
that we have a real chance. Today, he asks me if I am looking
forward to winning. He tells me that in 1992, when his victory
was looking likely, he dreaded it. While I wouldn't quite put it
like that, I do know exactly what he means.

To get myself in the mood for the big day, I watch Charlie
Brooker's *Election Wipe*. There's more sharp sense in one hour
than I've heard for weeks on end in the campaign. Not that I've
had time to watch much election TV, which in itself is one of
the best things about being a candidate. What I have seen has
been dreadful. Brooker's snap portraits are especially good: Ed
Miliband, a "PlayDoh IT man"; David Cameron a "bacon-faced
Bullingdon bore" and Nicola Sturgeon "that nice mum from
a biscuit commercial". Barely any mention of Clegg though;
there rarely is these days. It does feel as if the LibDems are
vanishing from sight. That may well make all the difference
tomorrow.

Election day, Thursday 7 May 2015,
1.45pm, Plaid office, Aberystwyth:
Elin had warned me that the loneliest experience she'd ever known was being a candidate on election day, and I am beginning to see what she means. My Twitter feed is full of Mark thundering around the county and visiting all the polling stations, which always seemed such a pointless election day activity to me. Mark is claiming that it's his way of thanking them, but actually, it's just to have one last thing to do, one final, exhausted challenge, to squeeze the last drops of adrenaline out of this interminably long day. Only now do I understand that.

Owen and I amble around Aberystwyth, and pop in on a couple of polling stations. They seem pleased enough to see us. Polling is fairly brisk, but there is no sense at all as to which way it is going. As we wander around the town centre, a few people wish me luck, some shake my hand and no-one shouts at me. All the aggro of the last month is seeping away, and fast. The deed is done, the boil is lanced, to everyone's enormous relief.

8.38pm, Aberaeron beach:
After picking Preds up from the station in Aberystwyth, we drive down to Aberaeron and book in for the night at the Harbourmaster. I am a bag of nerves, and can barely force my dinner down. We wander down to the beach to watch the sunset, and as it sinks perfectly into the horizon, I tweet a photo, with the message "Sundown on the beach at Aberaeron. What will the night bring?" Replies are numerous; most telling me that it will bring my election as the new MP for Ceredigion.

10pm, Harbourmaster Hotel, Aberaeron:
Lying on the bed, we're tuned in for the BBC exit poll. As it flashes up on the screen, we both gasp. They are predicting a massive Conservative victory, with nearly eighty seats more than Labour; that the SNP will win every seat bar one in

Scotland; that the LibDems will crash from 57 to 10; and that Plaid will nudge up by one seat to four. The guests in the studio are dazed by the figures, while Twitter has a collective cardiac arrest. My heart is racing: I'm going to win. It looks as if the tide engulfing the LibDems is one of those once-in-a-century inundations, and there's no way Ceredigion would be left high and dry as one of their few remaining islands. There are too many LibDem bastions in the south-west and the wintry north of England for that. Realistically, if there's a Plaid gain, it is only likely to be here or Ynys Môn. As ever, the island will be its perverse old self and buck any trend going; Labour will hang on there. Our gain is here, I'm sure of it.

Bloody hell. I'm going to be an MP. My life is never going to be the same again, and neither is Preds'. He is often so inscrutable, but right now, I can see a bubbling mix of pride, excitement, shock and terror in his eyes. He will, I know, rise to this latest challenge that I've thrown at him with calm poise, something I am going to need now more than ever. He said right at the outset that he wasn't going to be a political wifey, that there'd be no cake-judging in village halls for him and that if I were ever caught snorting coke off a rent boy's bottom, not to expect him to simper his forgiveness for the cameras at the garden gate.

On TV, the pundits, waiting for the first actual result, are still chewing over the exit poll in tones of hysterical incredulity. No-one really believes it; Paddy Ashdown says that if the LibDems actually lose that many seats, he will eat his hat.

I've been told to wait for a message from Owen, to let me know when we should make our way up to the leisure centre. He is insistent that we're not there too early, but the waiting is agony. The minutes tick by heavily, a cacophony of speculation on telly and Twitter, and a muted unreality in our room. For something to do, I shower and dress in my election night outfit: a new purple shirt, to go with a moss green jacket and pale green Levis. I've quite enjoyed the creative challenge of finding a look that works for me, yet is smart enough to pass muster. The colour green has been an unexpected boon to my wardrobe, and it's a happy nod to Plaid too. Green and purple is a colour combination that I've always loved; an earthy combination of nature and imperial ambition, one that stirs thoughts of the suffragettes (and, less pertinently, Wimbledon). I might have had to sacrifice my ear-ring, but throughout this whole process I've never once worn a tie. It is, I realise, a pathetically teenage victory, but that's politics for you.

At 10.43, the first text from Owen: "Swings in early booths indicate close one."

Me, 10.51: "Right! Those the local ones?"

Owen, 10.55: "Yes. Some disappointing ones in Llannon and Felinfach. Awaiting urban ones."

Owen, 11.06: "Rural ones disappointing. Eleven per cent swing to us in Llanfarian."

Me, 11.11: "When do you think we should come over?"

Owen, 11.16: "I'll ring soon. It's not looking great."

Me, 11.21: "OK, diolch."

He rings about half an hour later; his first words are "I'm sorry, Mike", and that is it. We've lost. Poor Owen is really quite distraught, whereas I'm numb, void, empty. Preds and I don't say anything; we hug silently and he's the only thing that feels real right now. Everything else is an out-of-body experience, the sensation that this is all happening to a parallel me, not the real one.

On the screen, the results are trickling in, and it seems that the exit poll was right. The LibDem vote has tanked, and there is a significant drift towards the Tories. I'm beginning to feel stir crazy, and really want to get it over and done with now. Unfortunately, Ceredigion is traditionally late to declare, and we are not expecting much before 4.00am. All the same, I call Owen and say that we'll walk up there in the next few minutes.

1.10am, Aberaeron Leisure Centre:
As soon as we arrive, I am aware that there is almost always a camera trained on me from some direction, so I keep my face neutral and comments light. Actually, there's no need to make a special effort, as the entire Plaid crew is bubbling on a cocktail of exhaustion and gallows humour, and it is surprisingly fun.

The only comparison I have for this feeling, the out-of-body sensation that is growing by the minute, is the bleary early morning hours at chemically enhanced all-nighters twenty years ago. Everything is so bright, so sharp, yet unfocused. I can't help but stare at the gaggle of LibDems, beams spreading ever wider across their faces. That despite the news coming through that they are losing seats by the shedload. Not this one, though. Aberaeron looks like being one of their very few safe harbours tonight.

On Twitter, people are still eagerly speculating that I have probably won. There is so much excited anticipation that I feel terrible for them, and for the grim news they will soon know, to add to the night's growing pile of distress. The initial exit poll is proving to be something of an underestimate: the Tories are steadily picking up votes and unexpected seats. There is even talk now of them gaining an absolute majority.

It is 1992 all over again, when the embers of racism were forensically fanned in the dying stages of the campaign, and to great effect. With one massive difference though: in '92, the panic button racism had to be silently released like a poison gas, in whispers and nods under the radar. This time, so far have the parameters of debate moved since then, it was all conducted in plain sight, trumpeted daily on the front pages and ricocheting ceaselessly around the broadcast and online media.

It is 1992 all over again, but without the tiny saving grace of a Plaid Cymru gain in Ceredigion. And for that, I feel personally culpable and truly sorry.

Time passes as if under water. I lose all sense of it, and fully expecting not to have the declaration this side of four o'clock, I'm suddenly aware that people are calling me and pointing towards the stage. I dimly recognise that my fellow candidates are already there, so dash for it, still eating the tangerine I'd just started. It is only just after 2.00am, and yes, this is the real thing.

In the BBC1 election studio, a heated discussion about devolution is interrupted as David Dimbleby says "We are going to a result, in Ceredigion". The nation joins us in the leisure centre, something I'm only aware of when my phone starts going crazy in my pocket. Whipping it out to mute it live on TV provokes a few sarky tweets.

Bronwen Morgan, Ceredigion council's chief executive, reads out the numbers:

Mark Williams (Liberal Democrat)	13,414	(35.9%; -14.2% on 2010)
Mike Parker (Plaid Cymru)	10,347	(27.7%; -0.6%)
Henrietta Hensher (Conservative)	4,123	(11.0%; -0.5%)
Gethin James (UKIP)	3,829	(10.2%; +7.7%)
Huw Thomas (Labour)	3,615	(9.7%; +3.9%)
Daniel Thompson (Green)	2,088	(5.6%; +3.8%)
Turnout	69.0%	(+4.2%)
Liberal Democrat majority	3,067	(8.2%; -13.6%)

As if to underline just how far Plaid are falling short tonight, on BBC1 they cut straight from the Ceredigion result to Kilmarnock, where the SNP swat aside a Labour majority of more than twelve thousand, and take 56 per cent of the vote. The Liberal Democrat there nets 789 votes, or 1.5 per cent. As that result is being read out, a red flash races across the bottom of the screen to tell us that Llanelli – one of the other potential Plaid hopes – is a Labour hold. It is actually much worse than that; Labour, on a catastrophic night for them, have almost doubled their majority over Plaid to more than seven thousand. In five minutes flat, Plaid hearts have been broken.

Ceredigion is a good result for everyone, except us. The electorate have spread their affection far and wide. Daniel is cock-a-hoop to have saved the Greens their deposit; it is their second best result in Wales. Gethin is thrilled too – the UKIP vote has gone up more than anyone else's, probably enough to secure him decent billing for a list seat in next year's Assembly election. Henrietta is smiling satisifaction, having kept third place; just imagine what she could have achieved had she put the tiniest bit of effort in. Huw quickly crunches the numbers and says how happy he is that the Labour vote went up by so much (5.8 per cent in 2010 to 9.7 per cent now), but he is evidently not best pleased to have come fifth, especially when he was in a fairly comfortable third after the postal votes.

Even we can squeeze some positive spin out of the result, as the headline swing figure is 6.8 per cent from the LibDems to Plaid. It's a supremely hollow statistic however, comprised entirely of the LibDems' collapse. Everyone thought that Penri's result five years ago was a freak lowpoint, but I've polled almost five hundred votes fewer than he managed, a drop of just over half a percent. I know that many hundreds – possibly a few thousand – people voted Plaid for the first time; most of them former LibDems and, in a fair few cases, people who hadn't voted for years, and some even who'd never voted at all. If that's the case, that means we have lost swathes of our bedrock vote. The news from the individual boxes confirms this: our vote plummeted in the rural south of the county, some going to Huw Thomas, but far more to UKIP. Unfathomably, they are picking up the votes of considerable numbers of *Cymry Cymraeg*.

Mark Williams of course is delighted. He is quite emotional, more so than I've ever seen him, especially as he is all too aware of how few colleagues he is going to be returning to. He was the first – and for quite a while, the only – Liberal Democrat to be re-elected, and in my speech I suggest that he may well end up party leader the way things were looking. I pay him a tribute that comes completely spontaneously, and I hope he knows that I mean it. For all his corny bluster, and the Addams Family around him, he is a thorough constituency MP, and I'm not surprised that the people of Ceredigion have plumped for him once more.

The hall empties with startling speed. The Plaid crew take some group photos, and a final swell of camaraderie sweeps through us with the sense of a job done as well as we possibly could. They are nearly all far more seasoned veterans of election campaigns than me, and can brush off a defeat with a well-practiced shrug. This one though will take some getting over for all of us. It was brutal.

I have to wait to do a couple of interviews, so there are hugs and smiles as the team leave Preds and me in the eerily quiet hall. Sara Gibson of the BBC records two radio interviews with me, one in each language. Her main question in both is a needling "Were you *really* the right candidate for this?" In Welsh, I bluster it out and say that yes, I think so, and that I don't think anyone else would have done much better. Then in English, I'm consumed by far more doubt, and snap that I just don't know if I was the right man for the job, and that's for other people to decide.

When I bought my new shirt for election night, I was mindful that it mustn't strobe on TV, but I never have to test it. There are cameras around, but no-one wants a chat with me. Yesterday's news already.

Mark is still doing interviews as we come to leave, so I wait to bid him goodbye, and to make him promise to look after his constituents. He tells me that his LibDem colleagues have gone down like ninepins, and that it is looking like a bloodbath in the south-west. He calls the Tories "utter bastards". And so they are, but then so they always have been. To everyone other than the LibDems, it was obvious that as soon as they hopped into bed with Flashman they would be royally buggered to within an inch of their lives.

I do feel slightly sorry for them, though. They were my first love, after all.

We get out of the leisure centre shortly before four. After the stale fug of the sports hall, the outside air is sweet and cold; I gulp it down. There is a distant glimmer of dawn far away inland, though on the silent Aberaeron streets, it is still neon-lit night reflected in cold puddles. A few seagulls are ransacking the bins, and somewhere a dog is barking. Preds and I walk in comfortable quiet, our footsteps echoing through the shadows.

I am walking taller and breathing deeper than I have in ages, for there is an enormous weight lifting from my shoulders, one that I hadn't even realised was there. I feel it rise, rise and drift away, a dark, dense shape against the lightening sky. I can't believe that the only words coming to mind are Tony Blair's cheesy soundbite from election night in 1997. "A new dawn has broken, has it not?" I say to Preds, and we laugh like losers.

Appendix

Was it the *Cambrian News* "wot won it"?

No, I don't believe that it was. It is important to state that I think we would still have failed to recapture the seat had the paper not behaved so disgracefully. The rightward drift of the campaign's last few weeks, which handed the Conservatives an overall majority against all predictions, played out in Ceredigion too, to the benefit of both coalition partners.

Likewise, the growing fear of the SNP effect, so ruthlessly deployed by the Tories and amplified by both of the other main UK parties and the media, unquestionably frightened some voters away from Plaid.

That said, I believe the result would have been considerably closer without the *Cambrian News*'s intervention. Towards the end of the colour section in the middle of this book, you'll find two maps, showing how the Plaid vote changed between 2010 and 2015 across Ceredigion. This is based on rough samples taken of the different area boxes from both election nights; a practice undertaken by all parties. They are only samples, and therefore far from precise, but it is quite possible to get a good general picture of the way the vote went in the various parts of the constituency. On the maps, the size of circles roughly corresponds to the number of voters in individual towns and villages, so that Aberystwyth is by far the largest.

At first glance, the rise and fall of support for Plaid appears fairly random. The only obvious patterns are that we did better in the north of the county than the south, and in towns rather than villages and more rural areas. There are significant rises in Aberystwyth, Aberaeron, Borth, and in the communities along the A487 to Machynlleth and in the Rheidol valley. More modest increases can be seen in Cardigan, Lampeter, New Quay and Llanarth, and the Ystwyth valley.

The sharpest falls in support came in Tregaron and nearby villages, Aberporth and the villages around Cardigan, Llandysul and the Teifi valley, the Aeron valley, Llannon and Llanrhystud and – in an apparent bucking of the north/south split – in Bow Street/Llandre. This is the home patch of the 2010 candidate Penri James; he had latterly been its local councillor, and it was probably his personal vote that led to the fall in 2015. There is another pattern there, which can be clearly seen in the second map, overlaid with the four different versions of the Nazigate edition of the *Cambrian News*, according to their different catchment areas. Remember these are front pages that sat there in hundreds of shops, garages, cafes and pubs for a whole week. Even people who didn't buy the paper would have seen them. It is quite clear that Plaid did far, far better in the one area of the county where the smear was relegated to the lesser, lower story on the front page. I do not believe that to be a coincidence.

*

My *Planet* article from 2001, entitled 'Loaded Dice', can be found in full online. Search for 'Planet Loaded Dice Mike Parker', or go to http://www.planetmagazine.org.uk/planet_extra/loaded-dice

For a textbook definition of the newspaper's actions, search online for "Godwin's Law".

Thanks and Thoughts

This has been a fascinating, if difficult, book to write. An intensely-fought election campaign goes at such a crazy and accelerating speed that it is hard to keep track of all that happens. Although I kept an extensive diary throughout, to get an accurate account of the last two months has required considerable unpicking of events, and much discussion with others. Thanks to all who gave so freely of their time and take on it.

Especial thanks to my many inspirational comrades in Plaid Cymru. First and foremost, my towering respect and affection for Leanne Wood, and her tireless work over the years to make Wales, and the world, a better place. The Plaid crew in Ceredigion were brilliant to work with, and great company too. I am especially indebted to Elin Jones, Owen Roberts, Gwenllian Mair, Matthew Woolfall-Jones and Mary Davies in the constituency office, and to my tenacious agent Richard Owen.

Hundreds volunteered in an upbeat and optimistic campaign; a mighty thank you to them all. Apologies for any that I've missed, but there are some whose commitment went way beyond normal: Aled Morgan Hughes, Cynog Dafis, Jordan Shapiro, Manon Elin, Llywelyn Williams, Nona Evans, Glyn Parry, Gareth Evans, Meg Thomas, Mererid Jones, Alun Williams, Mark Strong, Brendan Summers, Catherine Hughes, Meurig and Pat Jones, Sushma Lal, Marian Delyth, Elin Jones the Second, Emyr Jenkins, Guto and Sian ap Gwynfor, Caryl Wyn Jones, Lyn and Rhydian Fitter, Catrin Miles and Graham Evans, Jane Roche, Clive Davies, John Adams-Lewis, Dafydd Prys, Ellen ap Gwynn, Digby Bevan, Rob and Delyth Phillips, Bryan Davies, James Luchte, Gwilym Morus, Nigel Callaghan, Gwynfryn Evans, Jane Aaron, Lewis Griffith, Heledd ach Gwyndaf, and drivers Iolo ap Gwynn and Brython Davies. Diolch o galon i chi gyd.

Thanks too to those who have sifted my words and given such valuable feedback: Jasmine Donahaye, Helen Sandler, Emily Trahair and John Barnie; to the ever-helpful staff of the National Library and Ceredigion Archives, both in Aberystwyth; to Lefi, Eirian, Fflur and all at Y Lolfa.

The difficulties in writing this book have not just been practical. Re-living the campaign at its most brutal was extremely depressing, though it helped answer one of the big questions with which I came into this, namely can and should a writer, or indeed anyone with a extensive back catalogue, attempt to go into politics? I can't help but come to the conclusion that no is the answer, and that is a great shame.

The other big question for me was whether our political system is broken. I fear that it is, and for all the reasons so evident from this small story of one campaign in the west of Wales. Corruption, undue influence, a loaded media, a chronically limited debate, a discourse increasingly predicated on victimhood and synthetic outrage, short-termism, timidity and tribalism are all playing their unedifying part. I don't believe that I'd have come to a different conclusion had I won – indeed, I suspect it would have confirmed my worst suspicions, and provided me with plenty of new ones.

As I write (March 2016), the baying of the political media is once again in full throttle, this time over the impending EU referendum. If there is one thing we should have learned from the election of May 2015, and from the subsequent election of Jeremy Corbyn as Labour leader, it is that the tiny, self-selecting band of pundits and pollsters actually know very little. Yet they create and amplify their own tune, and demand that politicians and the public dance to it. Round and round they go in ever decreasing circles, and then they – politicians and media alike – wonder why people feel so disengaged from their shrill bleatings.

There is though one single change that would make a significant improvement: the first-past-the-post system must go. To have a majority government voted for by less than a quarter of the electorate is anti-democratic in the extreme, and only exacerbates the detachment so many feel towards politics. Had there been any sort of proportionality to the result, there would be a couple of dozen Green MPs, the LibDems would still have around fifty and UKIP about eighty. Much as the idea of eighty UKIP MPs horrifies me, I would far rather see their representatives in the bright light of proper scrutiny, where they would doubtless inflict the same kind of damage on themselves as have their MEPs in Brussels, than skulking in the shadows and using the fact that they only won one seat as yet more fuel for their destructive paranoia.

Standing in Ceredigion for Plaid Cymru was an honour and a privilege. It was also often great fun, and always interesting. I'd like to thank too my fellow candidates, and the people of Ceredigion who, for the most part, showed me great kindness. This is a very special part of the world, and it deserves far better than the deal it currently receives.

Most of all, my thanks and love to Preds. I was a bloody nightmare to live with at times during the campaign, and then again when writing about it. He bore all that, as he always does, with wisdom, compassion, strength and ego-busting good humour. Diolch am byth, cariad.

Mike Parker
March 2016

Also by the author:

Coast to Coast
Neighbours from Hell?
Map Addict
The Wild Rover
Real Powys
Mapping the Roads

www.mikeparker.org.uk
Twitter @mikeparkerwales

The Greasy Poll is just one of a whole range of publications from Y Lolfa. For a full list of books currently in print, send now for your free copy of our new full-colour catalogue. Or simply surf into our website

www.ylolfa.com

for secure on-line ordering.

TALYBONT CEREDIGION CYMRU SY24 5HE
e-mail ylolfa@ylolfa.com
website www.ylolfa.com
phone (01970) 832 304
fax 832 782